IMAGES
of America

KINGS MOUNTAIN

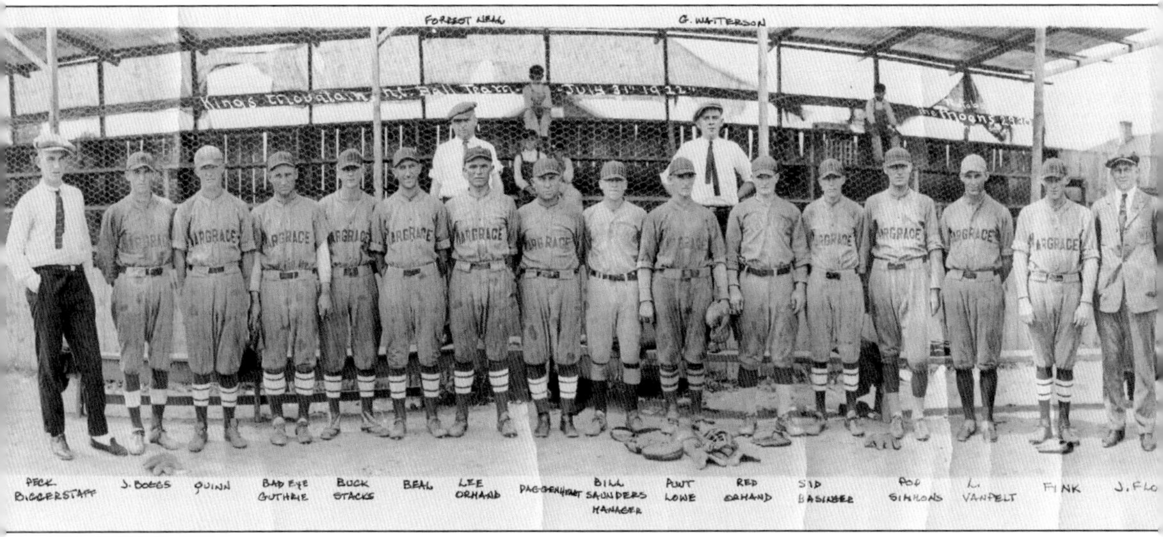

ON THE COVER: The American Textile League developed as Southern textile mill owners recognized a need to boost employee morale and offer social opportunities to their workers outside of the factory. Popular in the mill villages until the mid-1950s, the games became an event for the entire community, often creating fierce rivalries between neighboring mills. One of the mill teams in the area was the Margrace Mill baseball team. Shown posing for a photograph on July 21, 1922, are, from left to right, (first row) Peck Biggerstaff, J. Boggs, ? Quinn, "Bad Eye" Guthrie, Buck Stacks, ? Beal, Lee Ormand, Daggenheart, manager Bill Saunders, Punt Lowe, Hugh "Red" Ormand, Sid Basinger, Pop Simmons, L. Vanpelt, Fink, and J. Floyd; (second row) Forrest Neal and G. Watterson. (Courtesy of the Kings Mountain Historical Museum.)

IMAGES
of America

KINGS MOUNTAIN

Sharon Stack and Stephanie Walsh

ARCADIA
PUBLISHING

ISBN 978-0-7385-9797-3

Published by Arcadia Publishing
Charleston, South Carolina

Printed in the United States of America

Library of Congress Control Number: 2012942938

For all general information, please contact Arcadia Publishing:
Telephone 843-853-2070
Fax 843-853-0044
E-mail sales@arcadiapublishing.com
For customer service and orders:
Toll-Free 1-888-313-2665

Visit us on the Internet at www.arcadiapublishing.com

*To the past, present, and future friendly,
hardworking residents of Kings Mountain*

Contents

Acknowledgments

Just like the earliest settlers, we chose to come the area known as Kings Mountain. We have found the process of assembling this book educational as well as fun. We have wandered through time with photographs and family scrapbooks, visited with city residents and city staff, and been touched by the hardworking, friendly spirit of the people who have lived and still reside here.

We want to thank library assistant Landon Hulsey, who assisted with the scanning of the images. We also thank Nicholas Graham, program director of the North Carolina Digital Heritage Center, for digitizing the 1917 Kings Mountain map, the photograph of the Kings Mountain Business Men's Bible Class, and the 1974 commemorative centennial photograph.

We want to thank the Kings Mountain Historical Museum Board of Directors and staff, the City of Kings Mountain mayor and council, and the Mauney Memorial Library Board of Trustees and staff for allowing us the time to work on this publication.

Unless otherwise noted, all images appear courtesy of the Kings Mountain Historical Museum.

Introduction

The American Revolutionary Battle of Kings Mountain, called the "turning point of the war," put the area originally known as White Plains on the map and provided the name for the city. The appeal of good weather, soil, water, and later the proximity to roads and rail brought settlers and commerce to propel the area to success and prosperity.

The city is situated a few miles north of a 16-mile range known by the same name. Downtown Kings Mountain has a fine view of the range's highest peak, Kings Pinnacle. The battle was fought on the 10th peak below the pinnacle in South Carolina. As the railroad was built, the White Plains postmistress, in a patriotic spirit, named the new post office (and consequently the resulting town) Kings Mountain.

Kings Mountain was first inhabited prior to the American Revolution as Scotch, Irish, Dutch, and German settlers made their way down the Great Wagon Road and settled this area, with its good access to water and fertile soil. Solomon Beason, James Blythe, Alexander Dickey, John Husselberger, and Isaac Kimball received state and royal land grants for the land that formed the White Plains area. The commercial core of Kings Mountain and the adjacent area appears as part of Robert Falls's and Humphrey Parker's land after the initial generation of landowners sold. Other early landowners were Dr. James Wright Tracy and Ben F. Briggs. Dr. Tracy lived on Gold Street. His wife, Minerva, served as postmistress of the area (then White Plains) and was responsible for naming the town.

In the 1840s, Briggs was a landowner of 11,000 acres and was involved in iron ore mining. The operation necessitated the employment of many men, and Briggs maintained a supply store and saloon for his workers on land that would become part of the town of Kings Mountain. A chance discovery by his wife yielded another golden twinkle in the city's history. While fetching water for her family, Katherine Briggs dipped her bucket in a spring near her home and picked up a gleaming nugget of gold, deemed to be of the finest grade. The year was 1833, and a boom time for the area was set to begin.

This find brought the gold rush that began in North Carolina in the 1790s to the White Plains area. Local residents profited from the resulting growth in commerce, which included the arrival of boardinghouses, apartments, livery for saddle horses, and a grog shop, aptly called the Crow and Beam.

White Plains sent its young men off to the war that was developing between the states. Dr. Tracy served as Cleveland County's voting delegate to the secession convention. He served as a major and brigade surgeon under Gen. Robert E. Lee. White Plains muster ground, located south of El Bethel Church, served as the training area for Kings Mountain Company G, 49th Regiment. Capt. B.F. Dixon commanded Company G, 49th Regiment and the Cleveland Blues of the Confederate army.

Recognizing that incorporating as a municipality would provide advantages to the growing area, concerned citizens began the process of lobbying for this action, and Kings Mountain was officially chartered on February 11, 1874. W.F. Falls sold 25 acres for $1 for the area that would become the town. Additionally, he gave one acre for the purpose of a cemetery, reserving plots for his family. Members of the named council included D. C. Beam, Capt. Freno Dilling, W. F. Falls, W.A. Mauney, and Dr. J.W. Tracy. Mauney was chosen as mayor. Subsequent action appointed Jacob McGinnis as the first police officer and Emmanuel Patterson as the first constable.

With the town established, construction of the Charlotte Atlanta (Southern) Airline Railway opened the city for trade and transportation of goods and services to other markets. Brothers W.A. and Jacob S. Mauney had come to Kings Mountain on April 14, 1872, and subsequently opened the Mauney Brothers Store. Their cousins Marcus and A.P. Carpenter followed suit, opening Carpenter General Store. Additional businesses, such as the Ben Huff Wagon Factory and Beatty Millinery and Dressmaking Shop, quickly followed. Industry expanded with the 1882 construction of a steam-powered gristmill and sawmill known as Merchant Mills. The region was also rich in other minerals, such as tin, limestone, mica, feldspar, and more, which attracted additional industry to the area.

Cotton and its mills began to grow in Kings Mountain. From 1888 to 1920, a total of 10 cotton- and fabric-producing mills were built, along with the villages for workers and company stores. With the exception of the earliest mills, Enterprise (1892) and Dilling (1894), the owners named the mills after their own wives and daughters. They were called Cora (1900), Lula (1900), Bonnie (1900), Pauline (1910), Margrace (1914), and Sadie (1920).

The work sustained the community, and the town was able to hold on during the hard times of the late 1920s and 1930s. The 1930s were a time of growth for Kings Mountain, bringing the establishment of city departments, such as the fire department and the public library. The Kings Mountain Woman's Club built their permanent home on Mountain Street.

When the world war in the 1940s fueled further need for production, and with the men off fighting, the women went to work. Reba Odom Jolley remembers working during the war when a seemingly miraculous thing occurred; working various shifts in the cotton mills, she saved enough money to purchase a house. When her husband returned from war, he did not know where she and her son lived.

In 1965, John Henry Moss was elected as mayor of Kings Mountain. His 22 years in office saw improvements occur at the water and sewer treatment facilities. The lake that Mayor Moss envisioned became reality in 1973, assuring the city an abundant supply of water. The lake, named John Henry Moss Lake, is noted by the Cleveland County Chamber of Commerce as one of the top five most important events of the 20th century for Cleveland County. Mayor Moss was dubbed by *Newsweek* magazine as the "Mayor with the Midas Touch" for his ability to secure federal grants for the town during his service to the city.

Entertainment and distraction from daily life came in many forms for Kings Mountain residents. For children, the usual games of imagination and small toys led to "roly bat," a form of Roll-the-Bat, and hopscotch. Children enjoyed pets like chickens, ducks, and pigs as well as dogs and cats. In her memoir, Hazel Fryer (née Herndon) remembers riding the wagons and tricycles in the Carpenter General Store with her friends in the early 1920s. The mills provided entertainment in the form of baseball teams. Mill teams traveled regionally, and many were considered semiprofessional. A group of interested citizens from Gastonia and Kings Mountain developed Lake Montonia for recreation. The lots around the man-made lake were sold for $100 and were assigned in a drawing of numbers.

Worship was as important as breathing for settlers; it took place as the circuit rider ministers came through the area for camp meetings or services in brush arbors. Early churches organized in the area were Pisgah Associate Reformed Presbyterian Church (c. 1796), El Bethel United Methodist (1812), and Antioch Baptist (1813), which was founded in the Kings Mountain battleground area.

The congregation that would become St. Matthew's Lutheran Church began holding services in 1875 in town, and the church was chartered in 1876. According to Bonnie Mauney Summers, the first church building belonged to the Central United Methodist Church, erected on the northwest corner of Mountain Street and Piedmont Avenue. For African Americans, brush arbors and camp meetings gave way to their first churches, including the Bynum Chapel African Methodist Episcopal (AME) Zion Church, the first church built in town. The proliferation of congregations in town brought Baptist and Methodist churches on diagonal corners. It is said that when the church windows were open, the pastors could be heard preaching simultaneously. Once, as the Baptists were singing "Will there be any stars in your crown?" the Methodists could be heard singing, "No, not one! No, not one!"

Early efforts to educate the children in the area are recorded to the gold mining days and were carried out through homeschooling. Once the town was established, a more formal school system (which would grow to become the current accredited school system) was aided by the opening of Capt. William T. Reilly Bell's school, or Bell's Military Academy. This school was located in a frame building at the corner of Piedmont Avenue and King Street and was later moved to the Central School's site on Ridge Street. For African Americans, education in town began in a brush arbor behind the Bynum's Chapel AME Zion Church. The Compact School and the Davidson School were two early schools for African American children. Integration was fully complete in the Kings Mountain District by 1967.

Celebrations were frequent in Kings Mountain with everyday life marking weddings, birthdays, or even the passing of a grade in school. The city's namesake battle, fought eight miles to the south, has been remembered annually in celebrations held on or around October 7. The town has hosted the festivities, which have included parades and public speeches. These military commemorative events held at the battleground and within the city include the Centennial of the Battle in 1880, the erection of a monument in 1909, and the 150th anniversary of the battle, which brought Pres. Herbert F. Hoover, in 1930. Hoover's visit was the first time a president had visited a Revolutionary War site in the Southern theater.

Kings Mountain celebrated its own 100th birthday in conjunction with the October 6, 1974, celebration of the Battle of Kings Mountain with a grand series of events. A Centennial Commission created fun events, which included the growing of long beards for men and purchasing of buttons that entitled the wearer to daily liberties otherwise denied during the multiday event, a 100-unit parade, and a visit by the governor and other dignitaries. *Look to the Mountain: A Presentation to the Kings Mountain Centennial Commission* by Gary L. Welz was performed.

The ridgeline view and the city's very name are constant reminders to the area's residents of the historic battle fought eight miles south and of its importance to the birth of this nation. Equally enduring is the spirit of the people, with their willingness to fill the landscape with work, worship, learning, play, and, when the time is right, celebration of their promising future and continued success.

One

WORK

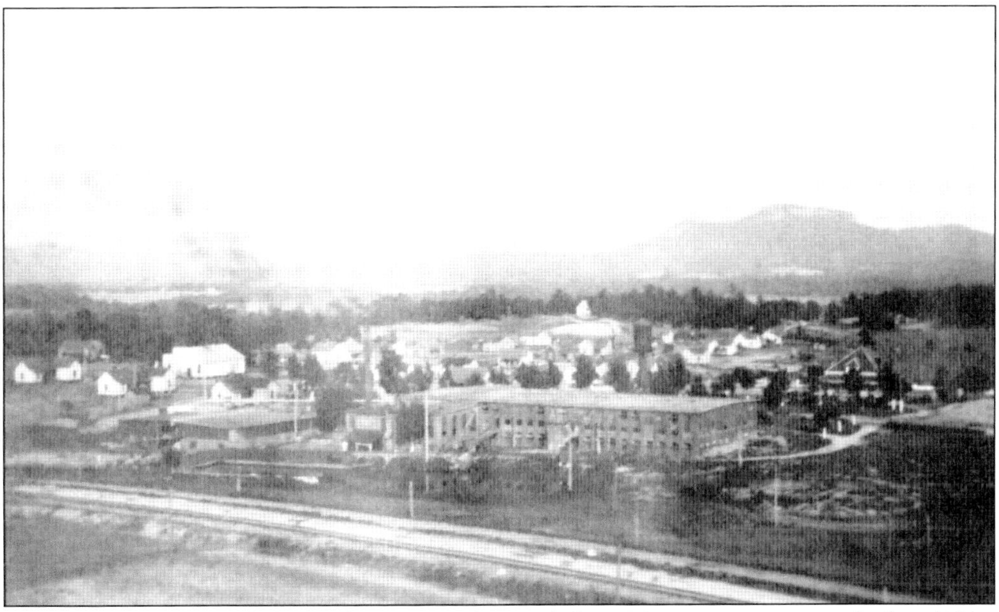

Textile mills began to fill the landscape in and around Kings Mountain starting in the late 1800s. The city's access to the railroad made it conducive for industrial growth. In 1920, Charles E. Neisler Sr. founded the Margrace Mill (named after his two daughters, Margaret Sue and Laura Grace). The Margrace Mill, shown in the foreground, operated in Kings Mountain until 1956. (Courtesy of Neisler Brothers, Inc.)

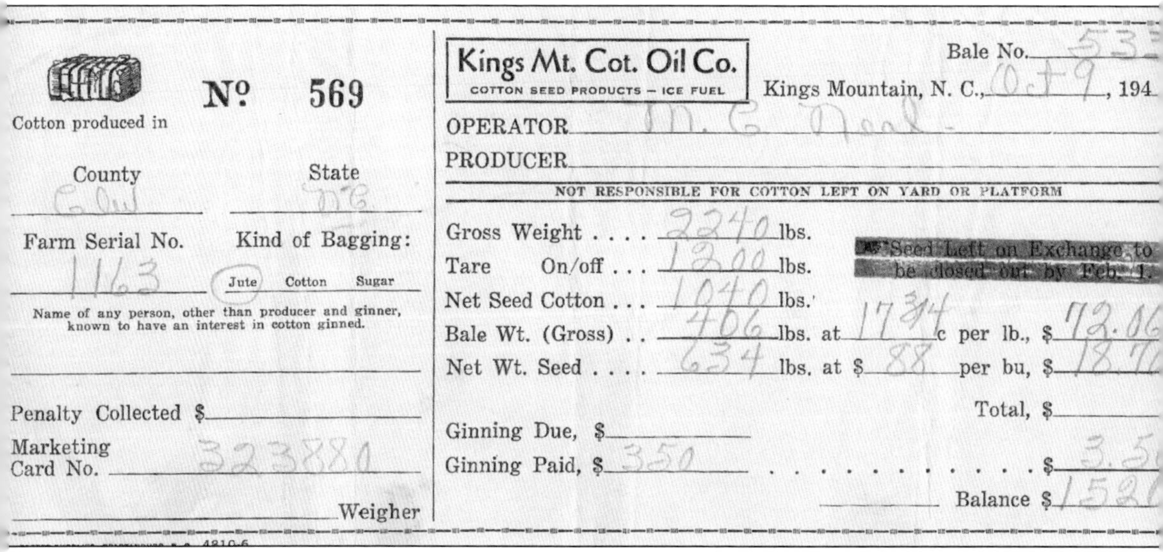
Cotton produced in

County ____ State ____

Farm Serial No. 1163 Kind of Bagging: Jute Cotton Sugar

Name of any person, other than producer and ginner, known to have an interest in cotton ginned.

Penalty Collected $____

Marketing Card No. 323880

____ Weigher

Nº 569

Kings Mt. Cot. Oil Co.
COTTON SEED PRODUCTS — ICE FUEL

Bale No. ____

Kings Mountain, N. C., Oct 9, 194_

OPERATOR ____

PRODUCER ____

NOT RESPONSIBLE FOR COTTON LEFT ON YARD OR PLATFORM

Seed Left on Exchange to be closed out by Feb. 1.

Gross Weight .... 2240 lbs.

Tare On/off ... 1200 lbs.

Net Seed Cotton ... 1040 lbs.

Bale Wt. (Gross) .. 406 lbs. at 17¾ c per lb., $72.0_

Net Wt. Seed .... 634 lbs. at $.88 per bu, $18.7_

Total, $____

Ginning Due, $____

Ginning Paid, $3.50 .... $3.5_

Balance $____

After the Civil War, cotton began to replace tobacco as the state's main income-producing crop. Cotton was picked by hand and put in sacks carried by the workers. Once a bale was ready, mules and wagons (and later trucks) transported it to the local cotton gin. Once at the gins, the cotton fibers would be separated from the seeds. As seen in this 1941 receipt from the Kings Mountain Cotton Oil Company, the cotton fibers and seeds were paid out depending on their individual weights. After the cotton was ginned, it was sold to the local textile mills; the seeds would either be replanted to grow new cotton crops, or converted into cottonseed oil for cooking. The production and manufacturing of cotton became a lucrative endeavor. In 1888, W.A. Mauney and Jacob S. Mauney, along with Capt. Freno Dilling, opened Kings Mountain Manufacturing Company, the town's first cotton mill. From 1888 to 1926, over 12 textile mills operated in the town of Kings Mountain. (Courtesy of Norma H. Drewery.)

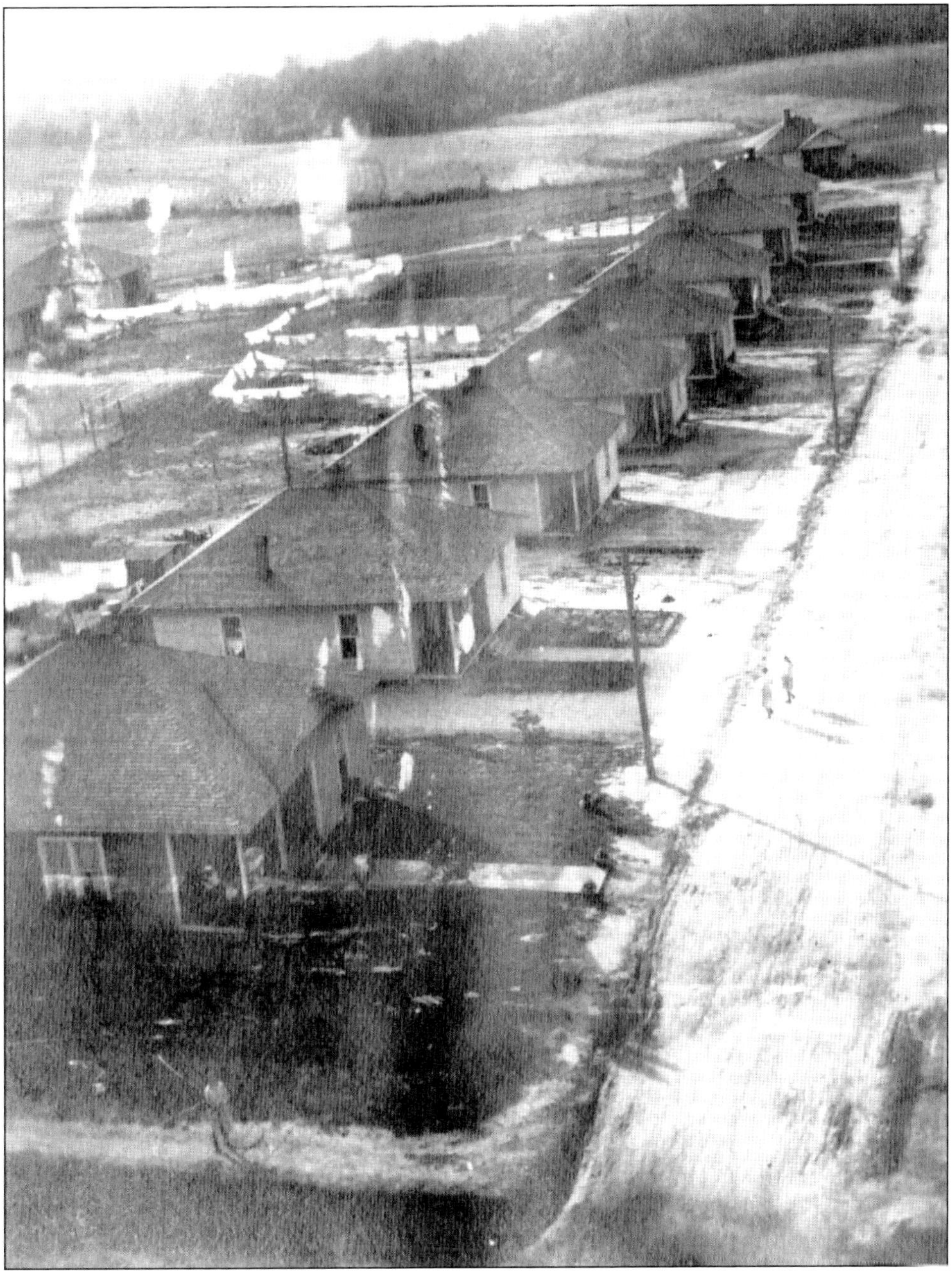

Along with the mills came men, women, and children from the farms and mountains. To accommodate the vast number of workers needed to operate these enterprises, and with the means of transportation limited, the mill owners began to provide essential services for their workers. As a result, newly built, small houses began to spring up around the mills. Set up by the mill owners, mill villages contained rows of small houses for workers and their families. These villages were tightly bound communities. Over time, the villages grew to include general stores, churches, and schools as well as recreational facilities, such as baseball fields and clubhouses. Pictured are the beginnings of the Margrace Mill Village; Charles E. Neisler Sr. had small houses with three to four rooms constructed near the mill for his workers. (Courtesy of Neisler Brothers, Inc.)

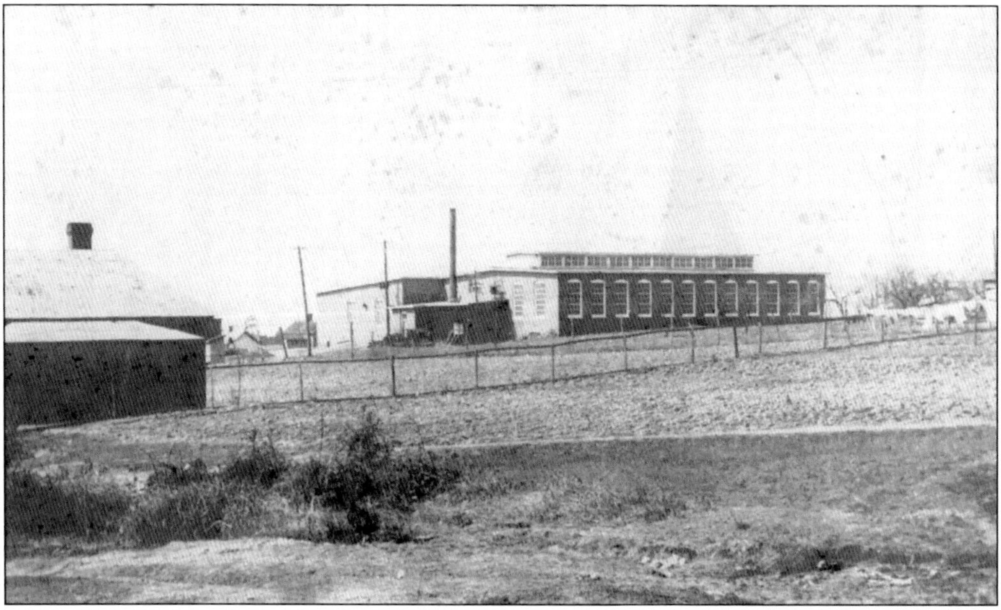

The Pauline Mill was founded by Charles E. Neisler Sr. in 1910. He named the mill for his wife, Ida Pauline Mauney Neisler. This mill was eventually combined with Neisler's Margrace and Patricia Mills under one corporate entity known as Neisco Mills. The Neisco Mills were eventually sold and ceased operation in 1955.

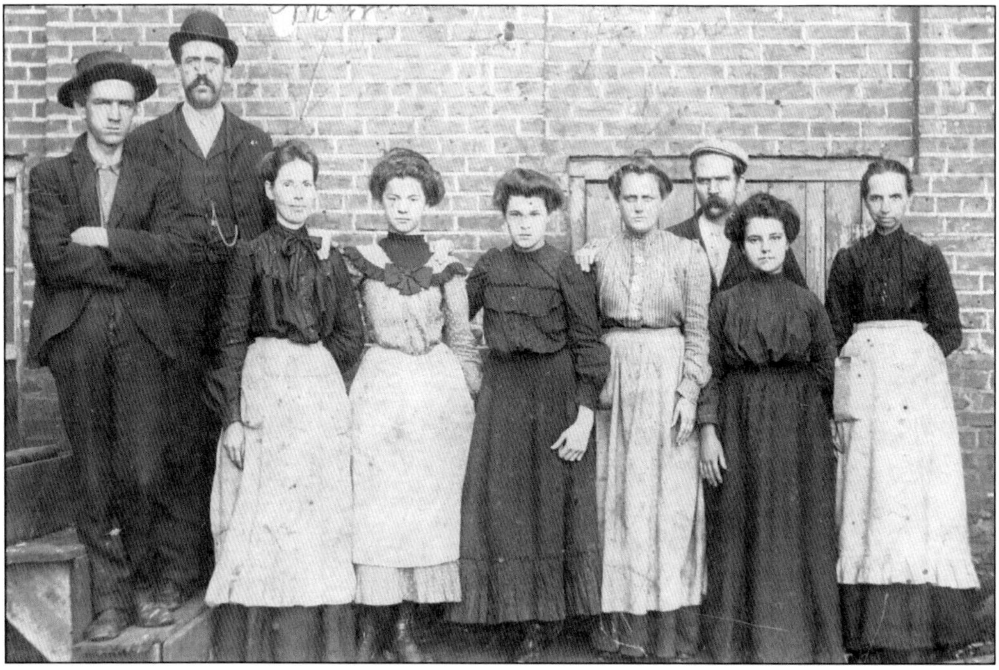

This photograph was taken in 1910 of the first employees of the Pauline Mill. Shown in the photograph are, from left to right, Will Purrish, unidentified, Maggie Long, unidentified, ? Long, Roselind Hartsro, and three unidentified workers. Over the years, as the mill grew, it became known as a major producer of damask table linens. At one time, the Pauline Mill operated 130 Jacquard looms.

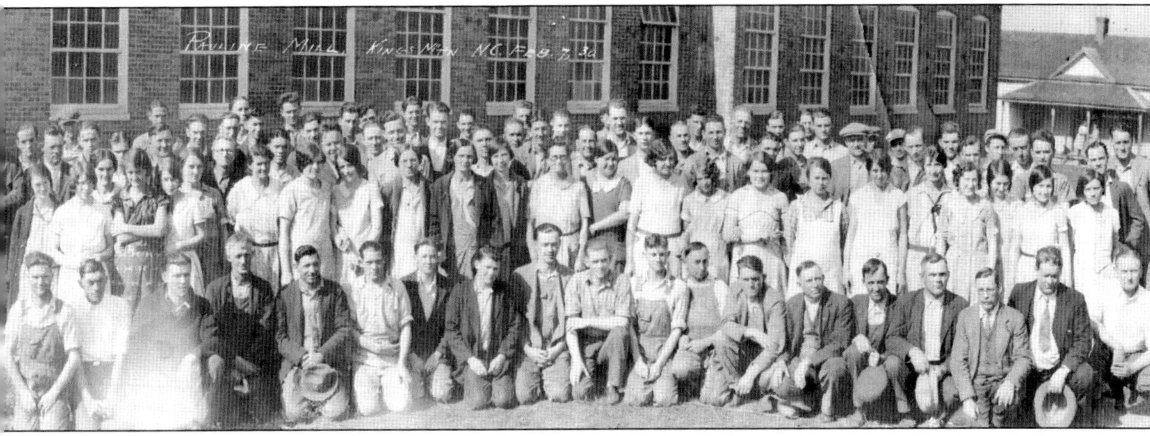

This group photograph of Pauline Mill employees was taken on February 7, 1930. This mill manufactured fine bedspreads, table napkins, and cloths, along with upholstery and drapery fabrics. During the hard times of the late 1920s and throughout the 1930s, Ida Mauney Neisler (wife of the mill's founder, Charles E. Neisler Sr.) suggested to her husband that during the years of economic hardship, the mills under Neisler control operate at a loss in order to continue providing the workers with a living wage. Later, in the 1950s, the Neisler mills produced fabrics for draperies for Radio City Music Hall in New York City. A production problem prevented the delivery pick up from taking place as scheduled, so rather than disappoint the customer, the Neislers drove the delivery through the night from North Carolina to New York.

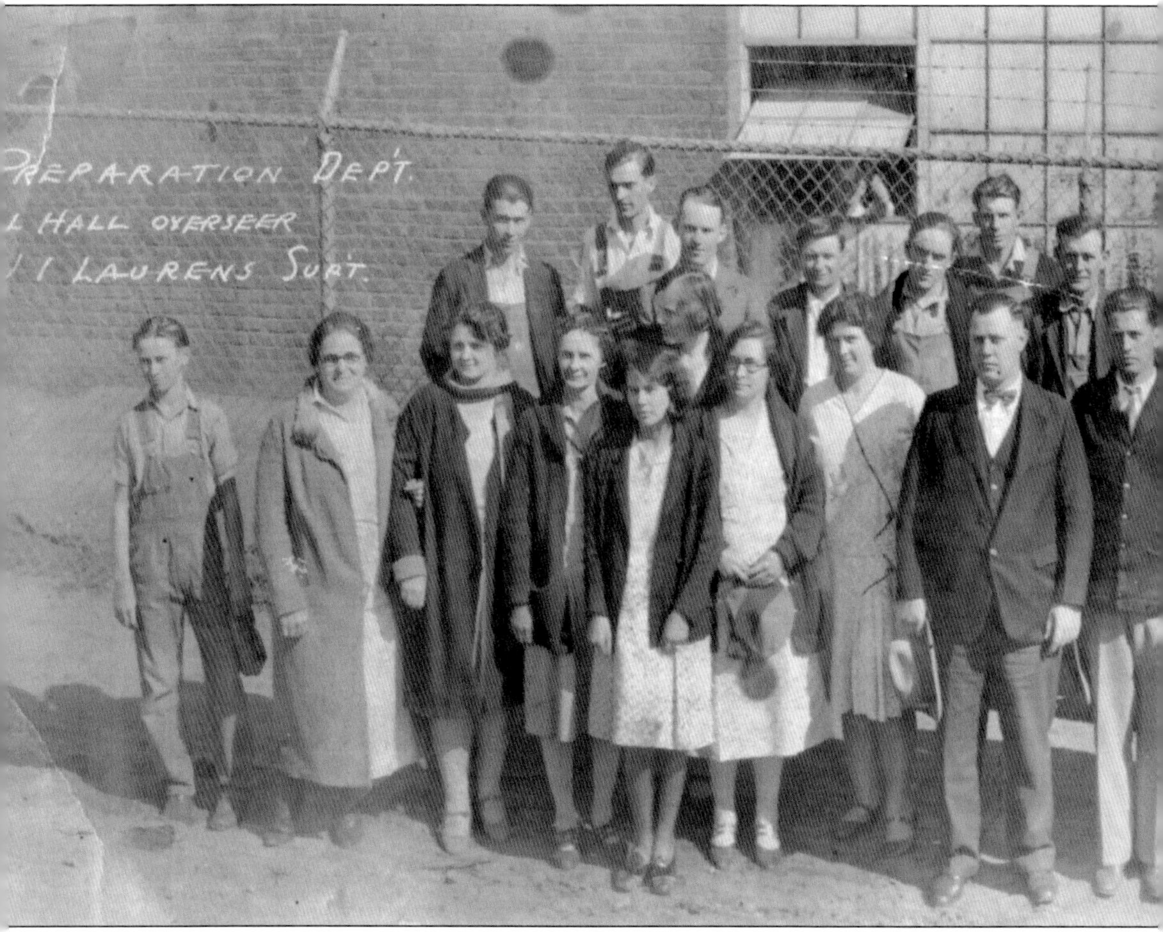

Capt. Freno Dilling founded the Dilling Cotton Mill in the late 1800s. It was later purchased by Burlington Industries, Inc. It is believed that in 1927, the Dilling Mill had the first telephone in Kings Mountain. Taken on February 11, 1930, this photograph shows the night force of the Dilling Mill. In the photograph are W.R. White, overseer of the Weaving Department, and I.A. Ball, overseer of the Preparation Department, in addition to members of the Carroll, Burton, and

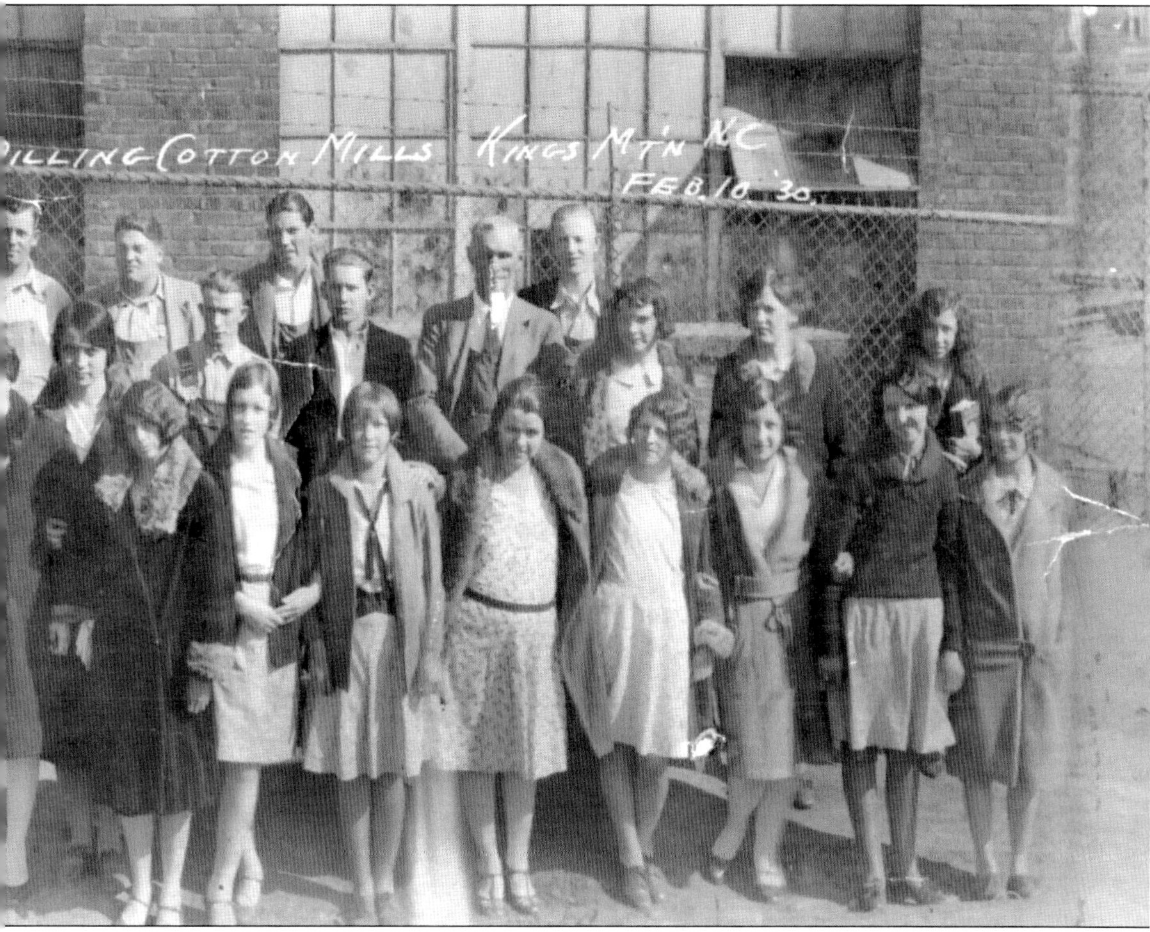

Hamrick families. The role of the overseer was to ensure that the shift started on time, manage the machines and the quality of the fabric under production, and provide reports to the mill's owners. The preparation and weaving process was one of the more skilled operations in the mill. (Courtesy of Mrs. Dewey Styers.)

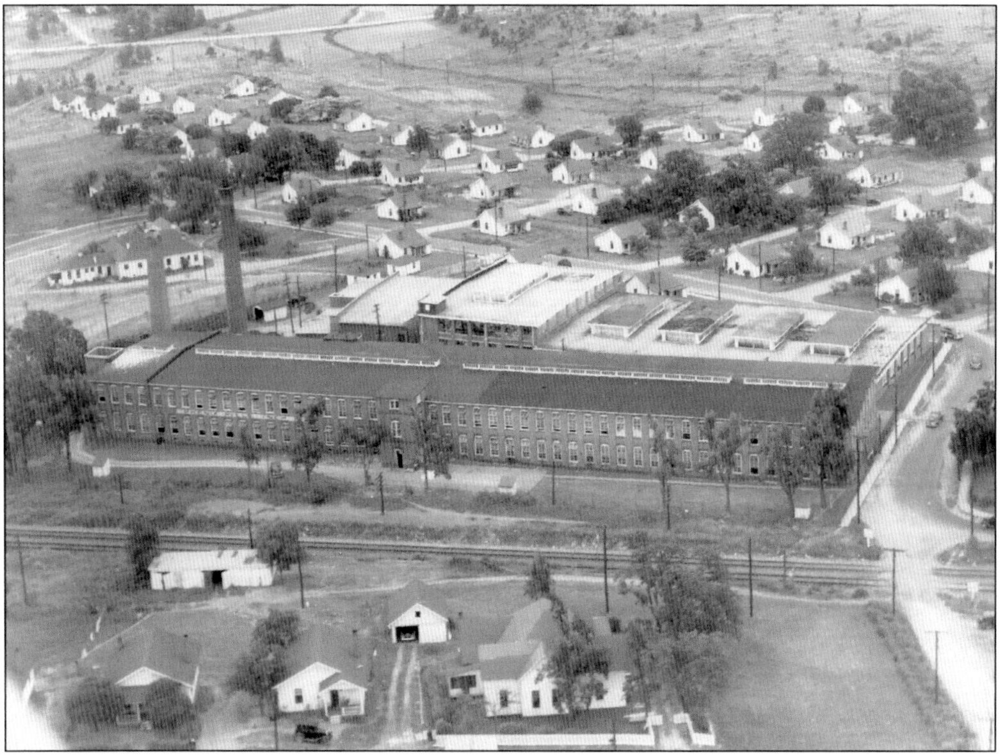

In the early 1890s, Capt. Freno Dilling founded the Dilling Cotton Mill. Located in the northern part of town, the Dilling Mill had 21,164 spindles and 150 looms. Weavers made a variety of cloths, such as broad cloth, silk dress cloth, and brazier cloth. The name changed to the Phenix Mill in 1940, after its sale to Burlington Industries. Almost 100 years after its opening, the mill closed in 1982.

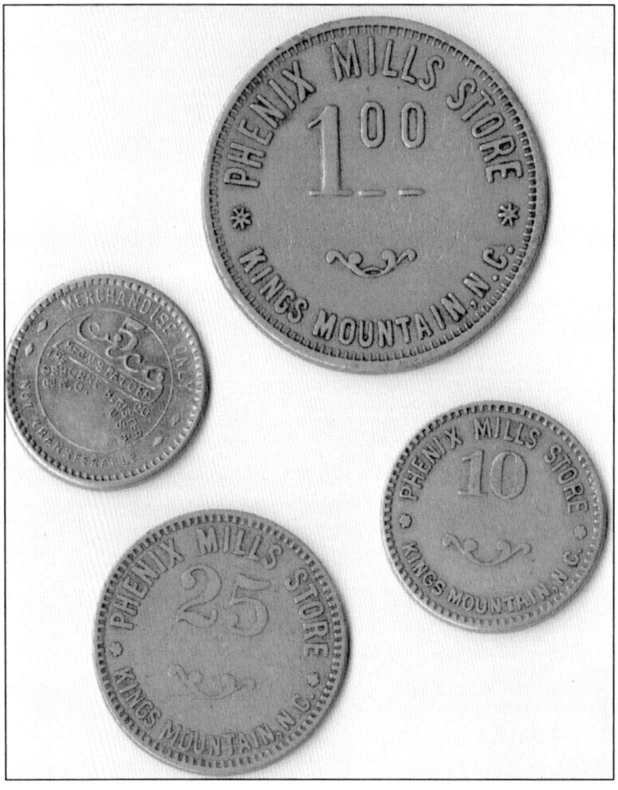

Googaloos were mill currency created by the textile mill owners for use in the company store. These particular metal tokens were issued to Phenix Mill employees as part of their weekly paycheck. The coins came in various denominations and could be used in exchange for merchandise only in the company store located in the mill village.

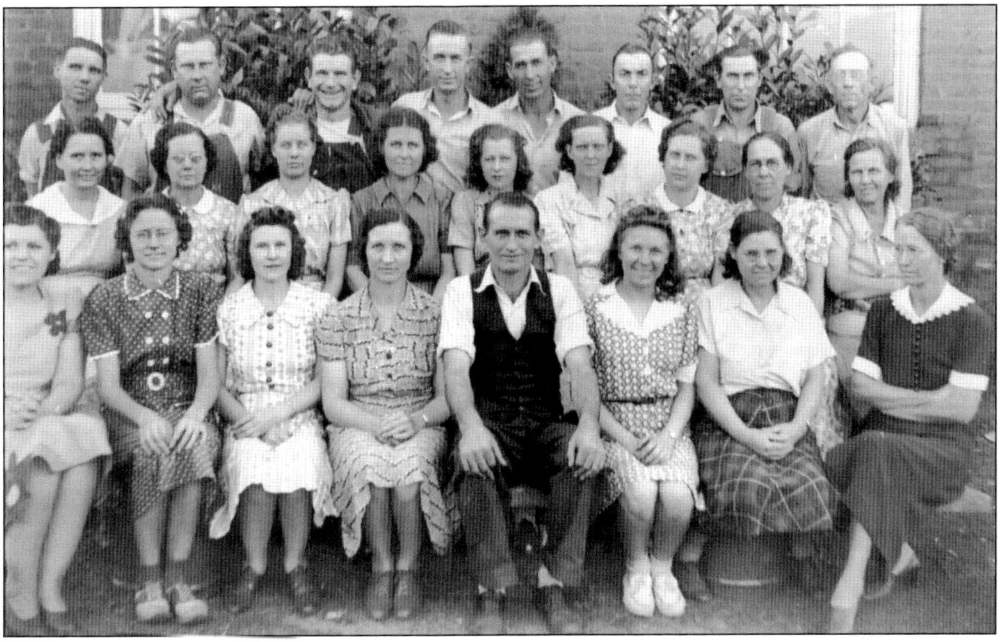

The Mauney Hosiery Mill began operation in 1929. The mill's first-shift workers in 1942 or 1943 are, from left to right, (first row) Bessie Crawford, unidentified, Myrtle Sanders, Lola Condry, Rufus Mitcham, Ida Yates, unidentified, and Ethel Mitcham; (second row) Cletie Randall, Lily Mitcham, Cubie Mitcham, three unidentified people, Viola Sanders, ? Randall, and unidentified; (third row) Lawson Houser, Charlie Randall, Gaither Hoyle, Nelson Ledbetter, Gaither Ledbetter, two unidentified people, and Charlie Randall.

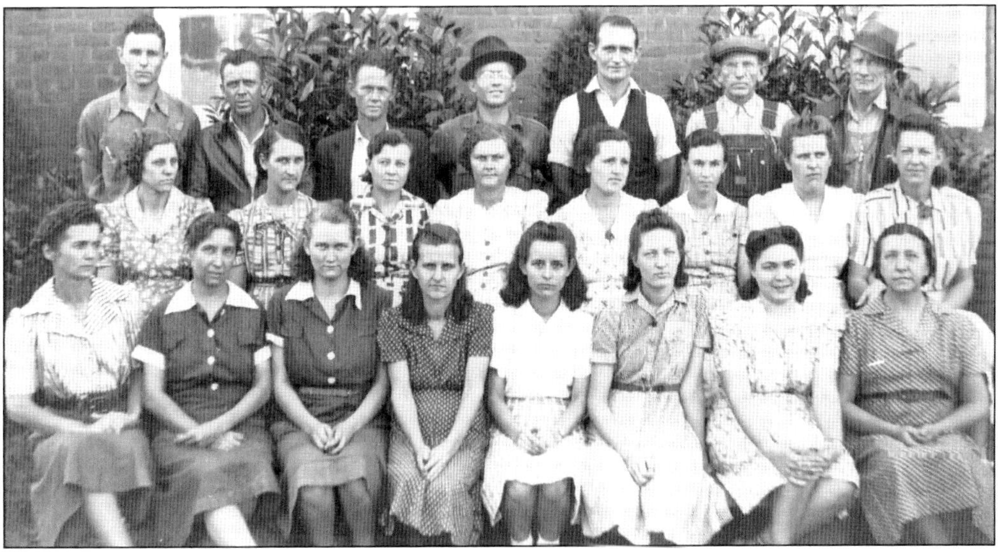

In this photograph are the Mauney Hosiery Mill second-shift workers around 1942 or 1943. Shown from left to right are (first row) Lola Ramsey, Fannie Jackson, Beulah Ligon, unidentified, Margaret Mitcham, Lorena Wilson, Gwen Hardin, and unidentified; (second row) Alma Whitesides, Onice Ramsey, Nola Morrow, Helen White, Reba Ledbetter, Bright Huff-Stickler, Juliette Uren, and unidentified; (third row) Hank Haynes, Paul Saunders, Willie Ramsey, unidentified, Rufus Mitcham, Meek Foster, and "Red" Ramsey.

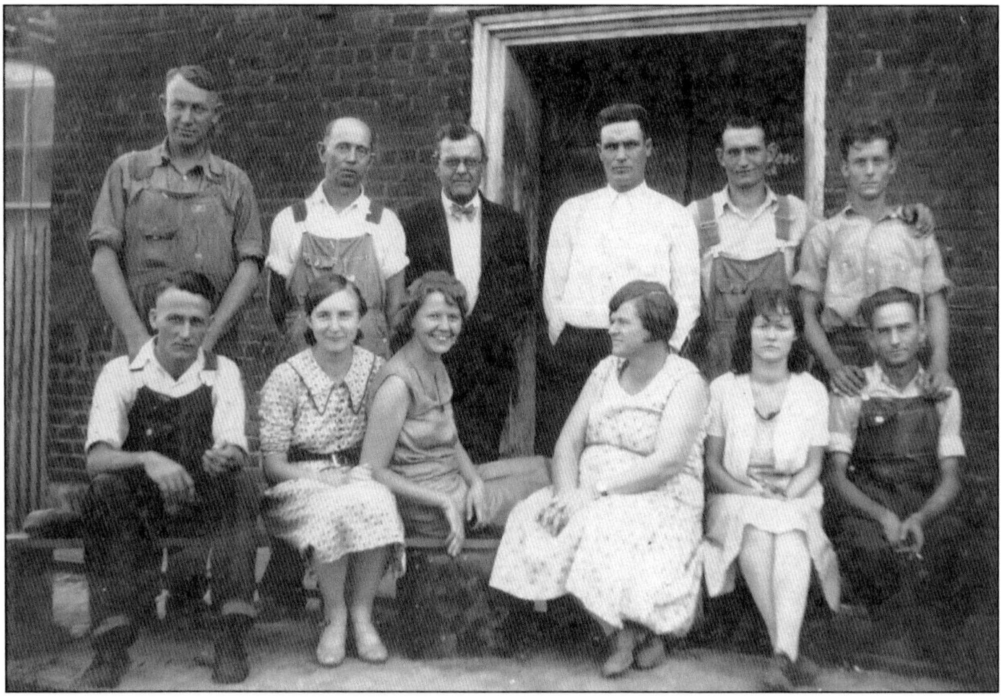

This image shows the Twister Room employees of the Bonnie Cotton Mill in 1927. The Bonnie Cotton Mill manufactured only yarn and was run with independent power, allowing for full production. These employees were responsible for twisting the fibers into yarn. Shown are, from left to right, (first row) Dewey Falls, unidentified, Myrtle McFalls, unidentified, Geneva McFalls, and Clarence Falls; (second row) Marshall Crowder, Pless Styers, C.J. Rhyne, Dewey Randall, Rufus Mitcham, and Lloyd Mitcham.

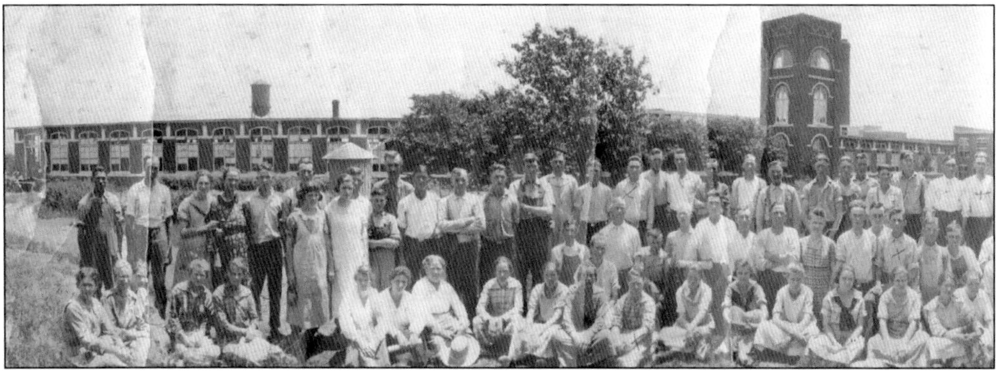

This photograph shows a group of Cora Mill employees outside the factory. Capt. Freno Dilling, Dr. O.G. Falls, and others founded Cora Mill in 1900. Sometime before 1947, the mill became Craftspun Yarns (where yarn was the primary product manufactured). In a newsletter from that year, the company challenged employees to produce the finest yarns, which could be run on a Nottingham Lace loom.

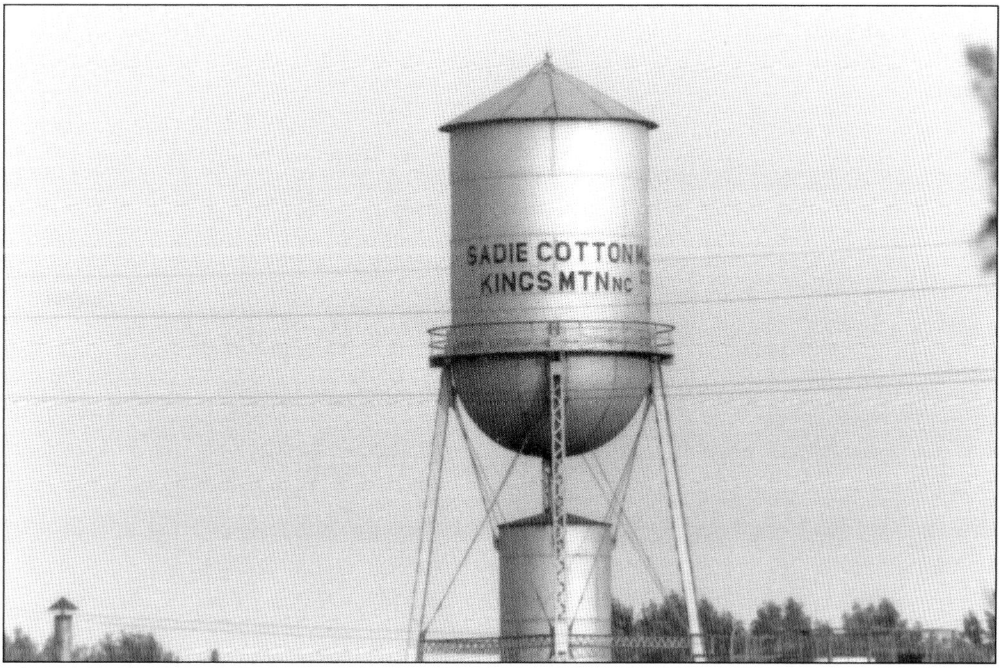

The Sadie Cotton Mill was built in 1920 by D.C. Mauney and L.A. Kiser, among others. Like most of the mills in Kings Mountain, Sadie Cotton Mill was named after a female relative of one of the founders; Sarah (Sadie) Elizabeth Fisher Mauney was the wife of D.C. Mauney. Located on East Gold Street, the company was later operated by the Burke Weaving Co. (Courtesy of Jane Talbert.)

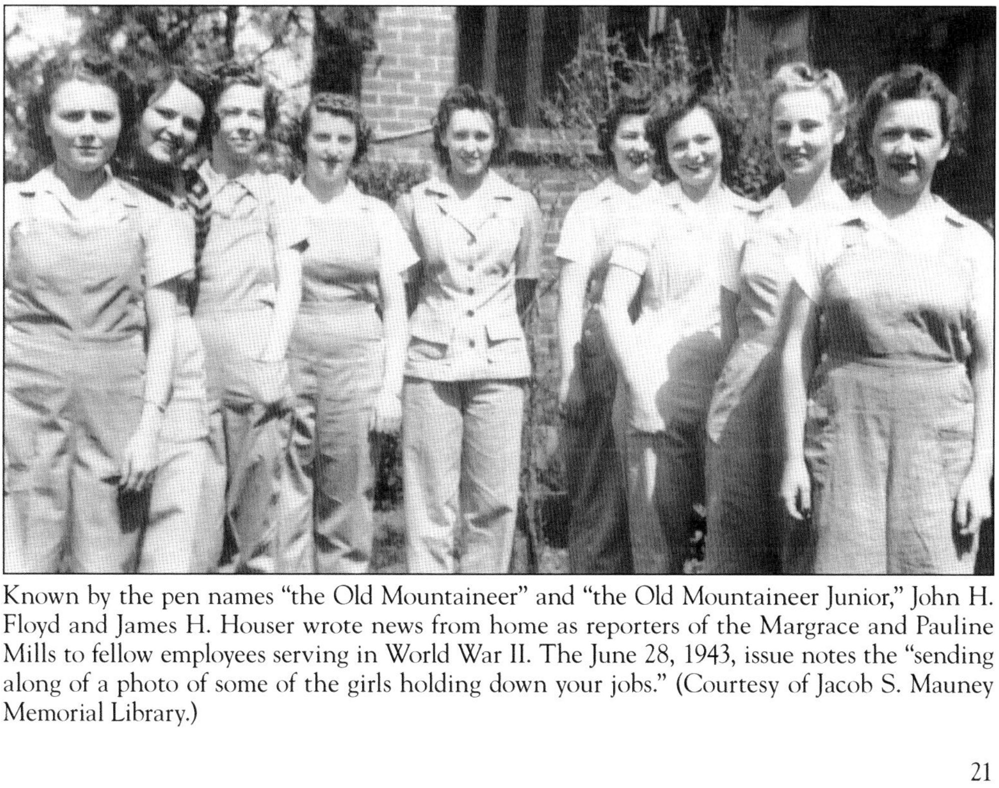

Known by the pen names "the Old Mountaineer" and "the Old Mountaineer Junior," John H. Floyd and James H. Houser wrote news from home as reporters of the Margrace and Pauline Mills to fellow employees serving in World War II. The June 28, 1943, issue notes the "sending along of a photo of some of the girls holding down your jobs." (Courtesy of Jacob S. Mauney Memorial Library.)

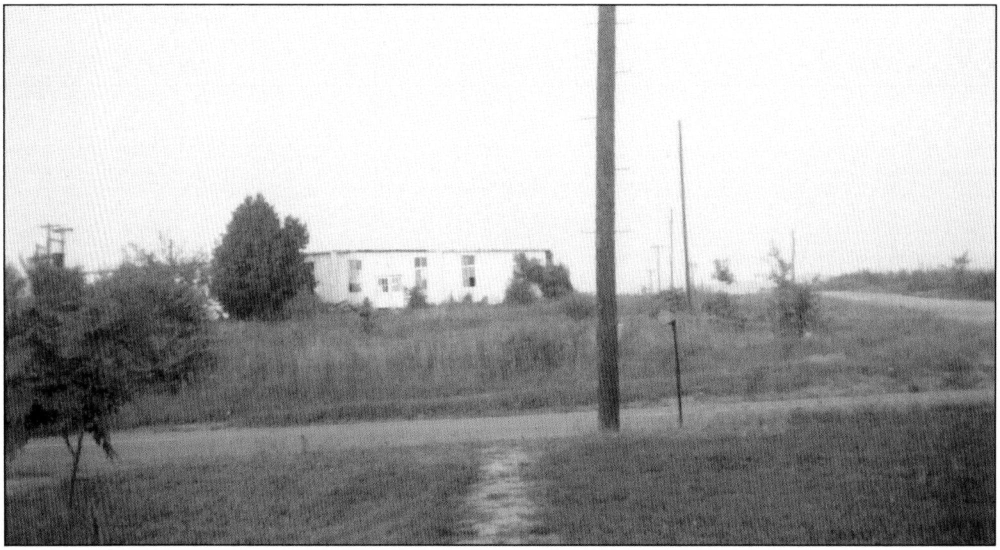

The Slater Mill, located off Highway 161 in Kings Mountain, employed approximately 75 people. A.J. Slater owned and operated the mill from 1951, while his son Robert Slater was general plant manager. The mill was modernized in 1961 to house weaving, dying, and finishing facilities. In 1964, a fire that started in the weaving room destroyed the mill. (Courtesy of Lydia Jane Edwards.)

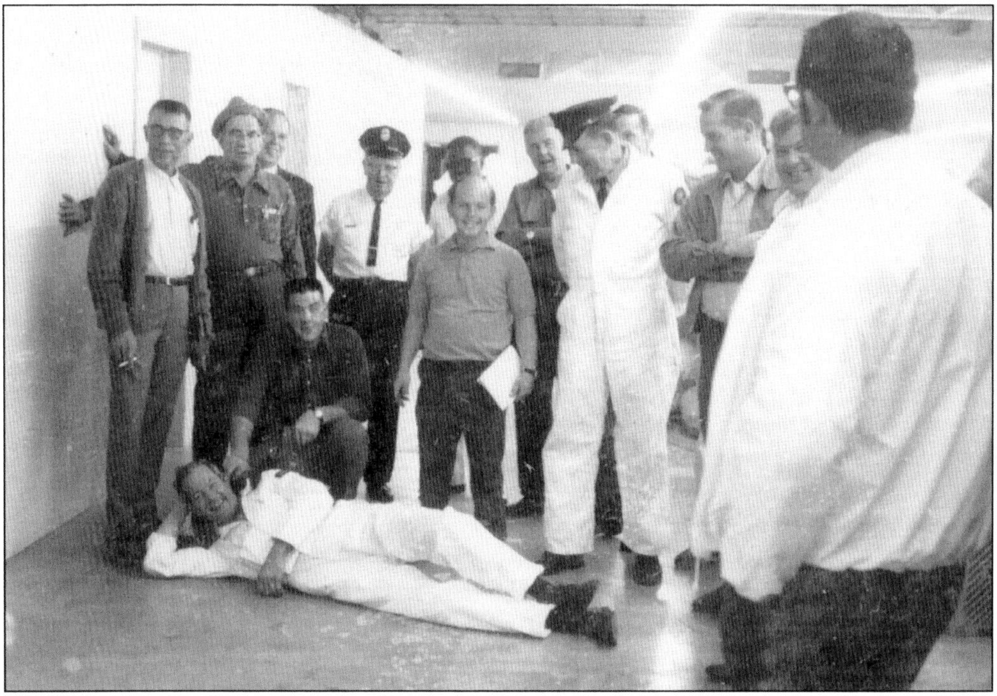

The photograph shows members of the Kings Mountain Fire Department with mill staff during a training exercise at one of the local mills during the 1960s. Pictured are, from left to right, (lying on floor) Gene Tignor; (kneeling) Jerry White; (standing) Harry "Dutch" Wilson, Charles "Red" Ware, Bennett Masters, "Red" McLee, Larry McDaniel, two unidentified, Tommy Pharr, Bob Hope, Jackie Barrett, C.E. "Bud" Ware, and unidentified (with back to camera). (Courtesy of the Kings Mountain Fire Museum.)

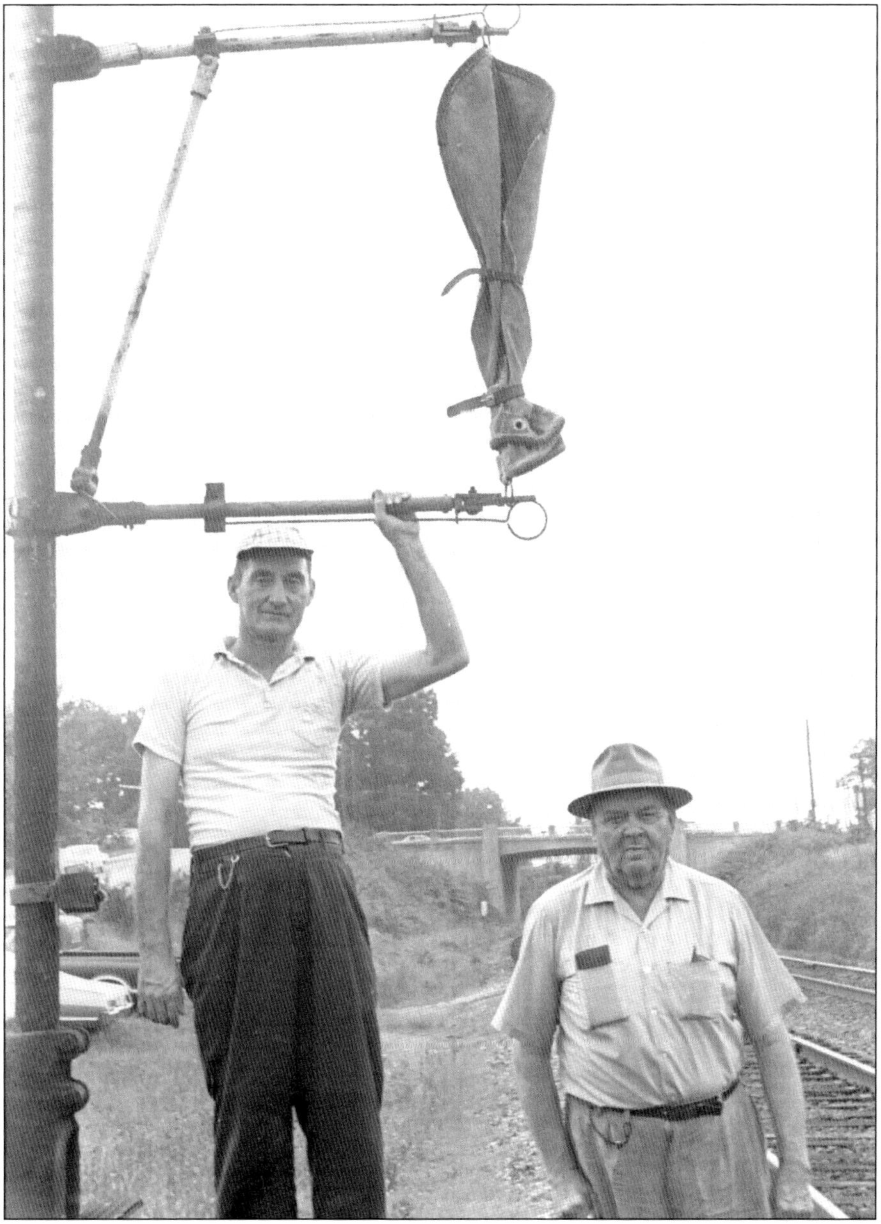

Postal service has long been associated with Kings Mountain. Before the town was officially founded in 1874, mail was delivered by horseback along the old post road, which ran from Cherryville to the El Bethel area. Rail transit arrived in Kings Mountain in 1872 with the Charlotte Atlanta Airline Railway, bringing with it faster mail service delivery. As the train traveled down the railroad tracks, a catcher arm was swung out from the passing train to catch the hanging pouch of outgoing mail. Mail being delivered to Kings Mountain was then kicked out of the railcar far enough that the mail pouch was not pulled back under the train. Postal employees would then retrieve the pouch and process it for local delivery. Shown in this photograph are postal workers Bob Ware (left) and Rufus Phifer (right) at a mailbag stop located at the intersection of Battleground Avenue and Mountain Street. In 1963, the city of Kings Mountain saw its final mail dispatch by rail.

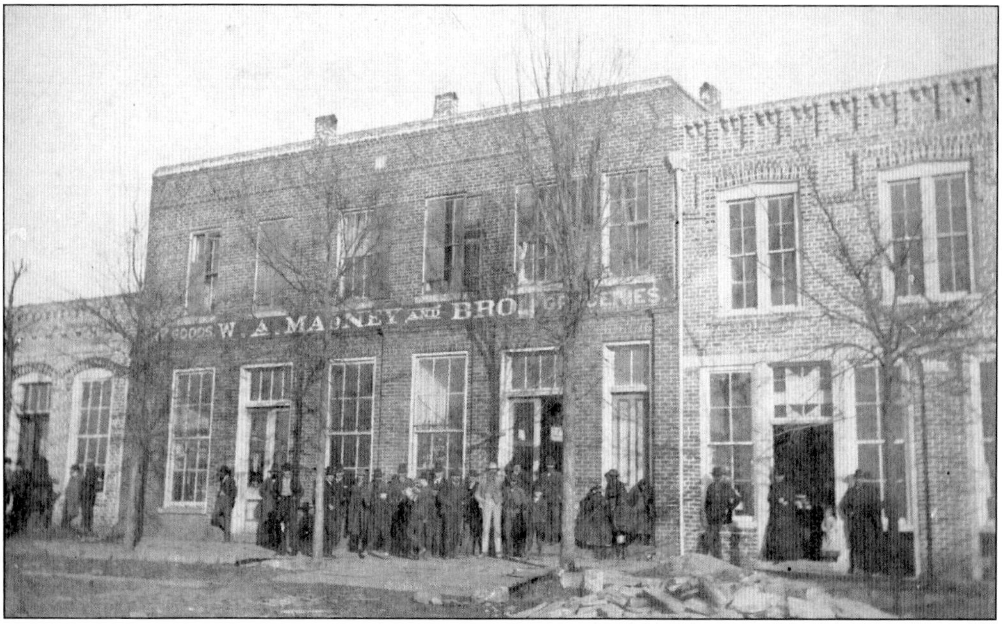

In 1874, W.A. Mauney and his brother J.S. Mauney moved their small general store closer to the railroad on the block between Mountain and Gold Streets. Three years later, they converted the wood-frame building into the two-story brick structure seen here. The store soon became home to the post office, and W.A. Mauney served as the postmaster for 17 years. (Courtesy of Neisler Brothers, Inc.)

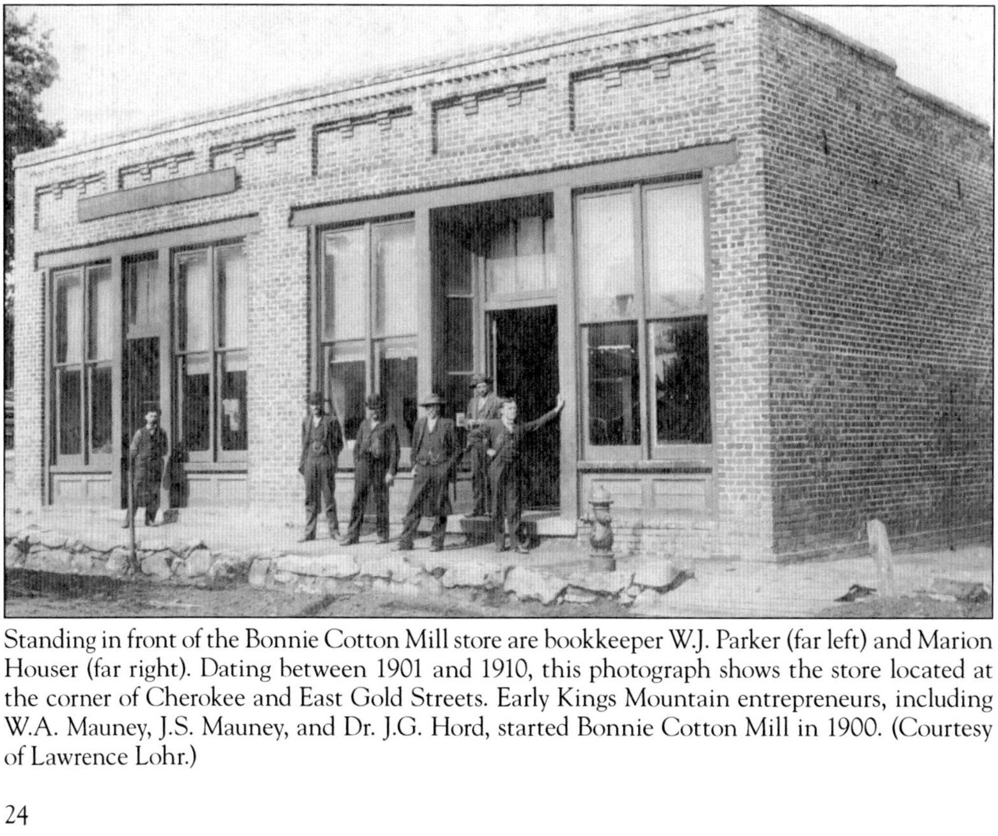

Standing in front of the Bonnie Cotton Mill store are bookkeeper W.J. Parker (far left) and Marion Houser (far right). Dating between 1901 and 1910, this photograph shows the store located at the corner of Cherokee and East Gold Streets. Early Kings Mountain entrepreneurs, including W.A. Mauney, J.S. Mauney, and Dr. J.G. Hord, started Bonnie Cotton Mill in 1900. (Courtesy of Lawrence Lohr.)

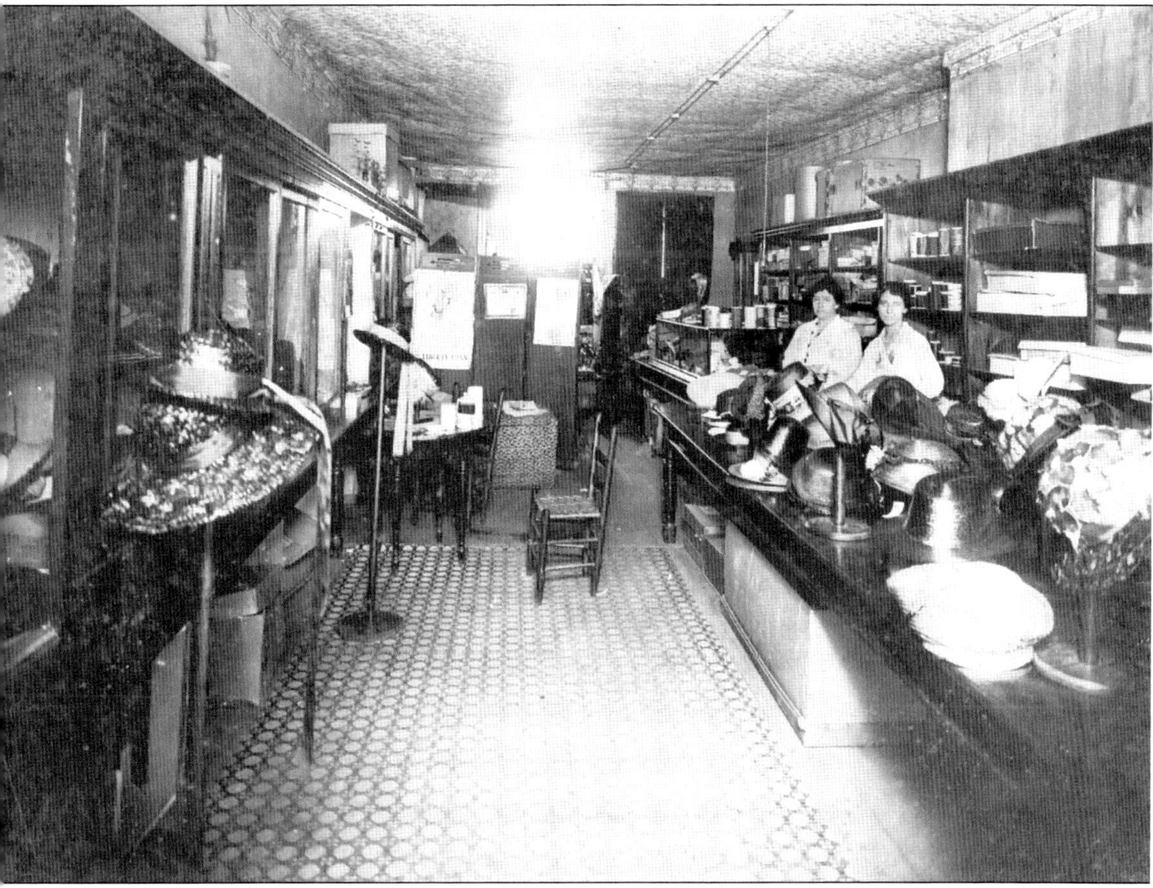

Prior to the turn of the 20th century, the Kings Mountain business community was comprised of a roller mill, a woodworking plant, two grocery stores, a millinery and dressmaking shop, buggy and wagon factories, and a cobbler. Many of the brick buildings on Mountain Street were erected after 1890, including the Beatty Millinery and Dressmaking Shop. A fire destroyed half the block in 1890 after lightning struck Willeford's Dry Goods Store. This photograph taken around 1910 shows Gussie Beatty and Enola Beatty inside their hat shop after the store was rebuilt.

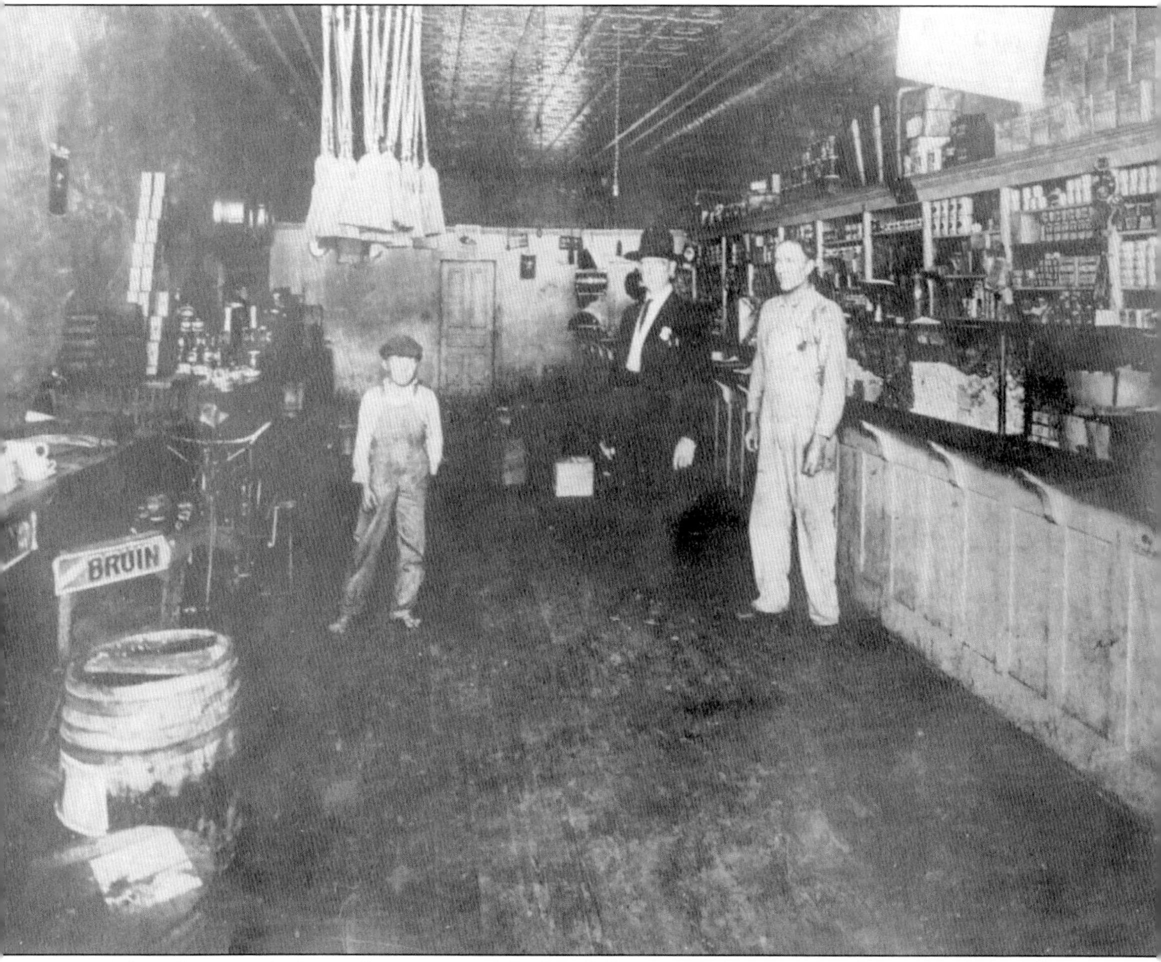

This photograph shows the interior of the Hord Grocery Store sometime between 1915 and 1918. During the early 20th century, shop owners were required to make the best use of their limited spaces, as demonstrated in this image by the brooms hanging from the ceiling and the boxes stacked up neatly against the wall. The Hord Grocery Store was located in downtown Kings Mountain on the upper side of Railroad Street. William Hord, also known as "Bill" or "Papa" Hord, owned and operated the family's store until 1945. In 1950, Hord passed away. Shown in the photograph are, from left to right, Hord's son (also called William); Eb Rhodes, the chief of police for the City of Kings Mountain; and Bill Hord. A boardinghouse was located on the street behind the store. (Courtesy of Martha Goforth.)

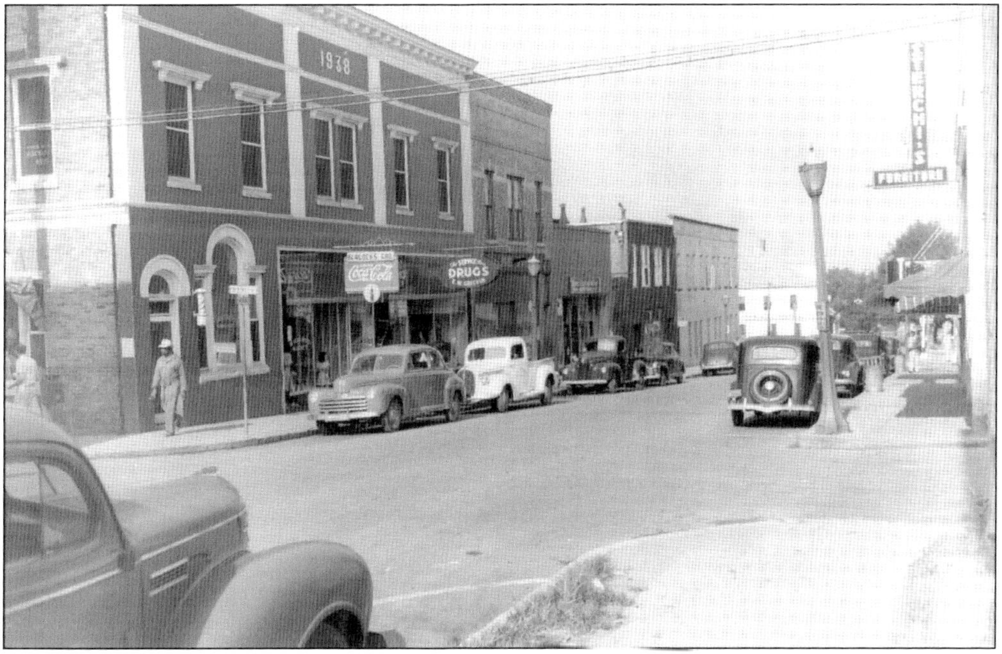

The 1950s-era Mountain Street was a showcase for the town's prosperity. A hub for the city's business activity, the downtown area flourished due to the railroads and textile mills. While many storefronts had been established prior to the town's inception in 1874, others developed because of the economic growth brought about after World War II.

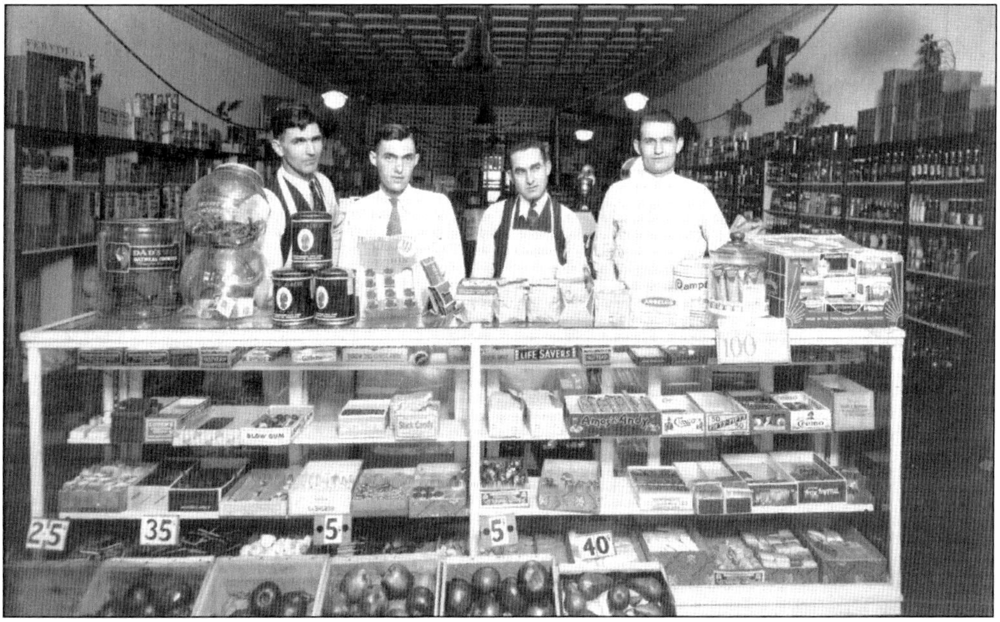

As the textile mills grew in size and operation, so did the downtown area of Kings Mountain. This photograph shows the interior of the Falls Store. Similar to other general stores in the area, the Falls Store supplied the community with items like canned goods, fresh fruit, and other necessities. Standing behind the counter are, from left to right, Lannie Dettmar, two unidentified men, and Rufus Mitcham.

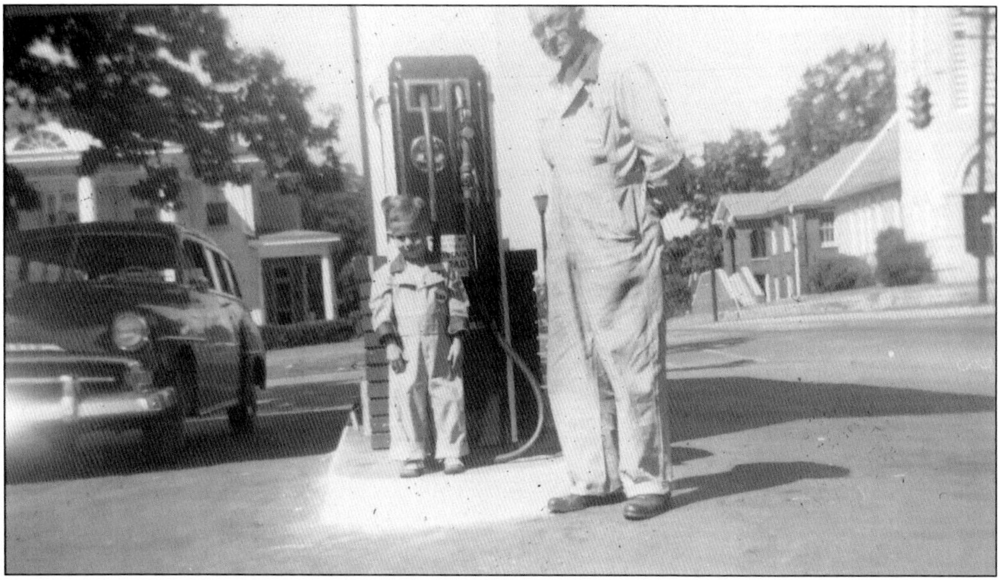

McGill's Service Station opened during the 1920s and served the city of Kings Mountain for 50 years. Pictured from left to right are five-year-old Jeff Mauney and Fuller McGill. Taken in October 1954, the photograph shows Mauney and McGill wearing matching Esso uniforms, as they were standard during the years McGill's Service Station was in operation.

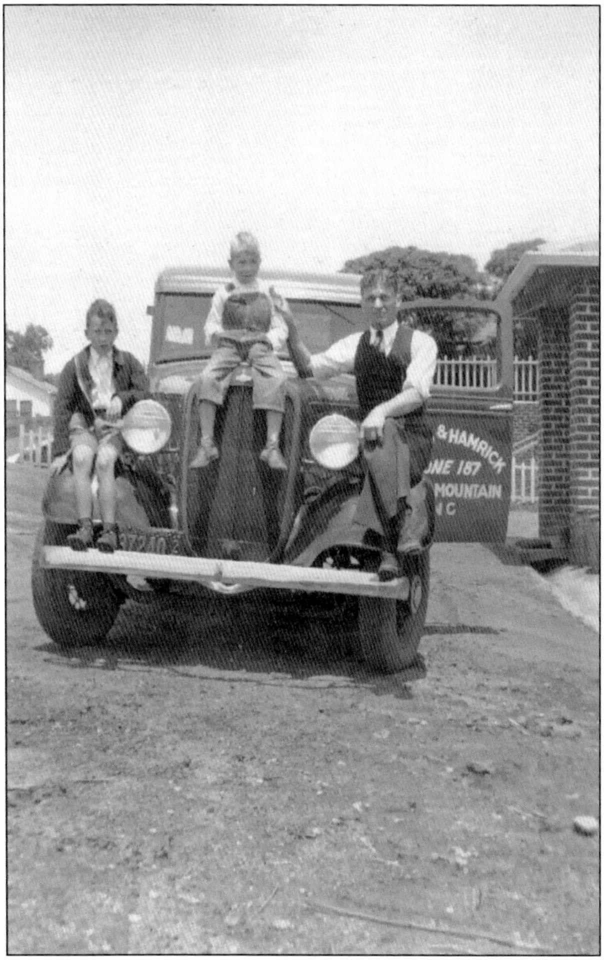

Parked outside the house of Glee A. Bridges on West Gold Street is the delivery truck for the Bridges and Hamrick Hardware Store. Glee A. Bridges owned the store with David Hamrick. In the 1950s, the business changed its name to Bridges Hardware after Glee's sons took over operations. Shown in the photograph from left to right are J.C. Bridges, Glee E. Bridges, and David Hamrick. (Courtesy of Norma H. Drewery.)

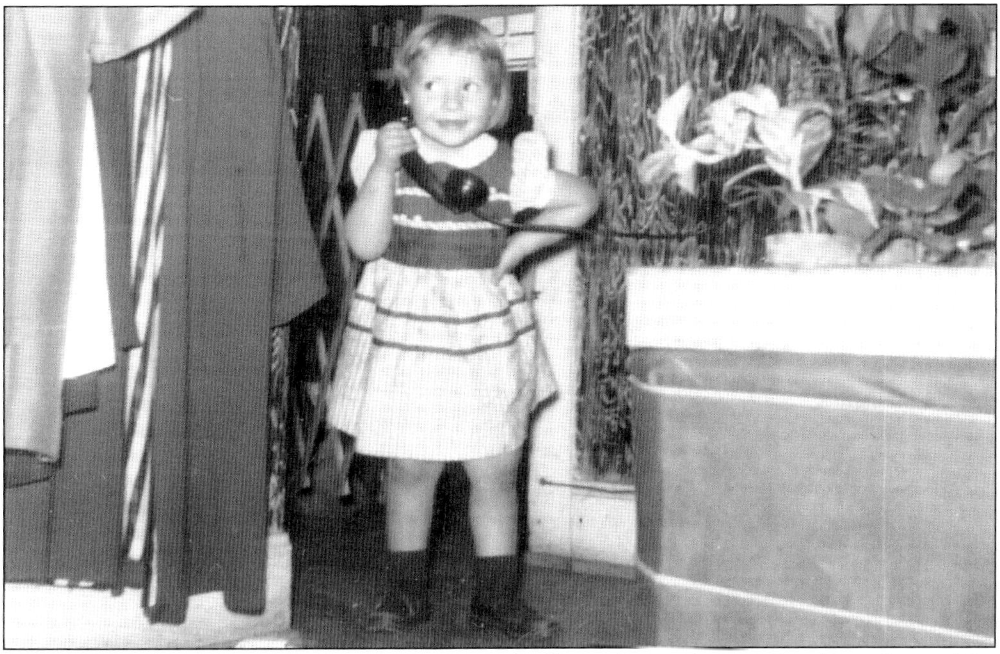

In February 1946, Grace and Selma Allen opened Allen's Flower Shop on East King Street. The business was operated by the two sisters and eventually with their husbands, until it was sold to Selma's daughter Cindy in 1989. This 1950s photograph shows Selma's daughter Rita Crawford as she answers the telephone for the flower shop. (Courtesy of Jane Talbert.)

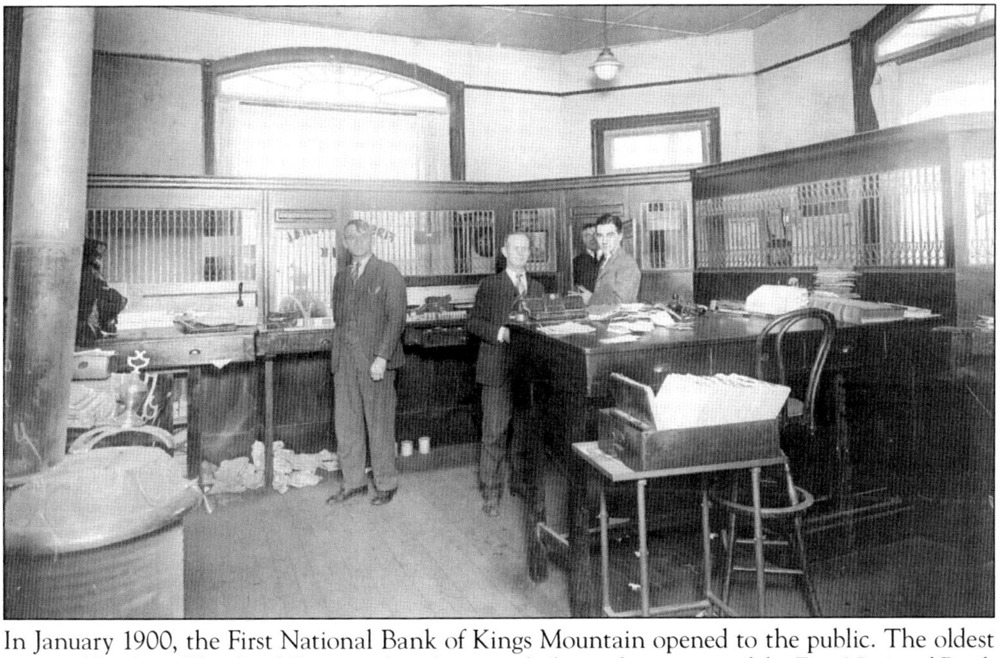

In January 1900, the First National Bank of Kings Mountain opened to the public. The oldest national bank in Cleveland County, this photograph shows the interior of the First National Bank when it was located at the corner of Battleground Avenue and West Mountain Street. Shown in the photograph are, from left to right, Wiley H. McGinnis, R. Lawrence Mauney, J.M. McGinnis, and an unidentified man. (Courtesy of Jeff Mauney.)

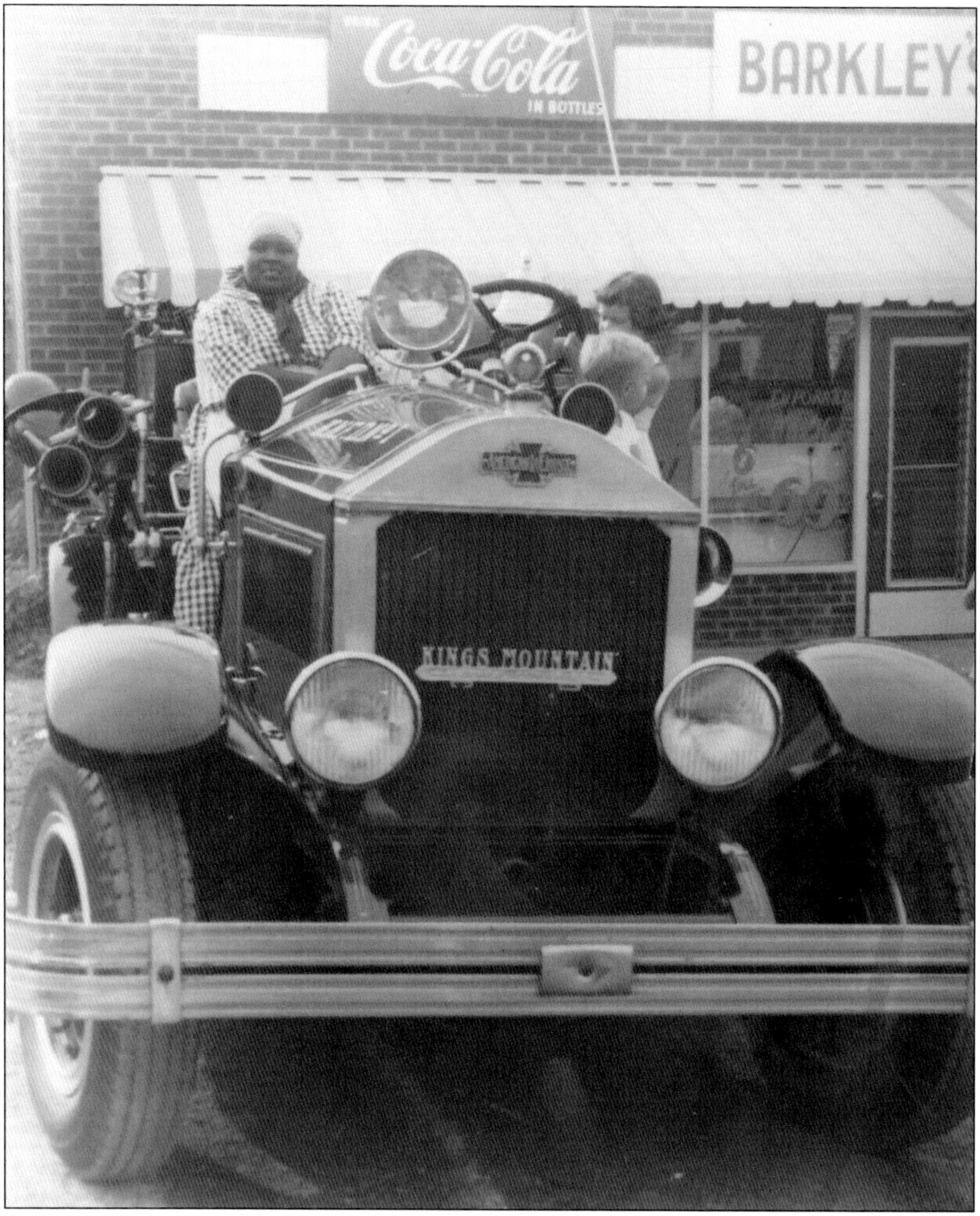

At the grand opening of Barkley's Food Services, which was located on York Road, the character Aunt Jemima from the Quaker Oats Company pancake flour and syrup advertisements was hired for the store's promotional event. During the event, customers could sit in the city's fire truck with Aunt Jemima and have their picture taken. (Courtesy of the Kings Mountain Fire Museum.)

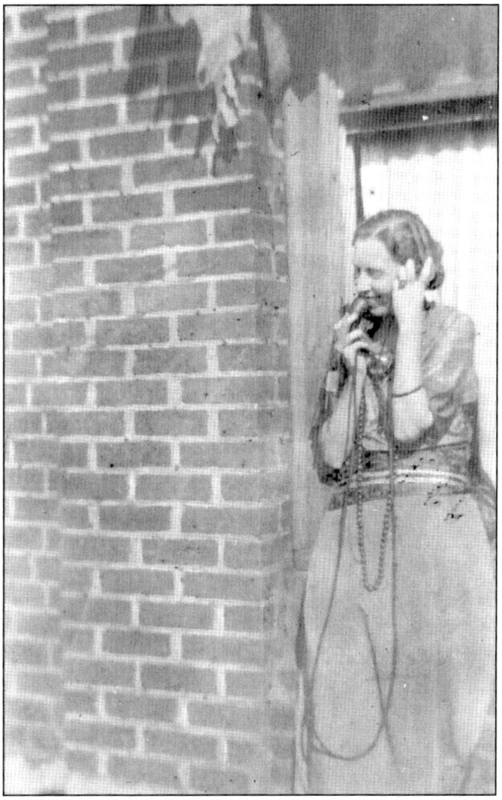

Ellen B. Falls was the chief operator for the Piedmont Telephone and Telegraph Company. The company was sold in January 1927, and its name was changed to the Southern Bell Telephone and Telegraph. In March 1950, the company converted to a dial system and, by the middle of the decade, had acquired and operated exchanges throughout Cleveland County. Taken in 1923, this photograph shows Ellen standing on the balcony of the building located on the corner of Mountain and Cherokee Streets. In 1922, Ellen Falls received a letter (seen below) and pin commending her for five years of service with the company. (Both, courtesy of Lydia Jane Edwards.)

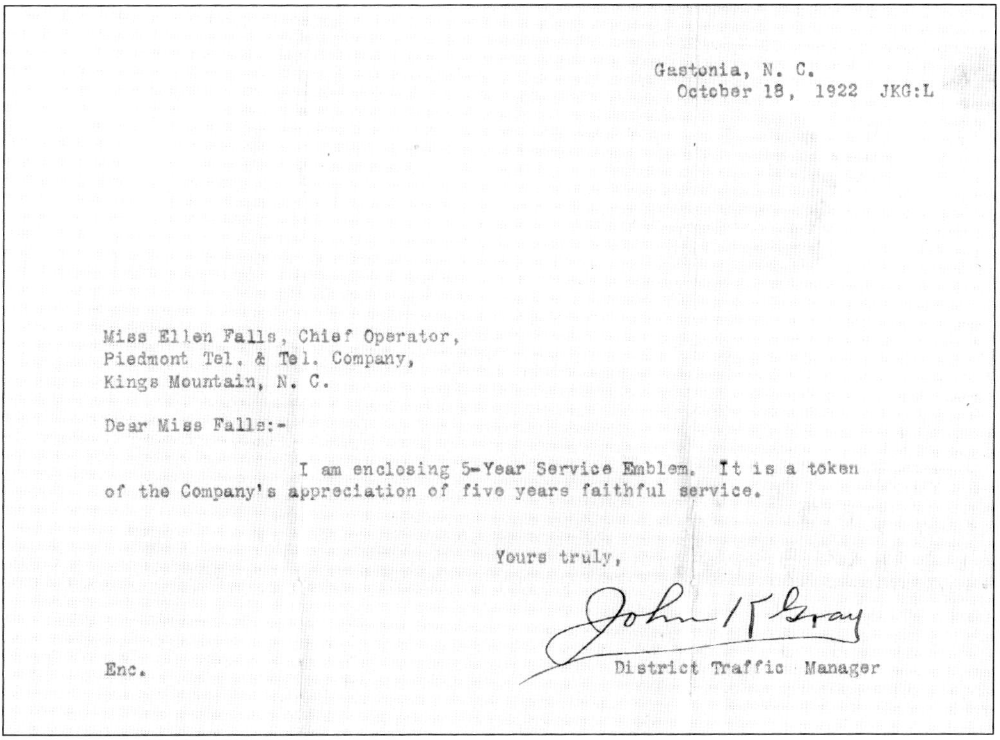

Gastonia, N. C.
October 18, 1922 JKG:L

Miss Ellen Falls, Chief Operator,
Piedmont Tel. & Tel. Company,
Kings Mountain, N. C.

Dear Miss Falls:-

I am enclosing 5-Year Service Emblem. It is a token of the Company's appreciation of five years faithful service.

Yours truly,

John K Gray

District Traffic Manager

Enc.

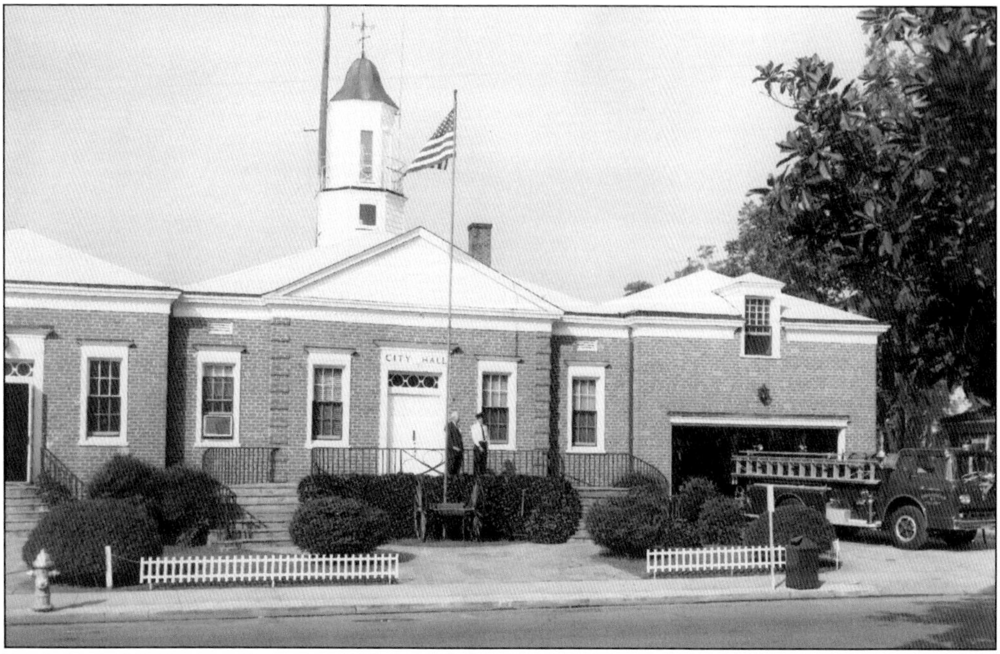

Built for $43,000, Kings Mountain City Hall found a home in this structure completed in 1937 at the corner of Piedmont Avenue and East Mountain Street. The building provided space for the recently formed fire department and library. Taken during the 1950s, this photograph shows Mayor Glee Bridges and fire chief Pat Tignor standing on the front steps. The building was eventually demolished in order to construct a new police station on this site.

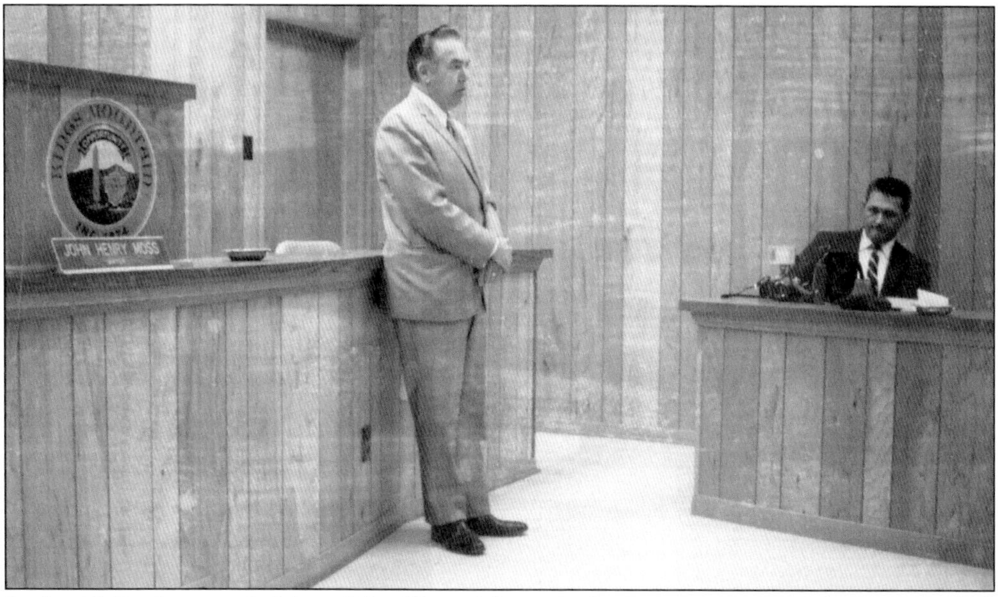

In this 1960s photograph, Mayor John Henry Moss presides over a meeting in the 1937 city hall council chambers while Jim McDaniel, the city's finance director, sits off to the right. John Henry Moss was first elected mayor of Kings Mountain in 1965 and served in office for 22 years. During that time, Moss successfully upgraded the city's water systems. (Courtesy of Kings Mountain Fire Museum.)

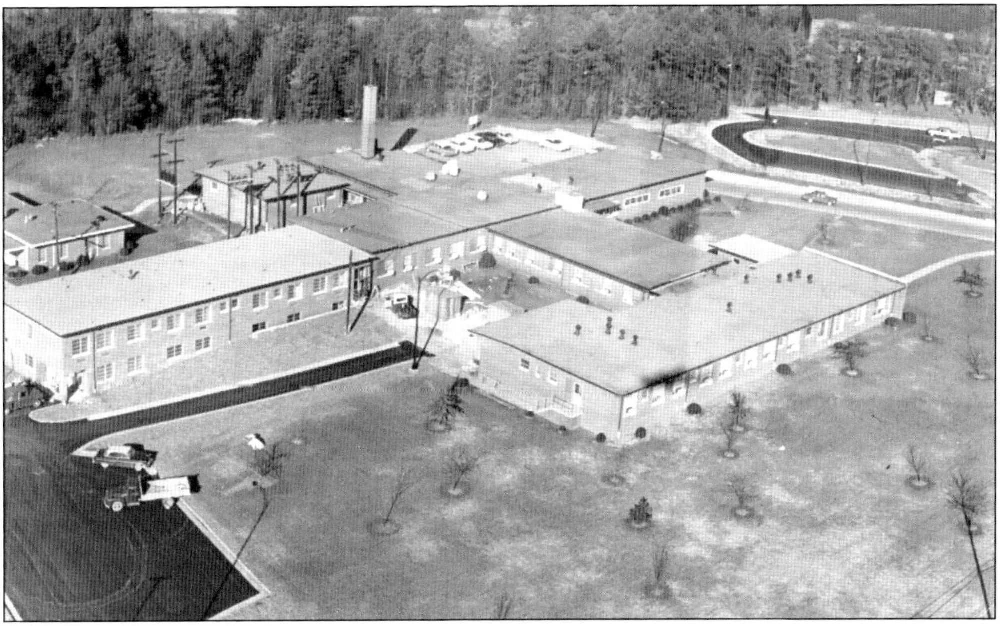

In April 1951, the Kings Mountain Hospital opened on King Street. Lottie Goforth, after her death in 1942, had bequeathed over $30,000 toward the construction of a hospital in Kings Mountain. These funds were the catalyst needed to construct the facility, along with the expansion of the Shelby Hospital. This funding was due to the enactment of the 1945 Hill-Burton Bill by Congress. Within the first five years of operation, the hospital grew from 24 to 50 beds.

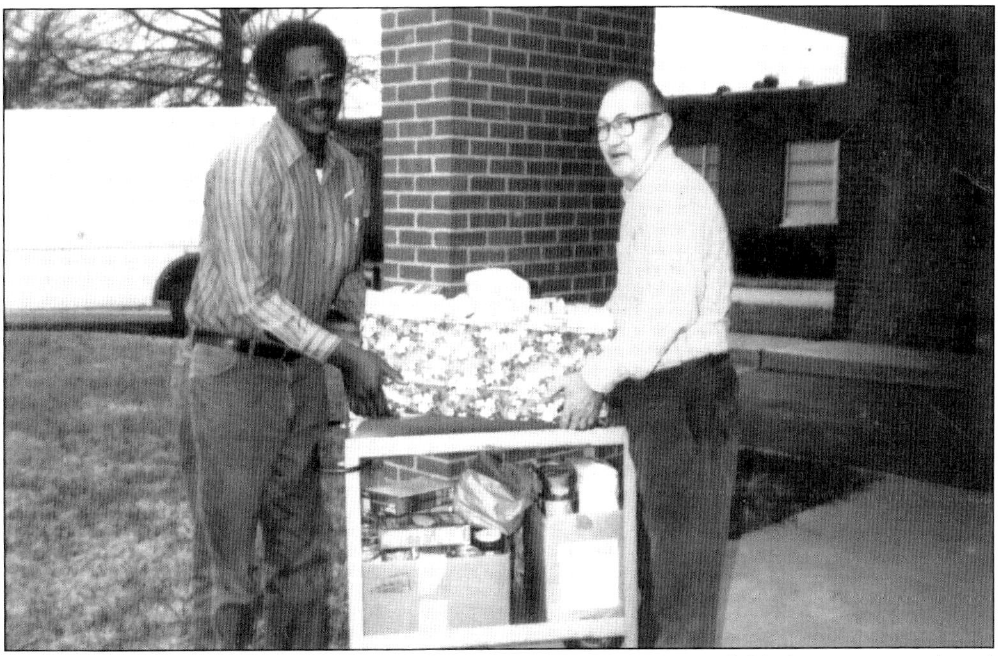

For 35 years, Lewis Curry Jr. (left) worked at Kings Mountain Hospital. He began as a cook and in 1954 became the hospital's maintenance chief. Known for his generous personality, Curry was helpful to the very end, seen here assisting a coworker in transporting supplies for his own retirement party. (Courtesy of Robert Curry.)

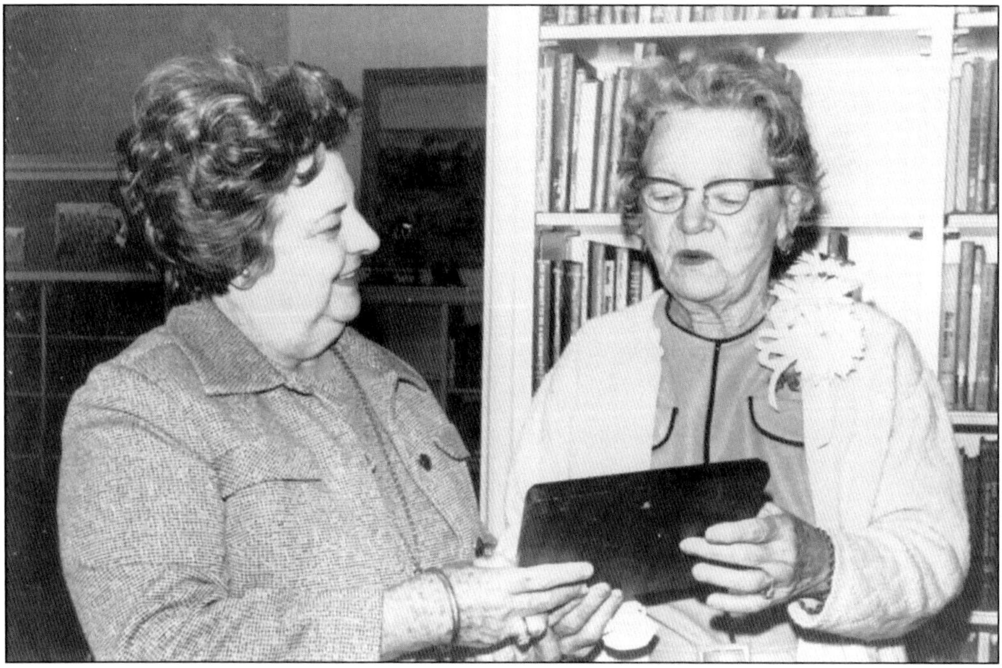

Laura Houser presents Willie Dilling with a service certificate at her retirement. Willie Dilling served as librarian at the Mauney Memorial Library between 1947 and 1972. (Courtesy of Jacob S. Mauney Memorial Library.)

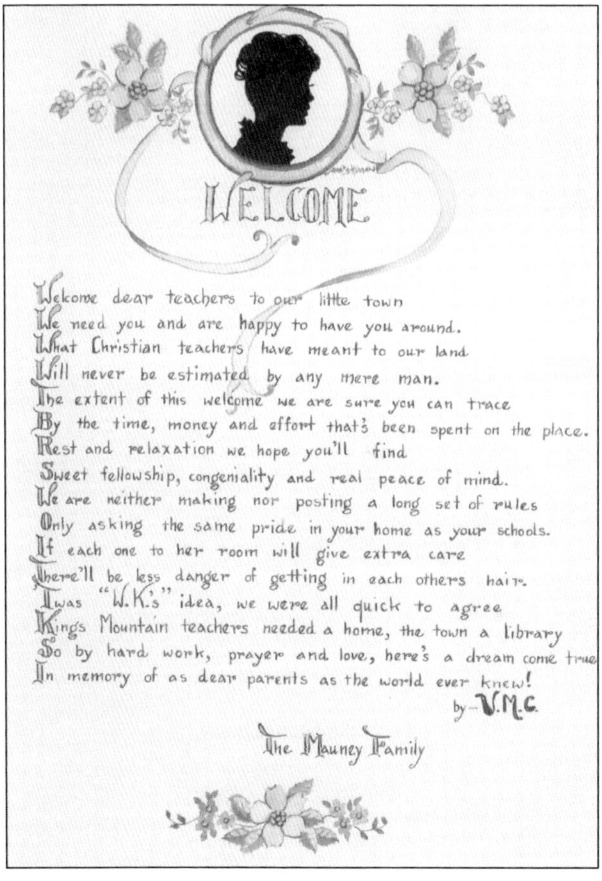

WELCOME

Welcome dear teachers to our little town
We need you and are happy to have you around.
What Christian teachers have meant to our land
Will never be estimated by any mere man.
The extent of this welcome we are sure you can trace
By the time, money and effort that's been spent on the place.
Rest and relaxation we hope you'll find
Sweet fellowship, congeniality and real peace of mind.
We are neither making nor posting a long set of rules
Only asking the same pride in your home as your schools.
If each one to her room will give extra care
There'll be less danger of getting in each others hair.
Twas "W.K.'s" idea, we were all quick to agree
Kings Mountain teachers needed a home, the town a library
So by hard work, prayer and love, here's a dream come true
In memory of as dear parents as the world ever knew!

by—V.M.C.

The Mauney Family

In 1947, the Mauney family gave the 1923 Hord Mansion to the City of Kings Mountain as a home for the Kings Mountain Library, formed 10 years earlier. The library occupied the front two rooms of the house, while the upstairs housed a teacherage for unmarried teachers who moved to the Kings Mountain area. Bertie Hughes Campbell was the town's first librarian, and her salary was paid with a Works Progress Administration grant. Rent money from the teacherage was used to pay the librarian's salary and to buy books. The poem and watercolor drawing was created to welcome teachers to the town. (Courtesy of Jacob S. Mauney Memorial Library.)

Two

WORSHIP

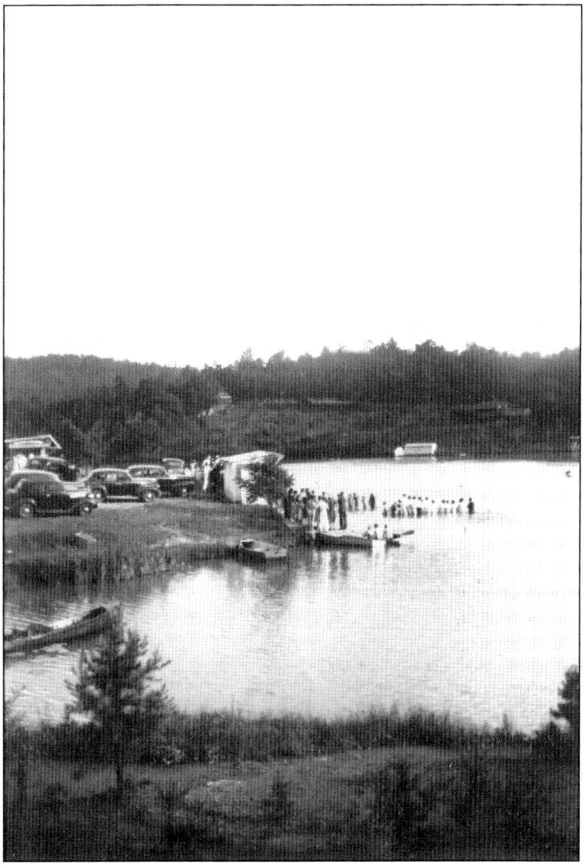

Baptism by immersion is a central part of the Baptist religion. The event is symbolic of baptism as detailed in the Bible. This photograph shows such a baptism at Lake Montonia in 1940. The bathhouse, or dressing room, was located in the building next to the water to provide private areas in which the newly baptized could change their clothes. (Courtesy of Mary Lewis Nantz.)

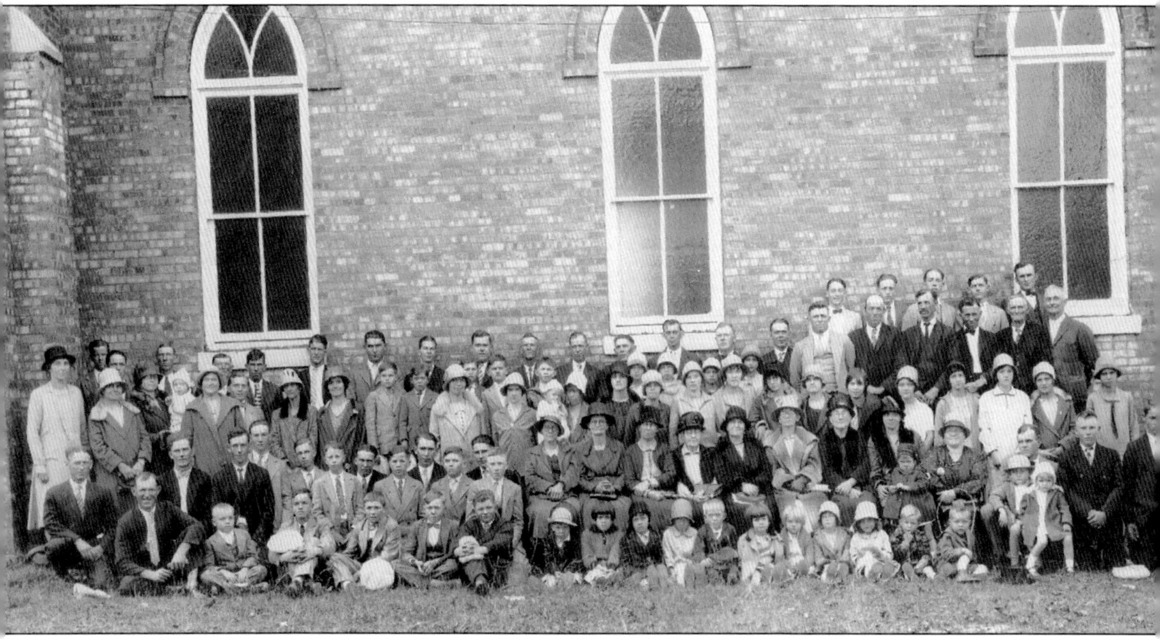

According to oral tradition, El Bethel United Methodist Church predates the city of Kings Mountain. The church began in 1812, when Methodist missionaries visited the area. During the first 20 years, members of the church met under a brush arbor or in individual homes. In 1832, the first church building was constructed on two acres of land donated by Samuel Collins. As the congregation increased in size, the need for a larger worship space became apparent. In 1875, Dr. J.W. Tracy purchased land on the east side of the property for the construction of a new church building. This building served the congregation until 1912, when it was replaced by a brick structure. The 1912 brick church is still in use today, having been enhanced over the years with the addition of a Sunday school unit (1931), a parsonage (1950s), an education building and fellowship hall (1960s), and a sanctuary renovation (1979). This 1927 photograph, titled "Homecoming Congressional Portrait," shows congregation members posing next to the church's side wall. (Courtesy of El Bethel United Methodist Church.)

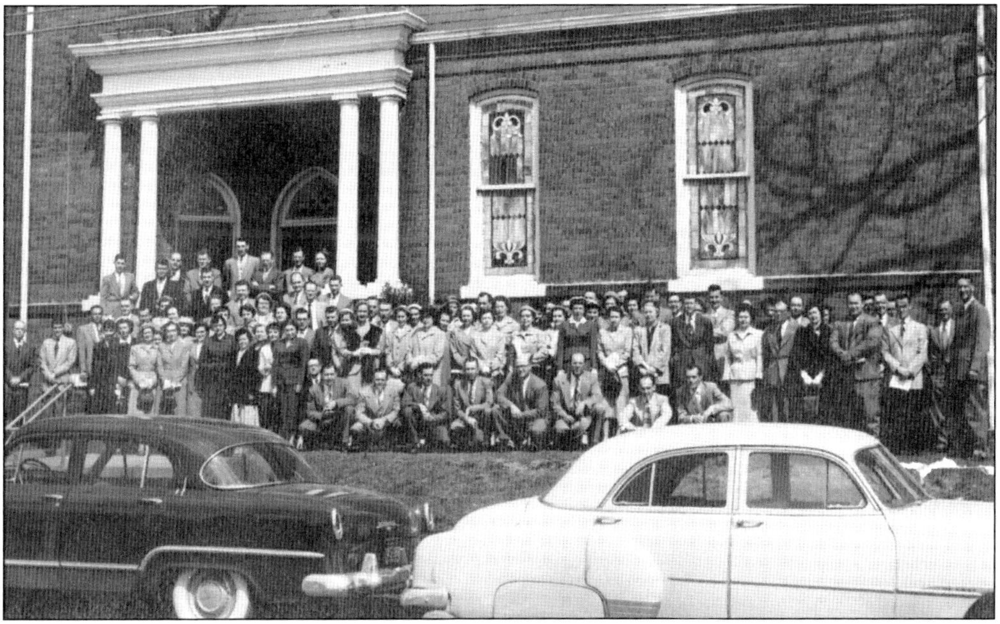

The history of Central United Methodist Church dates to the same year the city of Kings Mountain was established. In 1874, four families, new to the area, decided to organize a Methodist Church closer to their homes. This image lists the names of those members who participated in the 1940s adult fellowship class. (Courtesy of the *Kings Mountain Herald* and Central United Methodist Church.)

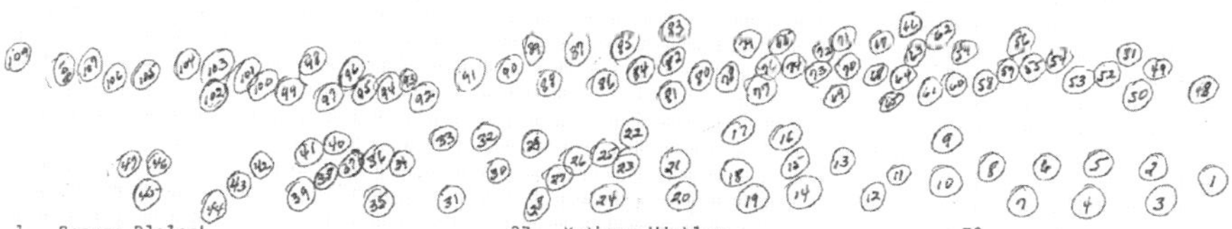

ADULT FELLOWSHIP CLASS - 1940's

1. George Blalock
2. "Mud" Poston
3. Arthur Walker
4. Bill Davis
5. Sally Davis
6. Pru Poston
7. Horace Walker
8. David Saunders
9. Edna Ruth Saunders
10. Clemensee McDaniel
11. Vivian Prince
12. Carl Logan
13. Carolyn Payseur
14. Zip Rhea
15. Mae Tignor
16. Margaret Cornwell
17. Ruth Cloninger
18. Bob Allran
19. Baxter Payseur
20. Lynwood Parton
21. George Ware
22. Inez Allen
23. Jim Cloninger
24. Ben Goforth, Jr.
25.
26. Martha Walker
27. Charlie Black
28. Tom Payne
29. Ruth McDaniel
30. C. J. Gault
31.
32. Vera Phifer
33. Eva Payne
34. Belvin Ware
35. Don Parker
36. Ruby Alexander
37. Kathryn Winkler
38. James Throneburg
39. Charles Alexander
40. Nell Parker
41. Lois Murray
42. Willie Patterson
43. Paul Walker
44. Buck Allran
45. Fred Wright, Jr.
46.
47.
48. Mary Grigg
49. Snooks McDaniel
50. Sudie Peele
51. Clinton Jolly
52. Margie McDaniel
53. Louise Blalock
54. Clarence Jolly, Jr.
55. Pink Ware
56.
57.
58. Dorcas Carpenter
59.
60.
61.
62. Sonny Peeler
63. Nancy Suber
64.
65. Grace Blanton
66. Sonny Peeler
67.
68.
69.
70.
71. Bill McDaniel
72. Chas. A. Goforth, Jr.
73.
74. Victoria Logan
75. Gail McDaniel
76. Nell Gault
77. Winnie Fulton
78. Edna Allran
79.
80. Nancy John Ware
81. Margaret Harmon
82.
83. Bill Gantt
84. Vernie Mae Allran
85. Jim Everhart
86. Madge Rhea
87. Meek Carpenter
88. Louise Hullender
89. Sam Howell
90. Neil Hullender
91. Willie Howell
92. Faye Goforth
93.
94. Carolyn Dilling
95. Mildred Wright
96. S. Jean Wright
97. Wilma Byers
98. Marvin Byers
99. Dot Hoke
100.
101. Ted Gamble
102. Charles Harrill
103.
104. Mary Black
105.
106.
107. Hilliard Black
108. Boyer Murray

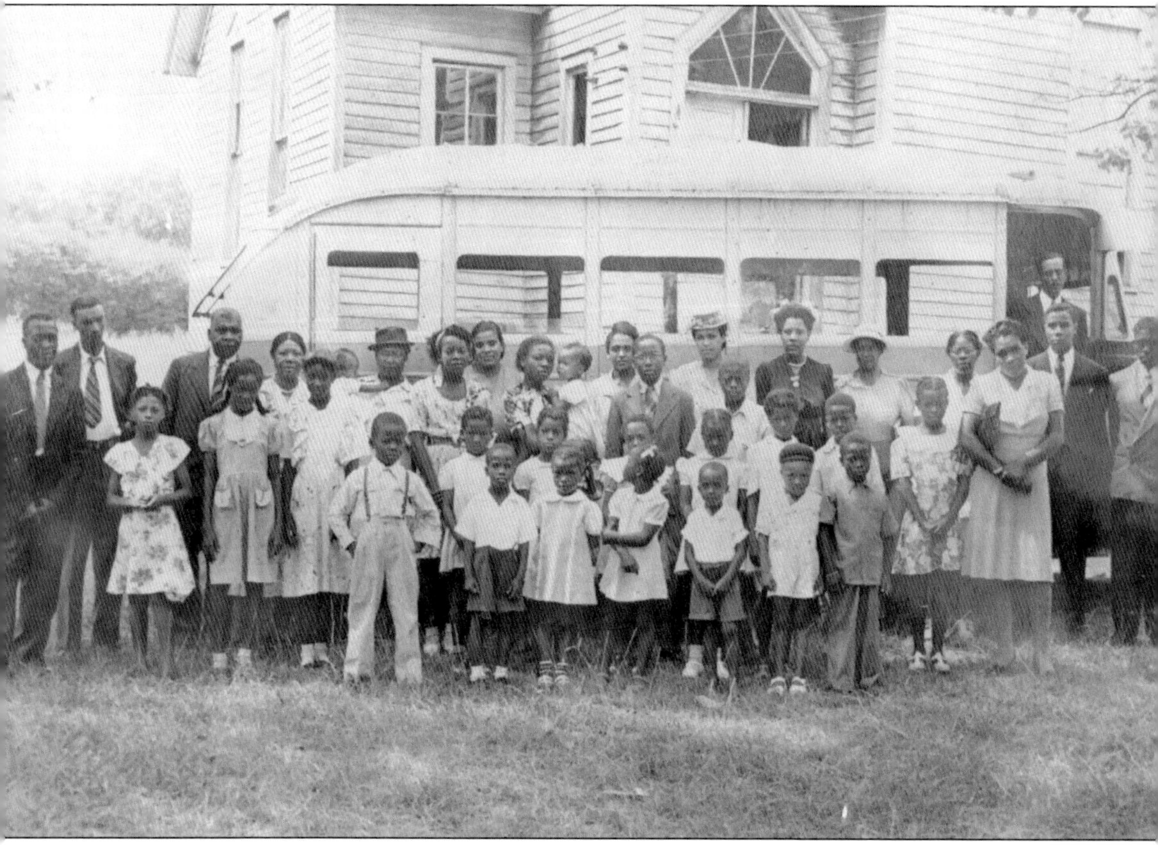

In 1913, Daisy Smith, along with the Bryant, Gamble, and Mayse families, founded St. Paul United Methodist Church. Having been members of Galilee Methodist Church, the group felt there was a need within the city limits for a Methodist church for the black community. A sanctuary was built on Ridge Street, where it served the congregation until 1955, when a block church was erected on Cansler Street. Over the years, improvements were made to the church, including the addition of brick walls and a basement. In 1979, construction began on a new brick and stone church, which was completed in 1980. Linda Bell (standing in front with her head turned) and O.V. Ellis Sr. (standing to the far left in the black suit) are among those shown in front of the church when it was on Ridge Street. (Courtesy of Linda and Belena Bell.)

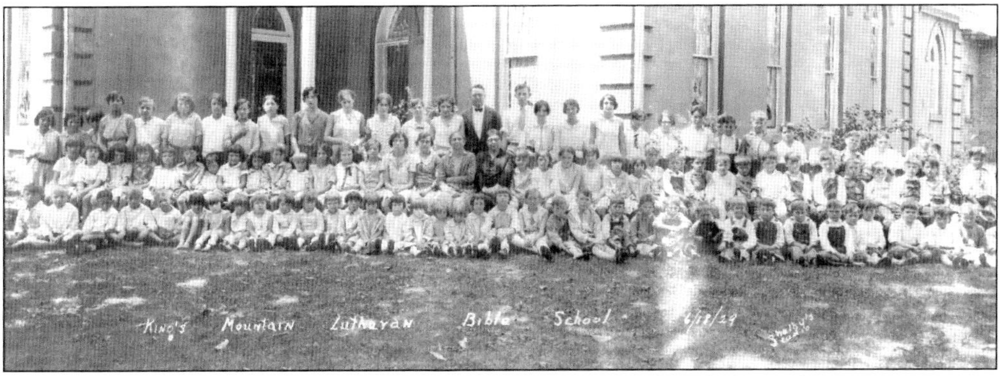

This photograph taken in front of the St. Matthew's Lutheran Church shows the Kings Mountain Lutheran Bible School on June 18, 1929. St. Matthew's Lutheran Church received its charter in 1876. Over the years, additional structures were added to the site to assist with worship and community programs. In 1922, St. Matthew's Lutheran Church initiated a Sunday school class for textile mill workers. (Courtesy of Jacqueline Queen.)

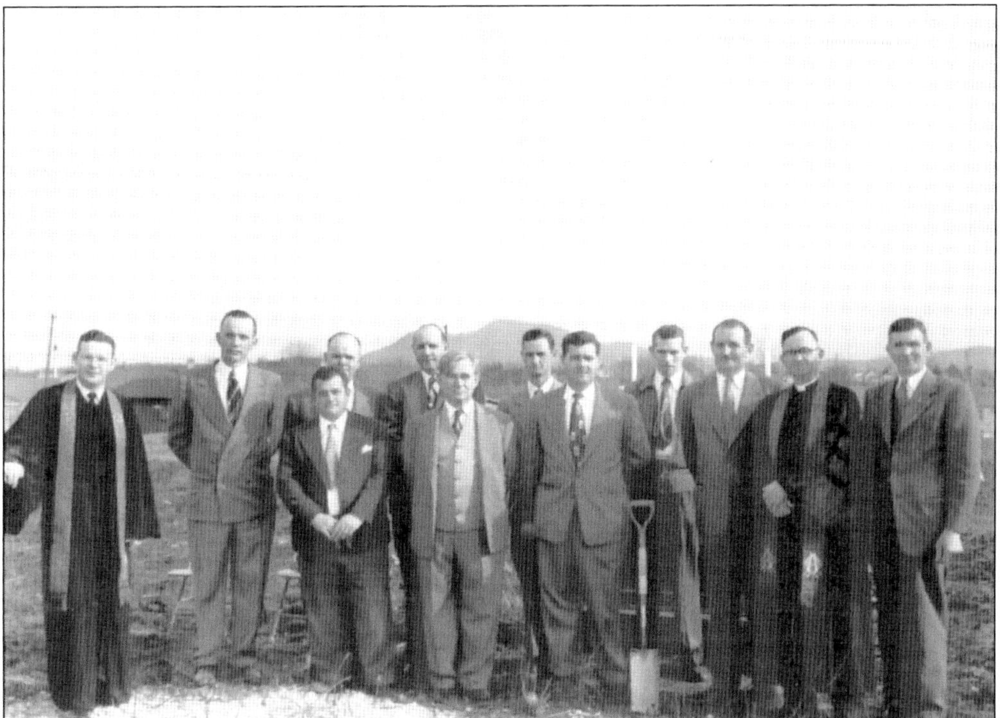

Resurrection Lutheran Church was founded in October 10, 1950, when 11 men from Kings Mountain met at Keeter's Department Store to discuss the idea of forming an Evangelist Lutheran church in the town. The proposal was heard enthusiastically, and four months later, a ground-breaking service was held at the church's present location. (Courtesy of Resurrection Lutheran Church.)

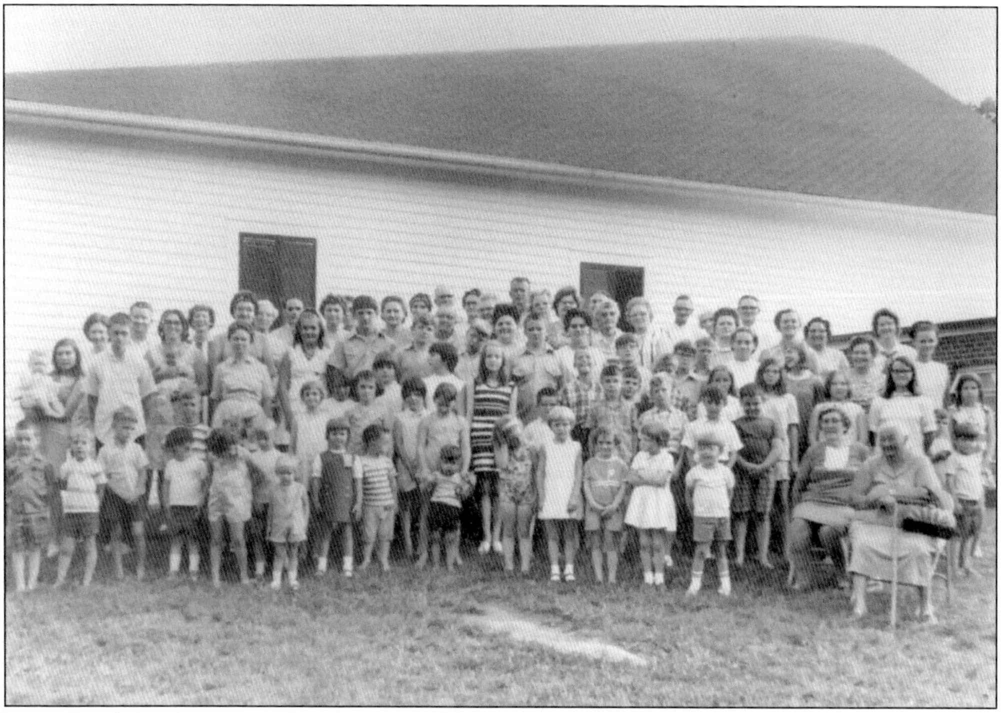

Long Creek Presbyterian Church was established in 1780. This group photograph was taken of the Bible school participants at Long Creek Presbyterian Church during the summer of 1970. The group includes both members of the church as well as individuals from the community who participated in the weeklong event. (Courtesy of Long Creek Presbyterian Church.)

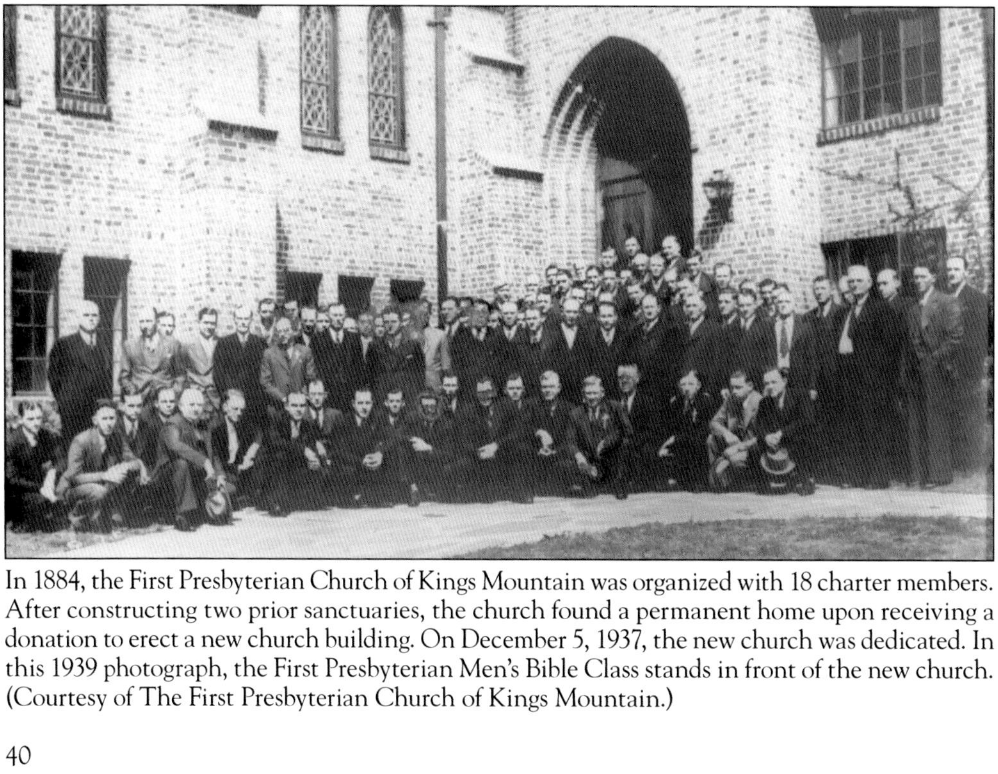

In 1884, the First Presbyterian Church of Kings Mountain was organized with 18 charter members. After constructing two prior sanctuaries, the church found a permanent home upon receiving a donation to erect a new church building. On December 5, 1937, the new church was dedicated. In this 1939 photograph, the First Presbyterian Men's Bible Class stands in front of the new church. (Courtesy of The First Presbyterian Church of Kings Mountain.)

On October 30, 1898, the congregation of Boyce Memorial Associate Reformed Presbyterian Church dedicated a new building on King Street and South Piedmont Avenue to replace the wooden structure they had previously used for worship. The church remained in this location, adding a parsonage and Sabbath school building to the property, until 1961. (Courtesy of Broad River Genealogy Society.)

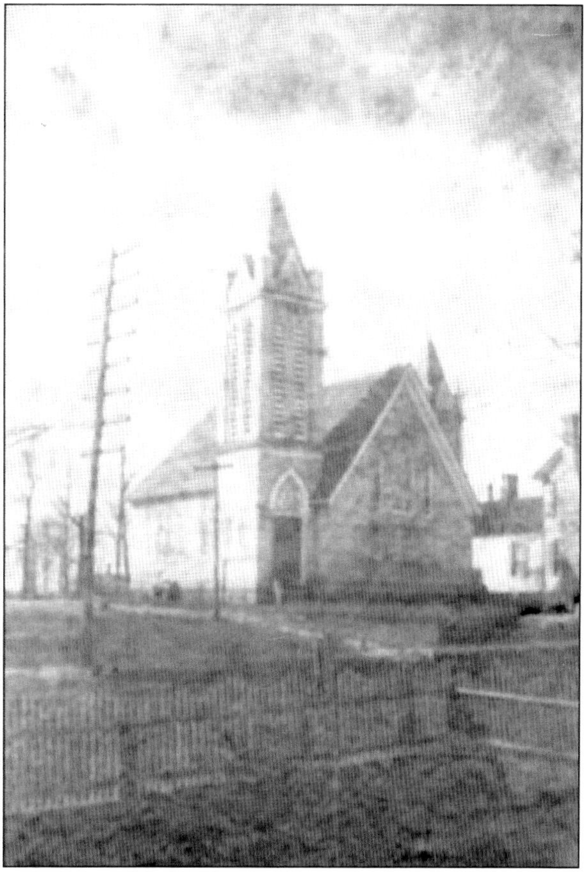

Taken on May 1, 1974, this photograph shows Mayor John Henry Moss speaking at the groundbreaking ceremony for the new Boyce Memorial Associate Reformed Presbyterian Church sanctuary on Edgemont Drive. The building was dedicated five months later. Also in the photograph are Rev. Charles Edward, Elizabeth Gamble at the piano, and Bob Cashion seated in the far right of the image.

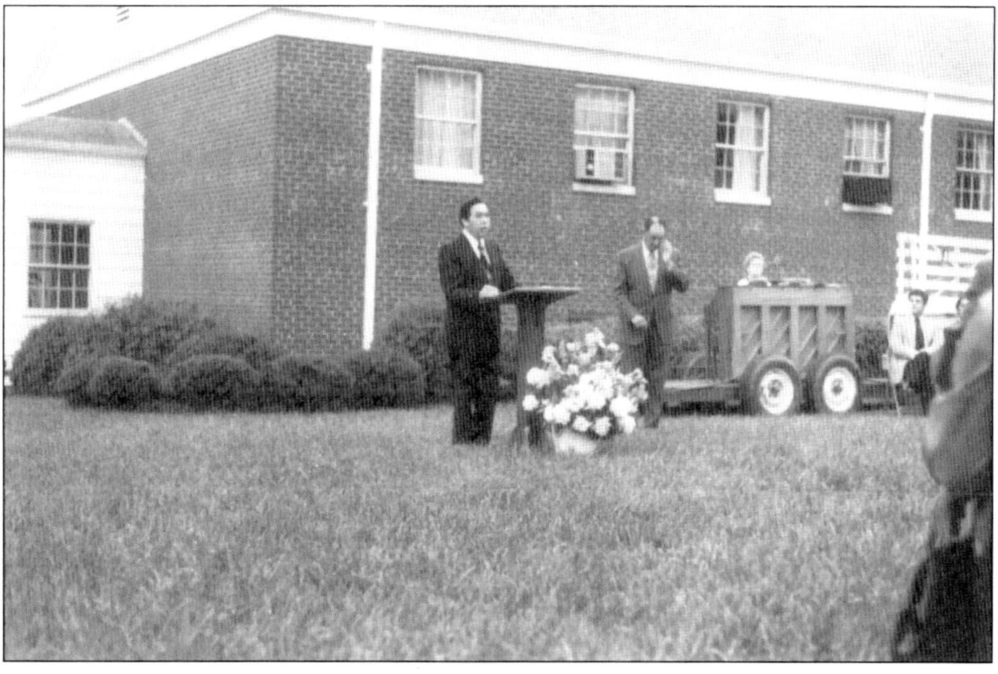

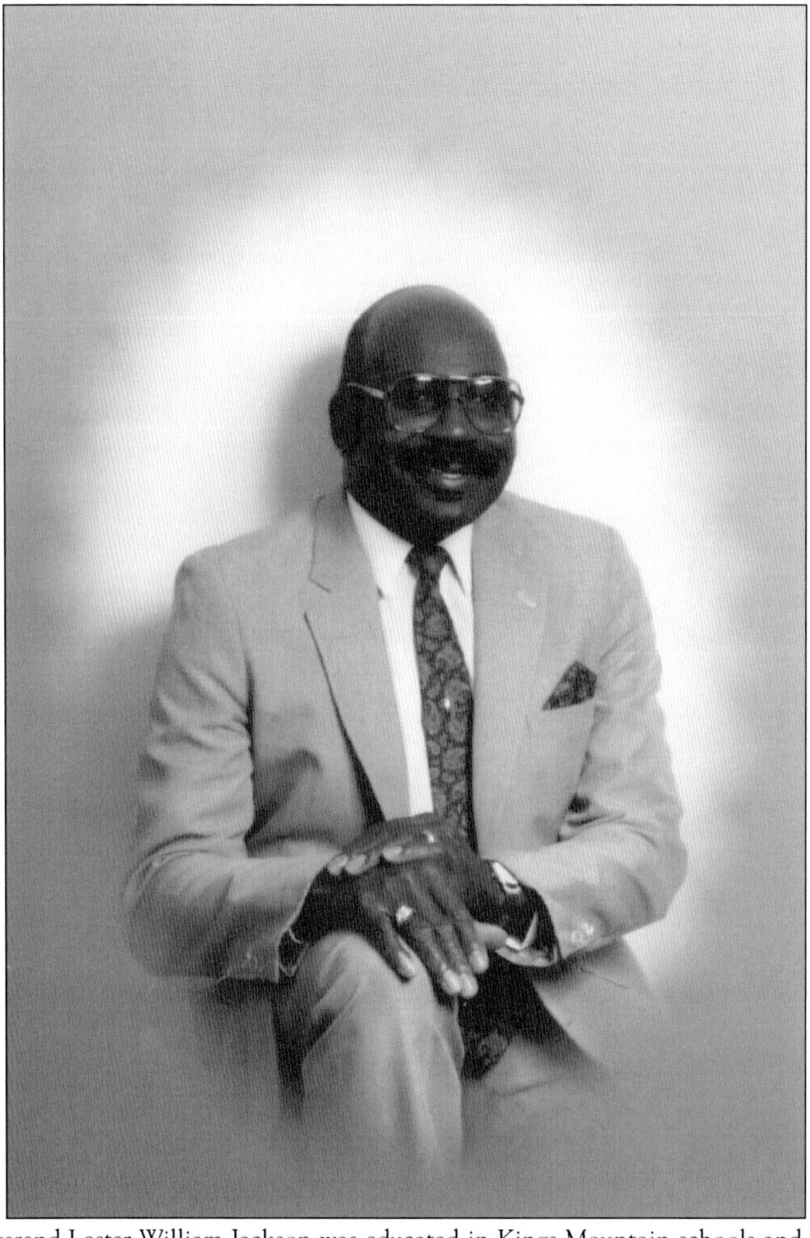

The Reverend Lester William Jackson was educated in Kings Mountain schools and is a 1957 graduate of the Davidson School. He has pastored the New Zion Church in Henrietta, North Carolina, for over 35 years. About 1924, the Davidson School began with the collaborative efforts of a cash grant from the Rosenwald Foundation. The cooperation of the black community to build the school and the agreement of the white community to operate it was unusual for its day. The school operated first as a four-room frame structure built on Ridge Street and was known as the Kings Mountain Colored School. Land purchases in 1925 and 1937 allowed the school to expand, and in 1934, Davidson became a high school It operated until 1967. The high school was demolished after 1968, and after desegregation, the remaining elementary school became the Davidson Alternative School, serving middle and high school students from around the county. (Courtesy of Robert Curry.)

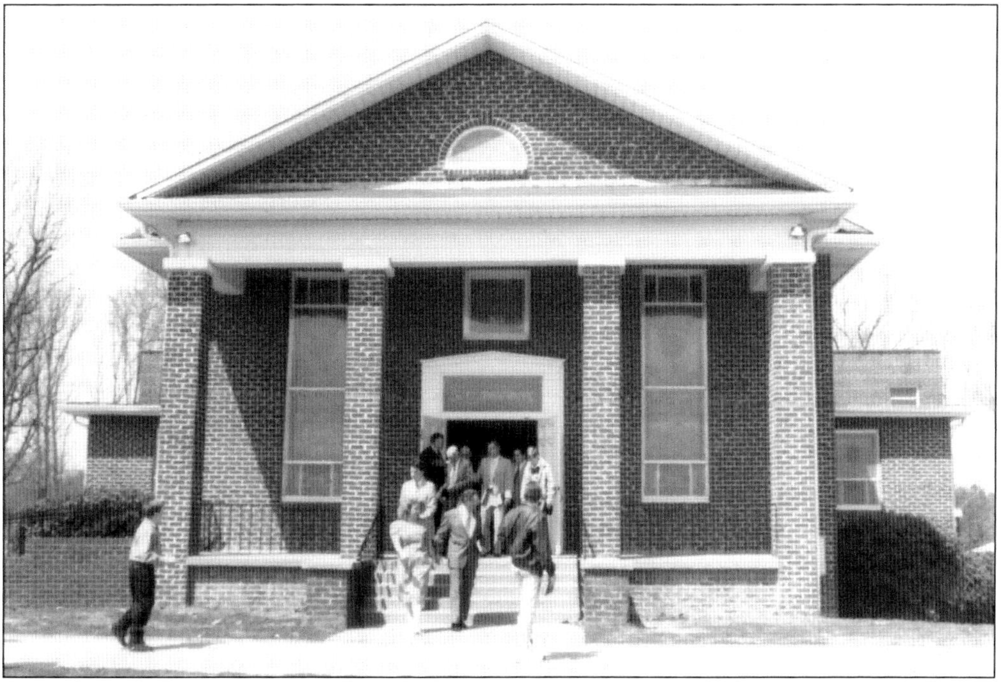

In 1841, Baptists in Kings Mountain sought to have a church near their homes. In order to receive and baptize members, they requested to become an extension of Antioch Baptist Church. Their request was granted, and on July 16, 1842, Bethlehem Baptist Church was officially organized. The congregation worshiped in the frame church until 1928, when construction began on the brick building seen in this photograph. (Courtesy of Margaret Ledford.)

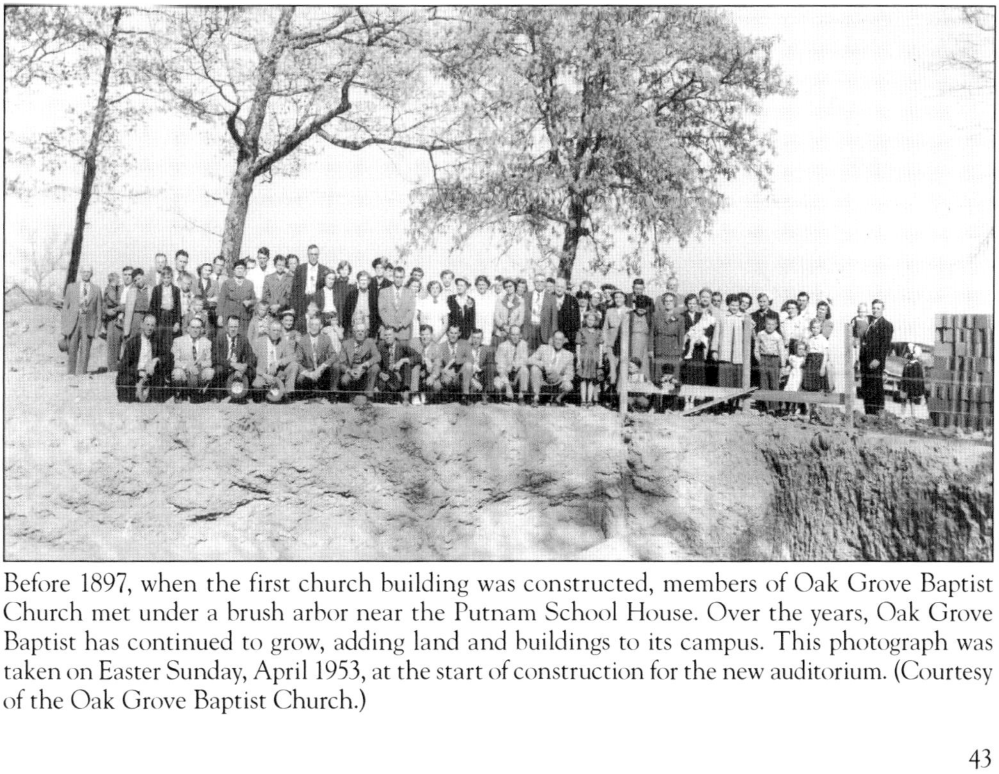

Before 1897, when the first church building was constructed, members of Oak Grove Baptist Church met under a brush arbor near the Putnam School House. Over the years, Oak Grove Baptist has continued to grow, adding land and buildings to its campus. This photograph was taken on Easter Sunday, April 1953, at the start of construction for the new auditorium. (Courtesy of the Oak Grove Baptist Church.)

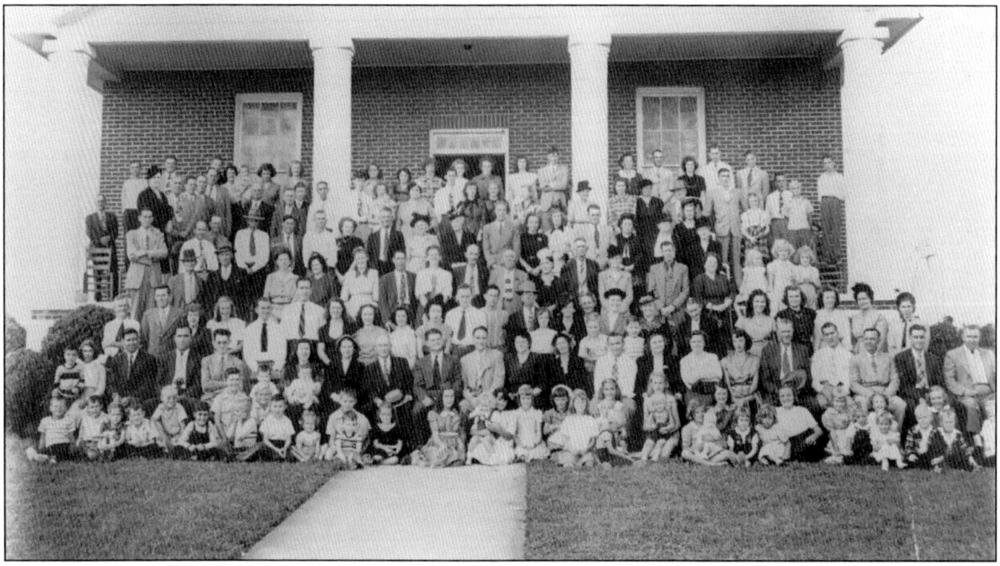

David Baptist Church was organized on October 9, 1938, due to the desire for a Baptist church located near Bethware High School. This 1949 photograph shows members of the congregation. Rev. N.S. Hardin and over 100 other members were present that Sunday for the congregation's portrait. (Courtesy of David Baptist Church.)

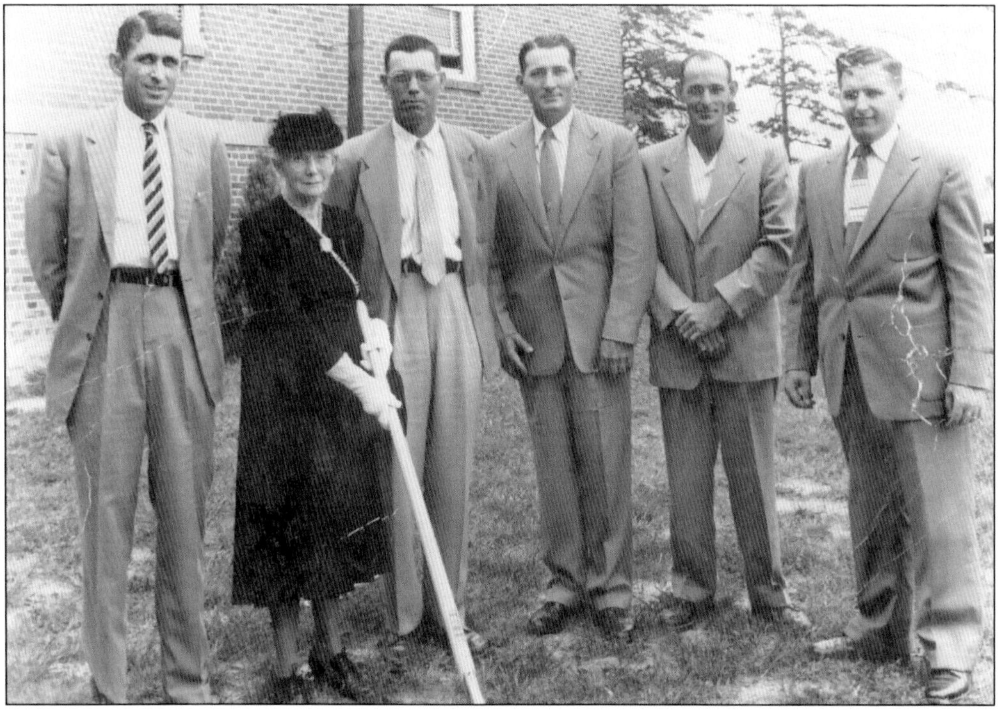

On November 15, 1884, Patterson Grove Baptist Church was established. An educational building was added to the campus in 1955. This photograph of the ground-breaking ceremony for the education building shows, from left to right, Frank Hamrick, Sarah Elizabeth Patterson Falls, Grady Scism, Edwin Moore, Max Putnam, and Rev. Jake Thornburg. (Courtesy of Patterson Grove Baptist Church.)

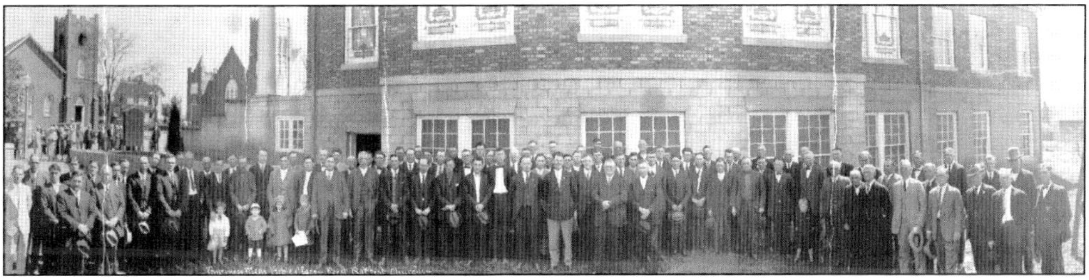

In 1890, the First Baptist Church was established with 36 charter members through the combined efforts of Frances Lucinda Smith Cornwell, Margaret Isabelle Nevitt Kendrick, and Callie Hoke Carpenter. This photograph shows the Baptist Men's Bible Class standing outside the church building. In the background are Central United Methodist and the First Presbyterian Churches. Whitney White is identified as standing at the far right of the photograph. (Courtesy of Steve Sanders.)

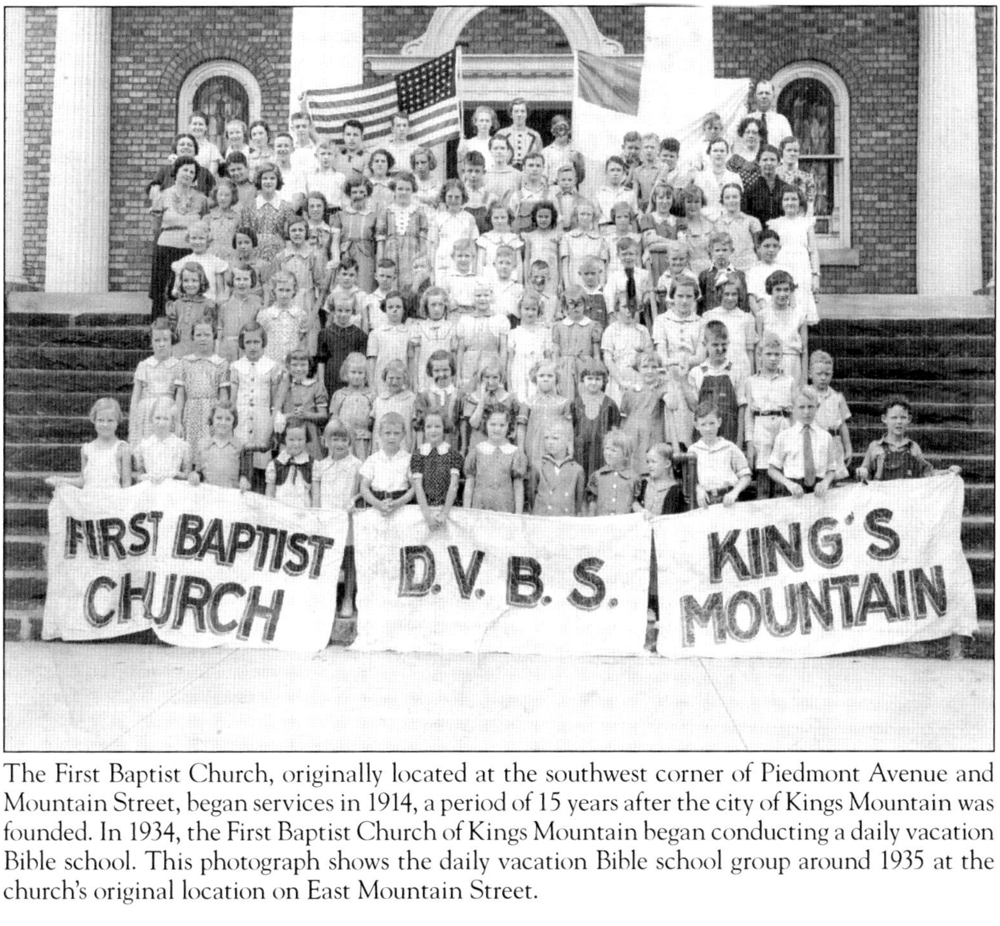

The First Baptist Church, originally located at the southwest corner of Piedmont Avenue and Mountain Street, began services in 1914, a period of 15 years after the city of Kings Mountain was founded. In 1934, the First Baptist Church of Kings Mountain began conducting a daily vacation Bible school. This photograph shows the daily vacation Bible school group around 1935 at the church's original location on East Mountain Street.

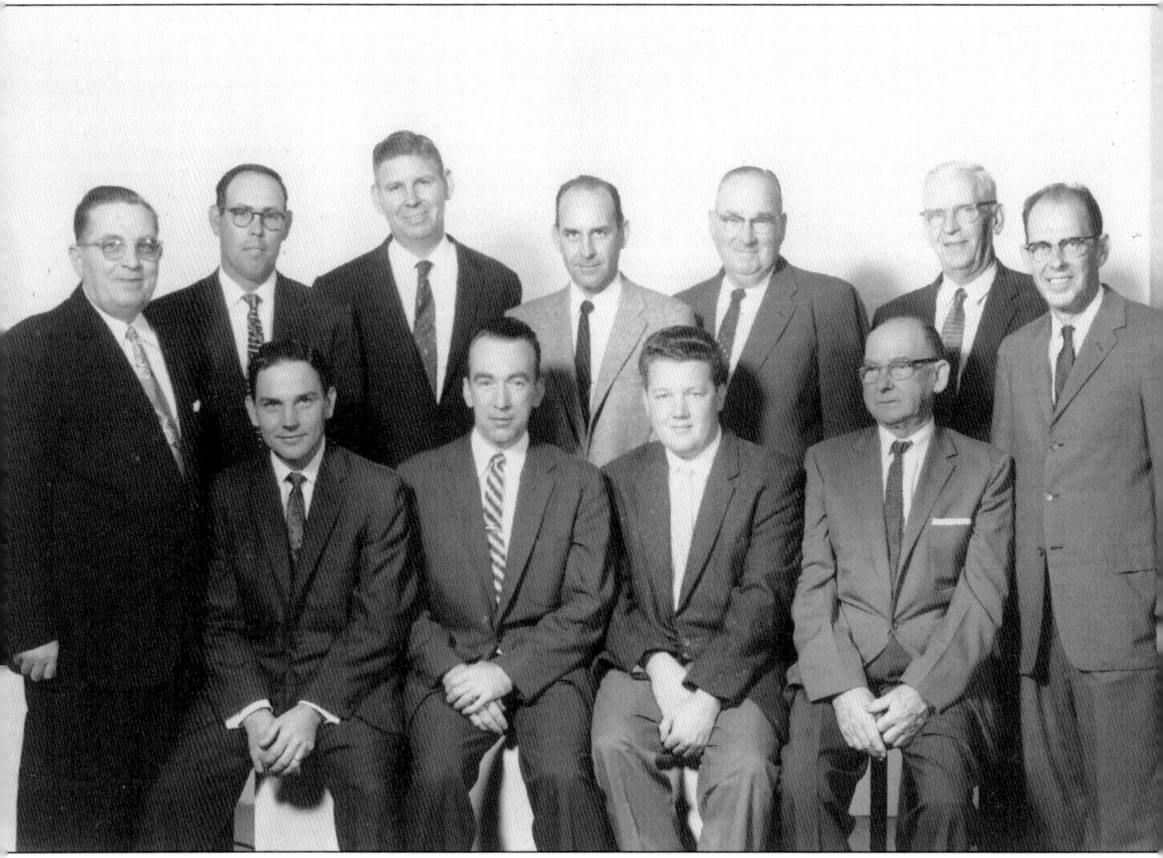

In 1957, members of the First Baptist Church of Kings Mountain decided to relocate from downtown to a new location on Kings Street. Over 200 members of the congregation opted to stay in their current location on Mountain Street and, in doing so, formed the Kings Mountain Baptist Church. In 1959, Rev. William Bumgardner became the first pastor, and the first deacons of the church were elected. Shown in this photograph, they are (seated) Atwood McDaniel Jr., J.C. Bridges, Gene Austin, and J.B. Keeter; (standing) Harold Crawford Sr., Odell Benton, Ollie Harris, Thomas Tindall Sr., W.T. Weir, Bryan Hord, and E.R. Roberts. Over the first year of operation, the congregation worked on updating the 1915 building. Between 1958 and 1959, air-conditioning, along with new paint and lights, were added to the sanctuary. Around the same time, a parsonage was constructed, and new concrete steps were added to the building's entrance. The congregation continued to improve upon the building, adding an elevator after 1978, purchasing land for a parking lot, and undertaking an exterior beautification project. In 1981, the sanctuary was again renovated. (Courtesy of Kings Mountain Baptist Church.)

Three

Live

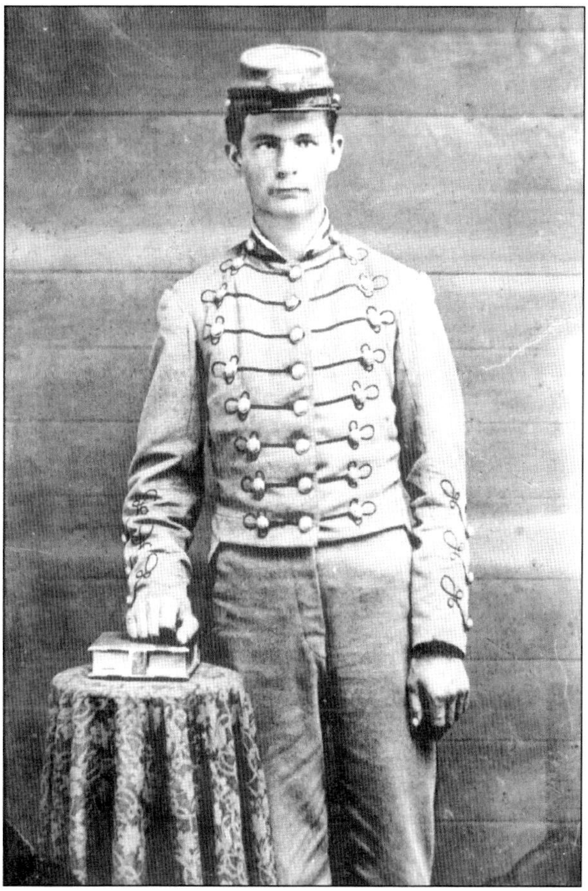

For the young men who came to Capt. William T. Reilly Bell's Military Academy, life consisted of lessons during the week. Boarding in nearby homes, the young men spent their recreational time playing sports on the school grounds. Jacob Quinn, shown wearing his gray Bell Academy uniform, went on to become a prominent lawyer as well as a leader in the church and civic life.

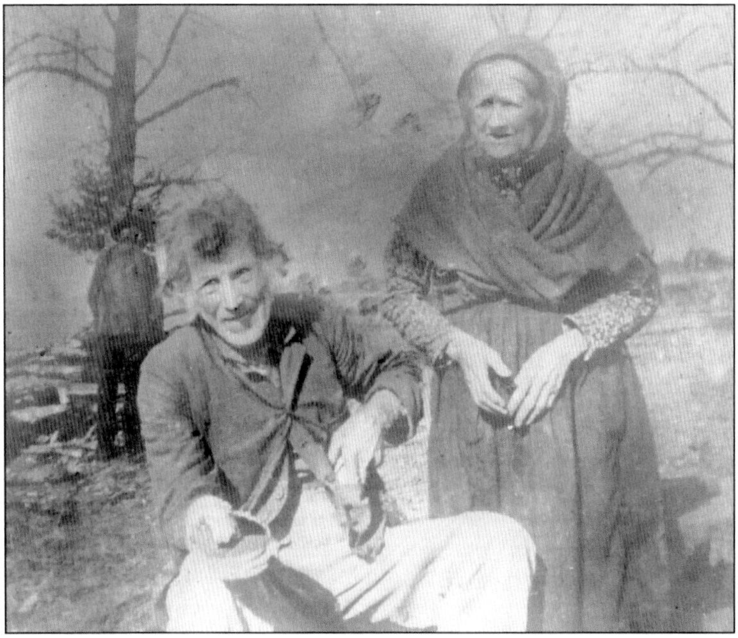

This photograph shows Christopher Hullender and his wife, Rebeca Kiser Hullender, around 1890. Both born in 1812, the Hullenders lived on Cherryville Road in Kings Mountain. The couple had four daughters, two of whom are buried in the "Old Hullender Graveyard." The cemetery was created by the Hullenders due to the lack of a burial ground near their home. (Courtesy of Jane Talbert.)

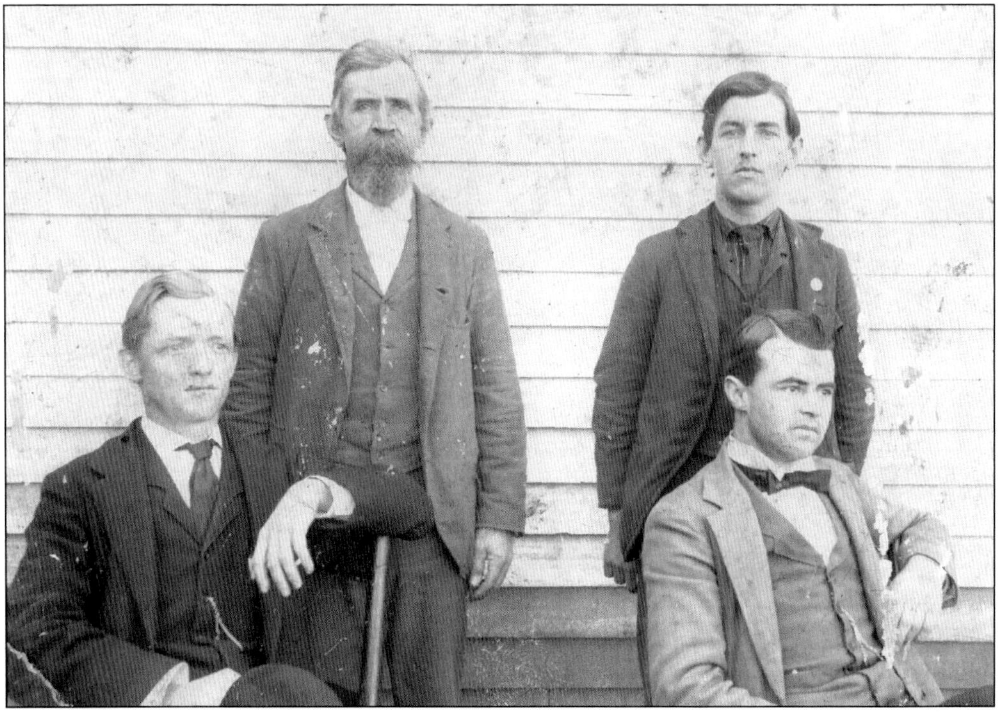

Two early settlers in the town of Kings Mountain were Jacob Simri Mauney (second from left) and Charles Eugene Neisler (left). Also in the photograph are two of Mauney's seven children, John David Mauney (third from left) and Samuel Augustus "Gus" Mauney (right). Jacob Mauney, along with others, organized the Kings Mountain Manufacturing Company in 1888 where C.E. Neisler served as superintendent and Gus Mauney worked as the bookkeeper. (Courtesy of Neisler Brothers, Inc.)

These wedding portraits commemorate the marriage of Sarah (Sadie) Elizabeth Fisher of Concord, North Carolina, to Dorris Carl Mauney of Kings Mountain, North Carolina, on September 1, 1904. The Mauneys had three children and lived in Kings Mountain until their deaths (Sadie's in June 1952 and Dorris's in October 1956). Dorris Mauney managed the Mauney Brothers Store upon returning from school at the Atlanta Business College. In 1918, Mauney formed a partnership with Larkin A. Kiser, and together the two men founded the Sadie Cotton Mill. Sadie and Dorris Mauney attended St. Matthew's Lutheran Church. Sadie Mauney, also active in civic life, was a member of the Kings Mountain Woman's Club, the Daughters of the American Revolution, Daughters of the American Colonists, and Daughters of the Confederacy. In 1913, she organized the Thursday Afternoon Book Club with Cora Rhyne.

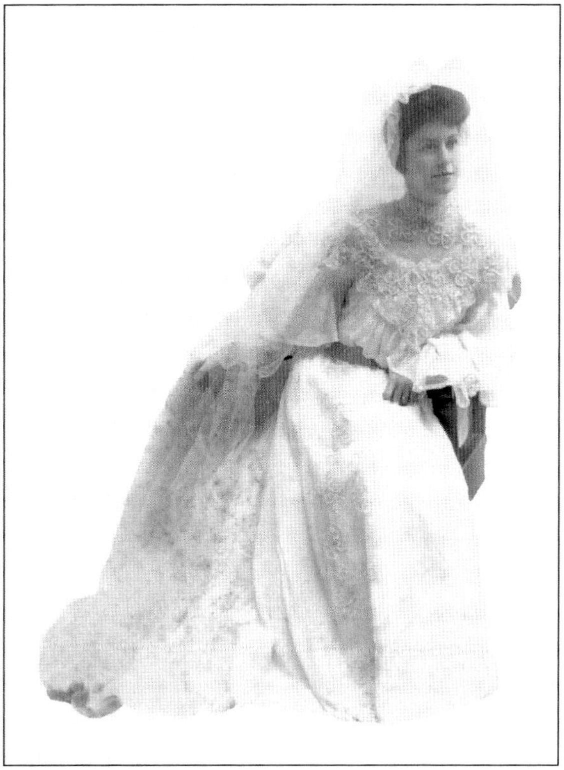

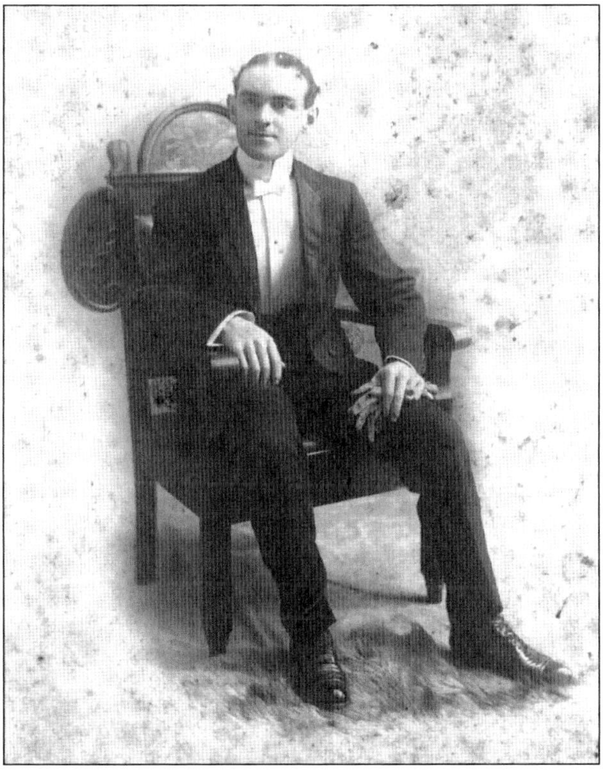

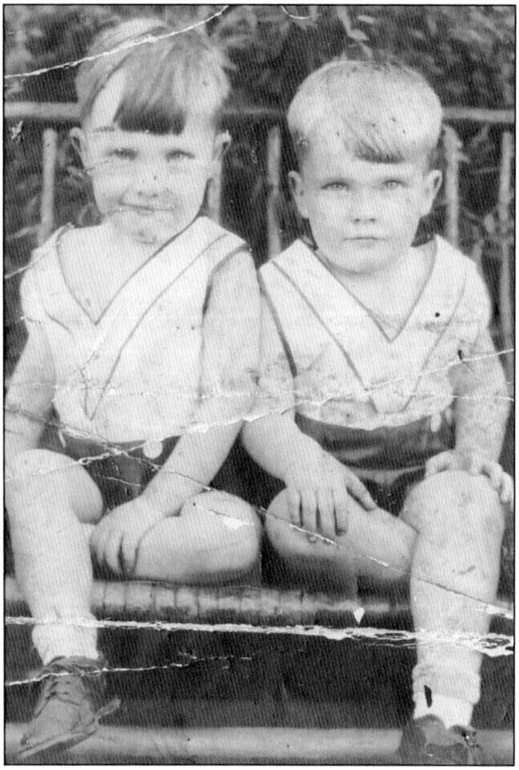

Twins Henry Parks Neisler and Charles Andrew Neisler were born on September 14, 1927, to Paul Mauney Neisler and Dicey Kathryn Moss. The two boys, along with their father and older brother, went on to found Dicey Mills, Inc., and Dicey Fabrics, Inc., in December 1956. (Courtesy of Susan Goforth.)

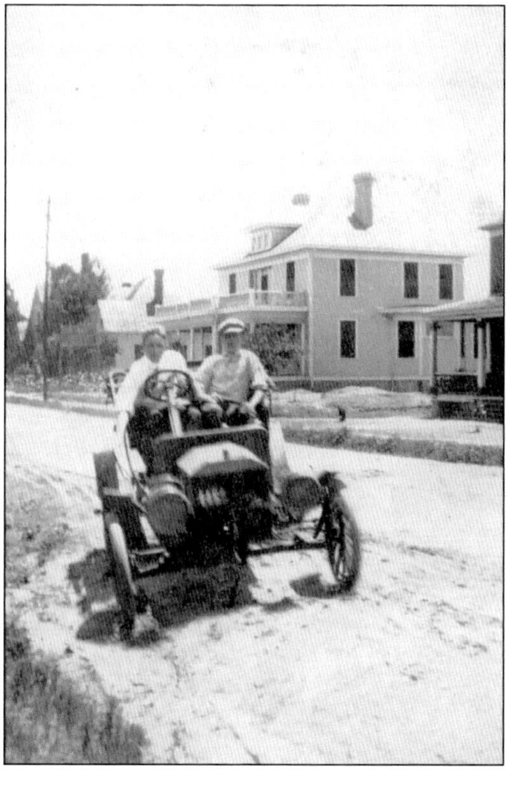

From 1908 to 1927, the Ford Motor Company produced the Model T. The automobile was considered the first affordable car for the middle class. Before the roads were paved, Kings Mountain residents would race their Model Ts up Mountain Street from the railroad tracks, trying to catch rings that were hung up along the way. (Courtesy of Neisler Brothers, Inc.)

Seen here are three of nine children born to Mary Catherine Harmon and Joseph Anderson Falls outside their home on East King Street in 1916. Joseph Anderson Falls used bricks made at his brick manufacturing company in the construction of his 1910 home. Shown in the photograph are, from left to right, Ellen, Oliver, and Ollie. (Courtesy of Lydia Jane Edwards.)

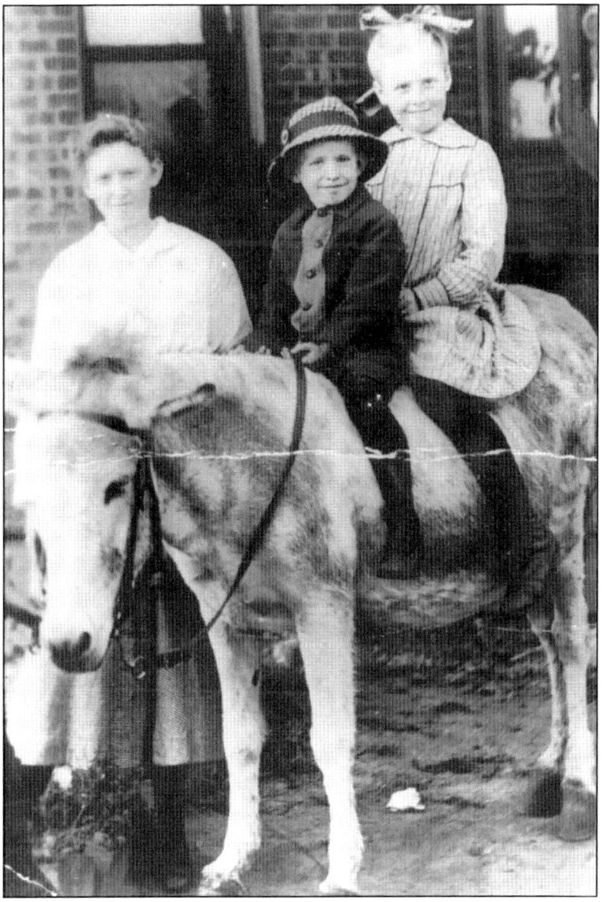

The John Jake Harmon family is shown in front of their home on Piedmont Avenue around the 1890s. In the photograph, Nancy Elizabeth Jane Thornburg Harmon is seated in front of her children, from left to right, Martha Adelaid Harmon Falls, Mary Catherine Harmon Falls, William Lee Harmon, Margaret Ann Harmon Lynn Howell, David A. Harmon, Elizabeth Jane Harmon Bridges, and Frances Regina Harmon Ford. (Courtesy of Lydia Jane Edwards.)

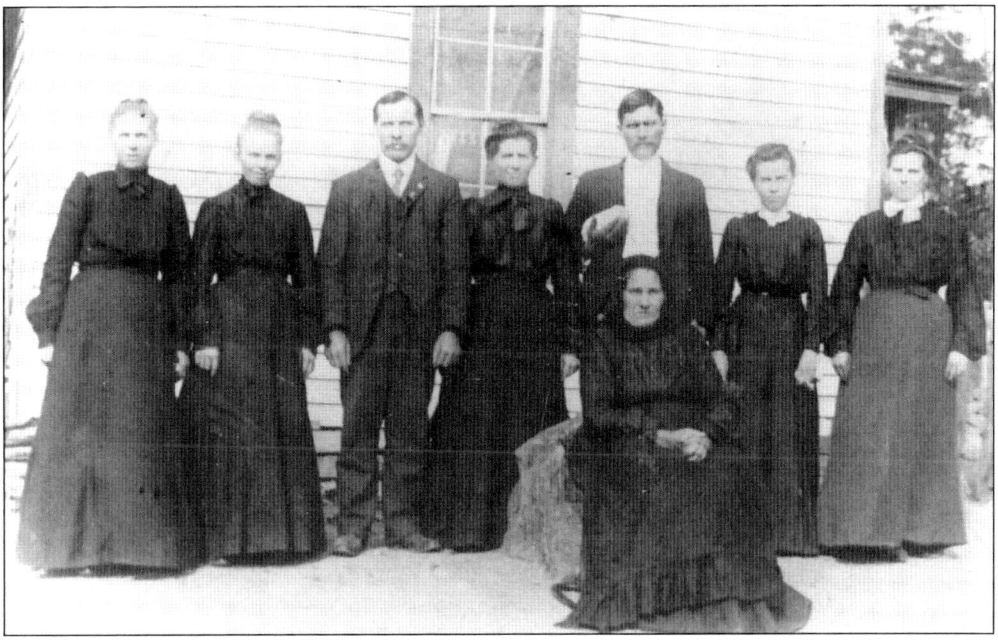

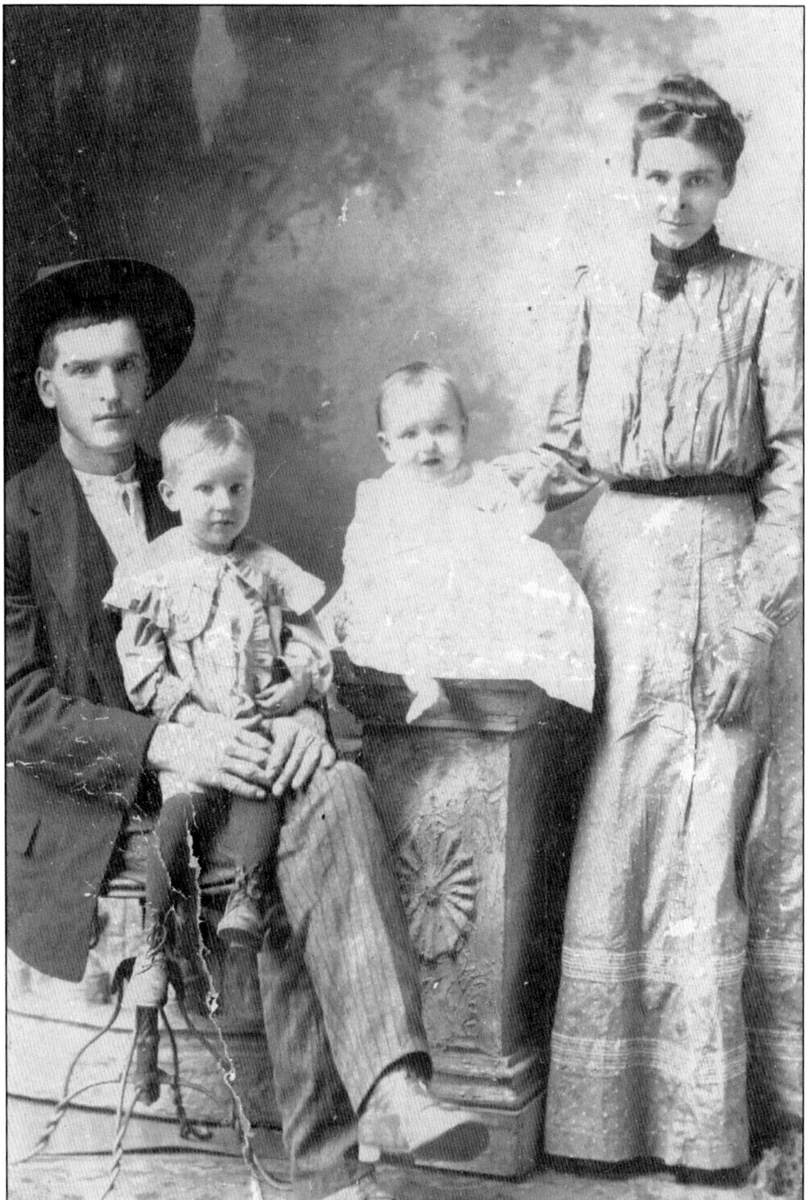

This photograph shows J. Marion Neal with his wife, Nancy Naomi (Ware) Neal, and two of their eight children. On July 10, 1865, J. Marion enlisted in the Confederate army as a private. He served with the Company C, 55th Regiment at the age of 19. Neal was captured during the Battle of Gettysburg and was initially held at Fort McHenry in Maryland. He was subsequently taken to Fort Delaware in Delaware and later to Point Lookout in Maryland before being released. Neal was able to negotiate his release after signing an oath of allegiance, or "loyalty oath," as it was called during the Civil War. In 1870, Neal married Nancy Naomi Ware from the White Plains area (now Kings Mountain), and the couple remained in the region until their deaths. The Neals lived several miles northwest of El Bethel Church. After Nancy Naomi's passing from tuberculosis in April 1889 and J. Marion's death in September 1907, the couple was buried near their home at El Bethel United Methodist Church. (Courtesy of Norma H. Drewery.)

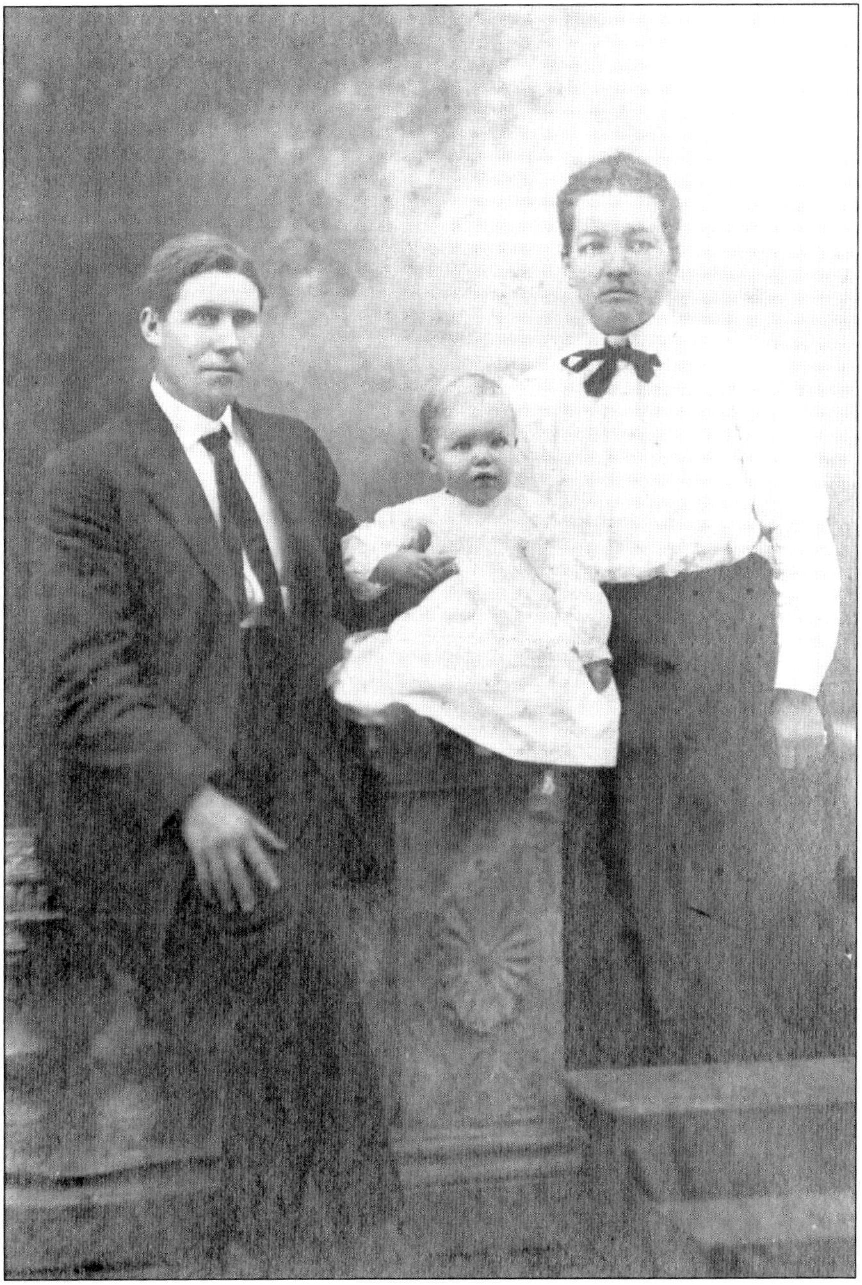

Monsieur "Montie" C. Neal, the youngest son of J. Marion and Nancy Naomi Neal, is shown in this 1910 photograph with his wife, Gertrude Dovie (Bowen) Neal, and their eldest son, Marion Hord Neal. Montie Neal owned a farm on El Bethel Road in Kings Mountain. In addition to farming, Montie operated a gristmill, which he used for grinding cornmeal and flour as well as ginning cotton. There was a sawmill on the property as well, and occasionally Montie operated a cane mill to make molasses. Dovie Neal enjoyed various methods of needlework, including crochet, knitting, and tatting. The couple had eight children and raised three grandchildren after the untimely deaths of their parents. Montie passed away in 1957 and Dovie in 1972; both are buried in the cemetery at El Bethel Church. (Courtesy of Norma H. Drewery.)

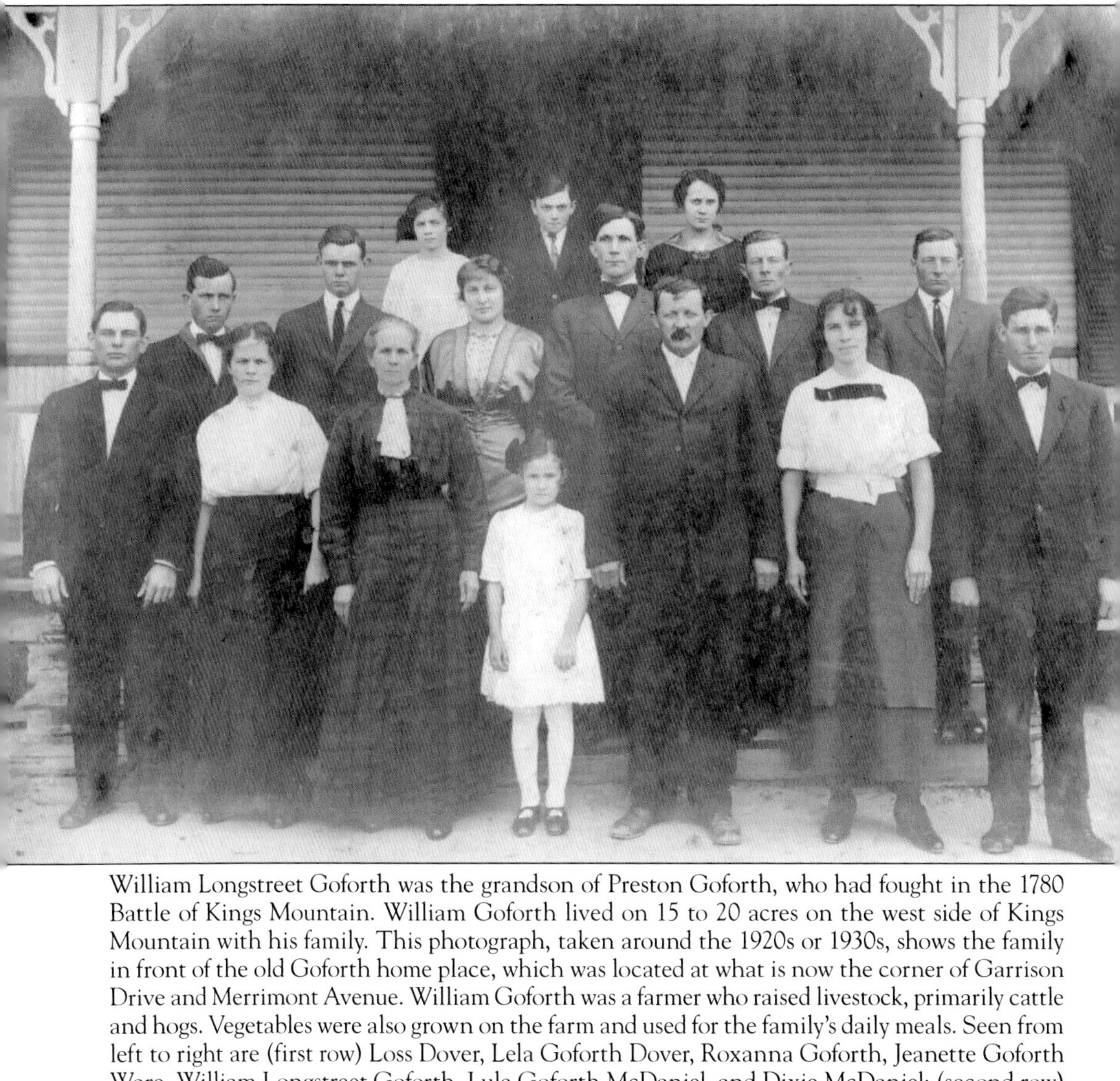

William Longstreet Goforth was the grandson of Preston Goforth, who had fought in the 1780 Battle of Kings Mountain. William Goforth lived on 15 to 20 acres on the west side of Kings Mountain with his family. This photograph, taken around the 1920s or 1930s, shows the family in front of the old Goforth home place, which was located at what is now the corner of Garrison Drive and Merrimont Avenue. William Goforth was a farmer who raised livestock, primarily cattle and hogs. Vegetables were also grown on the farm and used for the family's daily meals. Seen from left to right are (first row) Loss Dover, Lela Goforth Dover, Roxanna Goforth, Jeanette Goforth Ware, William Longstreet Goforth, Lula Goforth McDaniel, and Dixie McDaniel; (second row) Marvin Goforth, Joe Goforth, Mae Morrow Goforth, Dee Goforth, Brady Goforth, and Grady Goforth; (third row) Emma Mae Goforth Dye, Hall Goforth, and Angie Goforth Goforth. (Courtesy of Susan Goforth.)

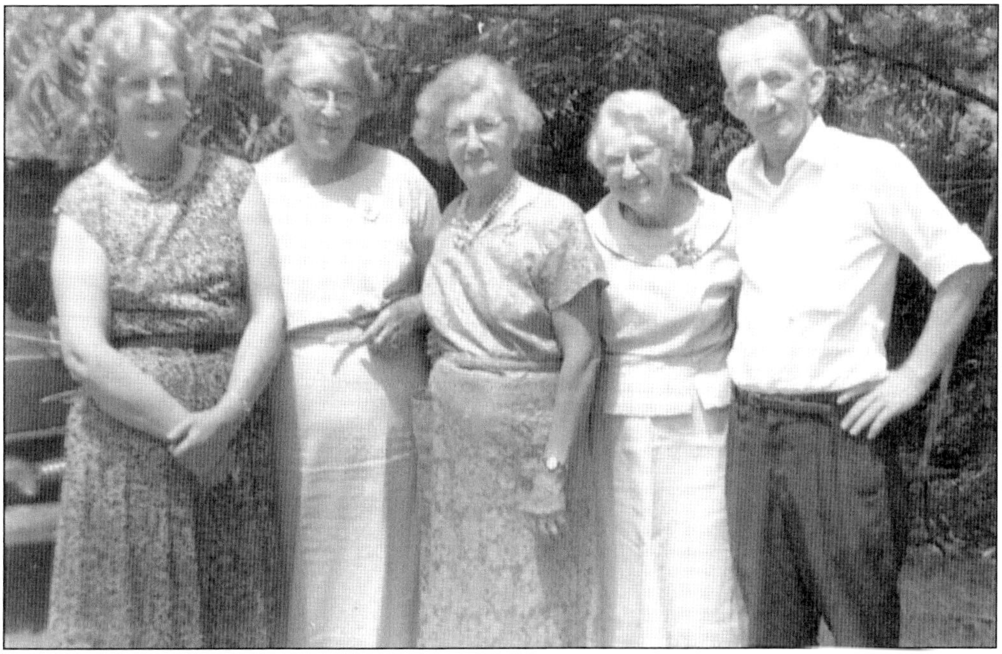

Taken in 1965, this photograph shows the remaining five of Joseph and Mary Harmon Falls' nine children at a celebration for Leola Falls's birthday. Pictured from left to right are Ollie Falls Whittemore, Bessie Falls Beam, Leola Falls Hendricks, Ellen Falls Petrosino, and Oliver Falls. (Courtesy of Lydia Jane Edwards.)

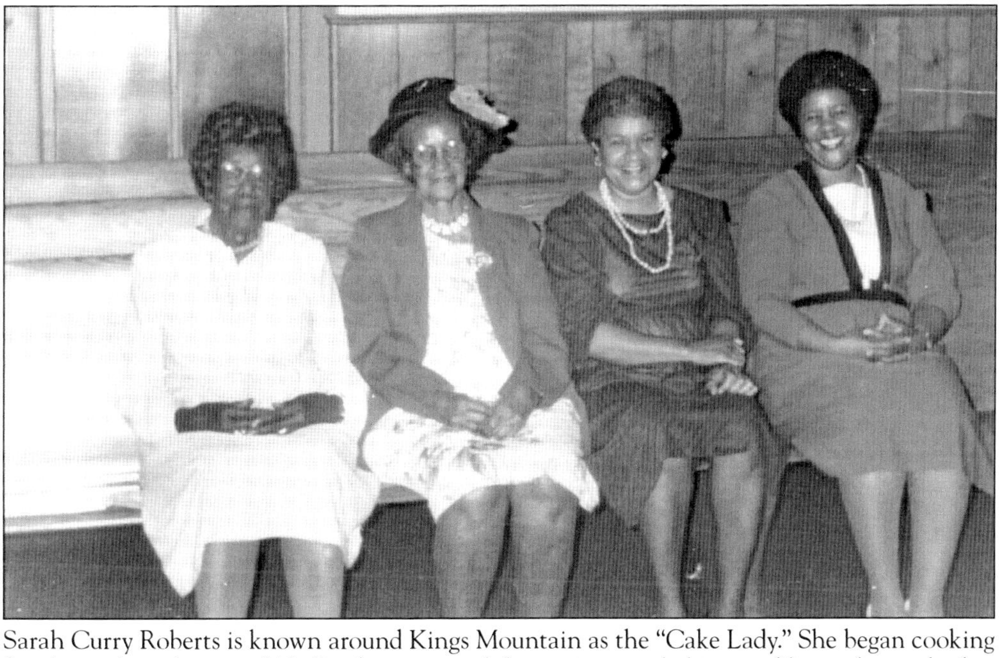

Sarah Curry Roberts is known around Kings Mountain as the "Cake Lady." She began cooking family meals at the age of 12. Sarah now spends her retirement baking wedding cakes and other sweet treats, shipping them to customers throughout the country in hatboxes. Shown in this photograph are, from left to right, Venice Mae Kilgore, Lillie Bell Curry, Rebecca Kilgore Curry, and Sarah Curry Roberts. (Courtesy of Robert Curry.)

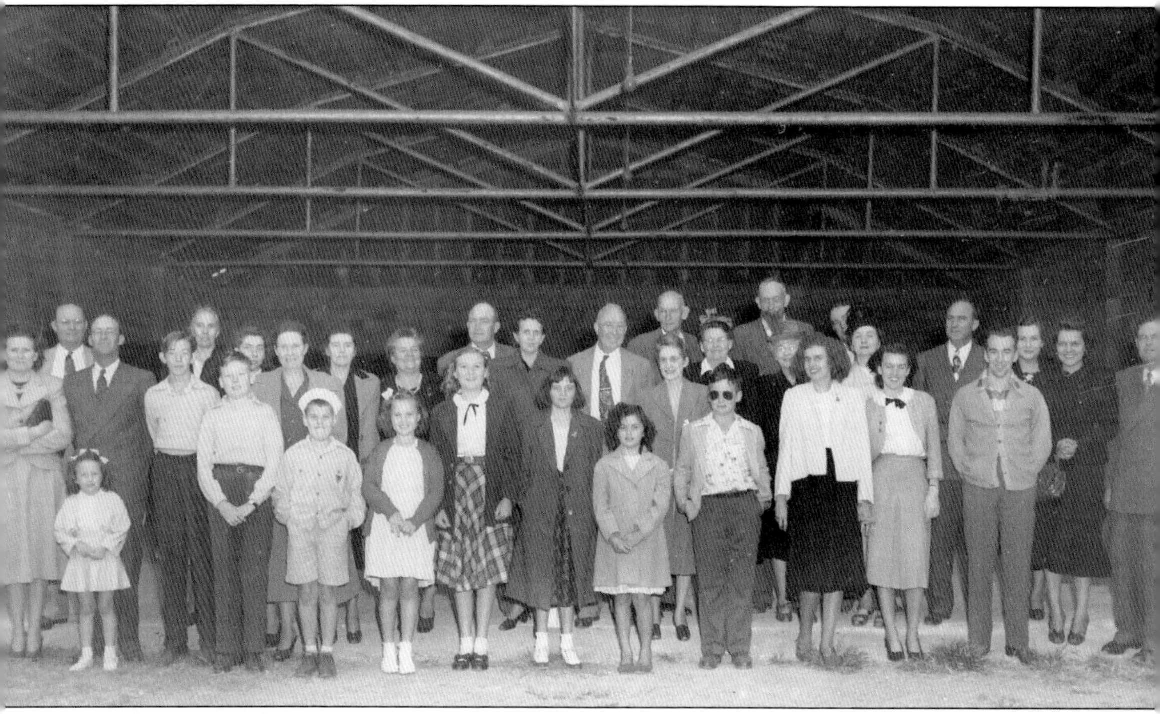

Glee Acor Bridges was one of 16 children, 13 of whom lived through adulthood. Every year, the siblings and their spouses and children would come together at the Kings Mountain Airport for a family reunion. Identified in this September 1948 photograph are Ben Bridges, Tony Bridges wearing the sailor hat, Durham Bridges, Glee A. Bridges, Malin Bridges, J.C. Bridges, Edith Bridges, and Elmo Bridges. Glee A. Bridges constructed the Bridges' airport on his family farm in the 1940s, about three and a half blocks from Kings Mountain's downtown business district. Bridges and his children all eventually received their pilot's licenses. Many people remember Glee A. Bridges taking his plane out and flying over playgrounds and other areas frequented by children. Before going out, Bridges would wrap bubble gum in toilet paper and then drop it from the plane to the children as he flew overhead. At times, he would take a child up with him to help with the distribution.

Hazel Herndon Fryer served as a Red Cross girl during World War II. After a two-week training period at American University in Washington, DC, Herndon was sent to Fort Meade, Maryland, before moving on to London and then Germany. In Germany, she met Frank Milton Fryer. The two married there on August 25, 1945. After returning to Kings Mountain, Hazel Herndon Fryer was involved with various civic activities.

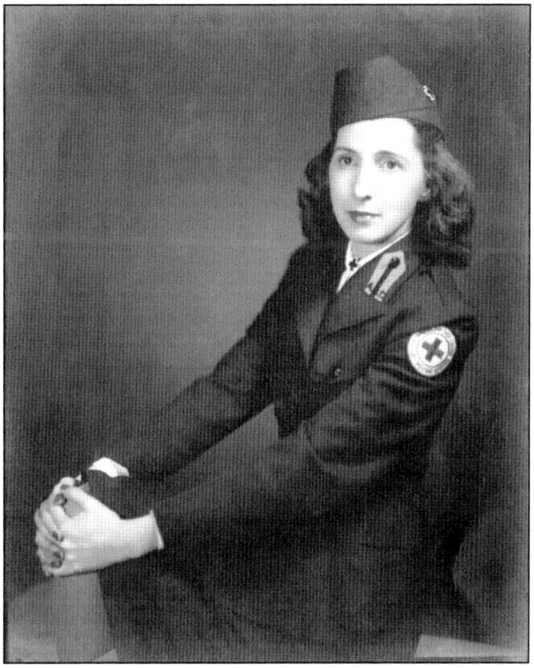

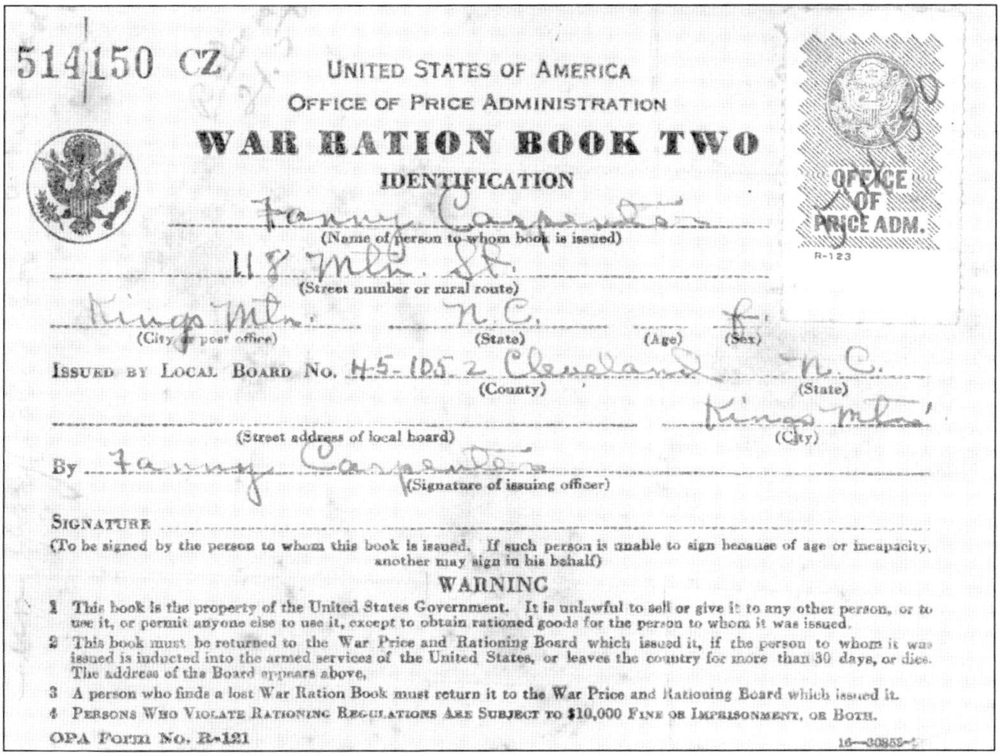

514150 CZ

UNITED STATES OF AMERICA
OFFICE OF PRICE ADMINISTRATION

WAR RATION BOOK TWO

IDENTIFICATION

Fanny Carpenter
(Name of person to whom book is issued)

118 Mtn. St.
(Street number or rural route)

Kings Mtn. (City or post office) N. C. (State) (Age) F. (Sex)

ISSUED BY LOCAL BOARD No. 45-105 2 Cleveland (County) N. C. (State)

(Street address of local board) Kings Mtn. (City)

By Fanny Carpenter (Signature of issuing officer)

SIGNATURE
(To be signed by the person to whom this book is issued. If such person is unable to sign because of age or incapacity, another may sign in his behalf)

WARNING

1 This book is the property of the United States Government. It is unlawful to sell or give it to any other person, or to use it, or permit anyone else to use it, except to obtain rationed goods for the person to whom it was issued.
2 This book must be returned to the War Price and Rationing Board which issued it, if the person to whom it was issued is inducted into the armed services of the United States, or leaves the country for more than 30 days, or dies. The address of the Board appears above.
3 A person who finds a lost War Ration Book must return it to the War Price and Rationing Board which issued it.
4 PERSONS WHO VIOLATE RATIONING REGULATIONS ARE SUBJECT TO $10,000 FINE OR IMPRISONMENT, OR BOTH.

OPA Form No. R-121

16—30852-1

OFFICE OF PRICE ADM.
R-123

During World War II, the shortages of many products, such as gasoline, tires, and nylon, were becoming commonplace for American citizens. Ration books were the government's answer to the shortage and an attempt to distribute goods fairly. Every person received a book containing ration tickets. After one book was completed, an additional book would be distributed.

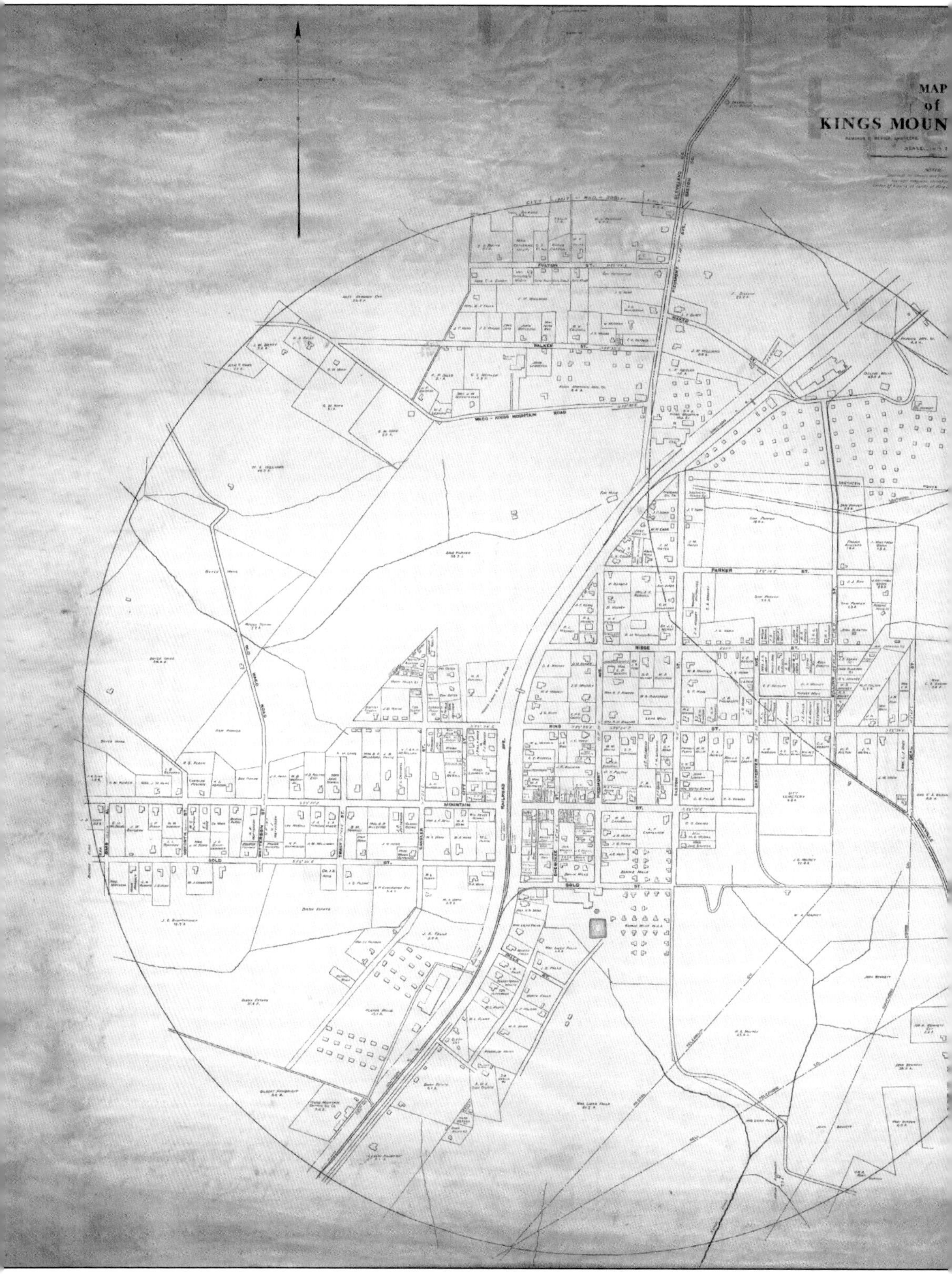
MAP
of
KINGS MOUN

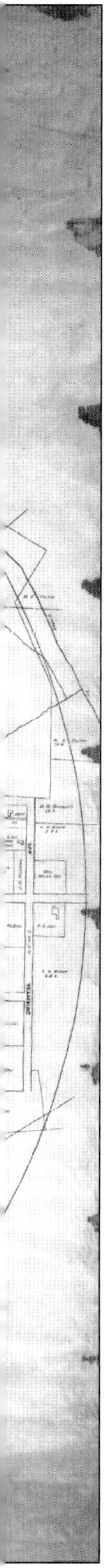

Until 1917, the city of Kings Mountain straddled both Cleveland and Gaston Counties. In 1915, a special election was held to adjust the county line to accommodate Kings Mountain solely in one of the two counties. The election resulted with 341 in favor of Cleveland County and 270 for Gaston. However, in 1917, Gaston County representatives in the North Carolina General Assembly attempted to nullify the vote. After a speech by Cleveland County representative W.A. Mauney on behalf of his county, the vote was upheld. Surveyors drew off the lines, and the commissioners of both counties adopted them during a meeting in October 1918. Over the years, and as the town grew, the city of Kings Mountain once again straddles both Cleveland and Gaston Counties. (Courtesy of Ed Anthony.)

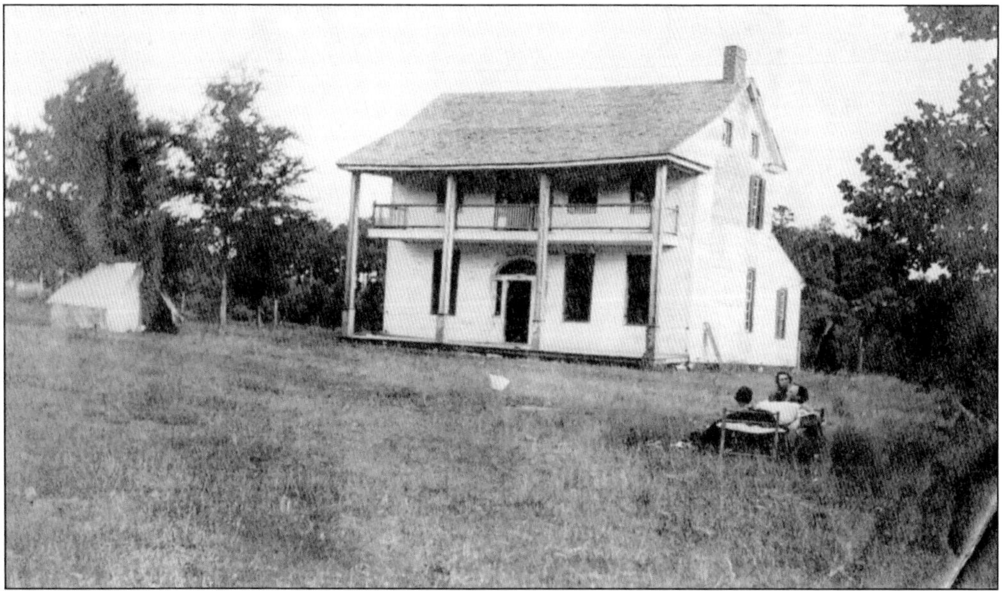

Anderson P. and Marcus M. Carpenter relocated to Kings Mountain from Gaston County. In 1874, the men opened general store on Battleground Avenue. While still bachelors, the brothers built a two-story frame house on the corner of Mountain Street and Piedmont Avenue. Marcus was the first brother to be wed. Due to an agreement between the brothers, Marcus and his bride, Fannie Rudsill, resided in the house. When A.P. married Caroline "Callie" Hoke in 1887, the couple built their house on the corner of Mountain and Gaston Streets. A.P. and Callie's daughter Lula married Marion E. Herndon. In 1921, the Herndons built their house on property between the existing structures.

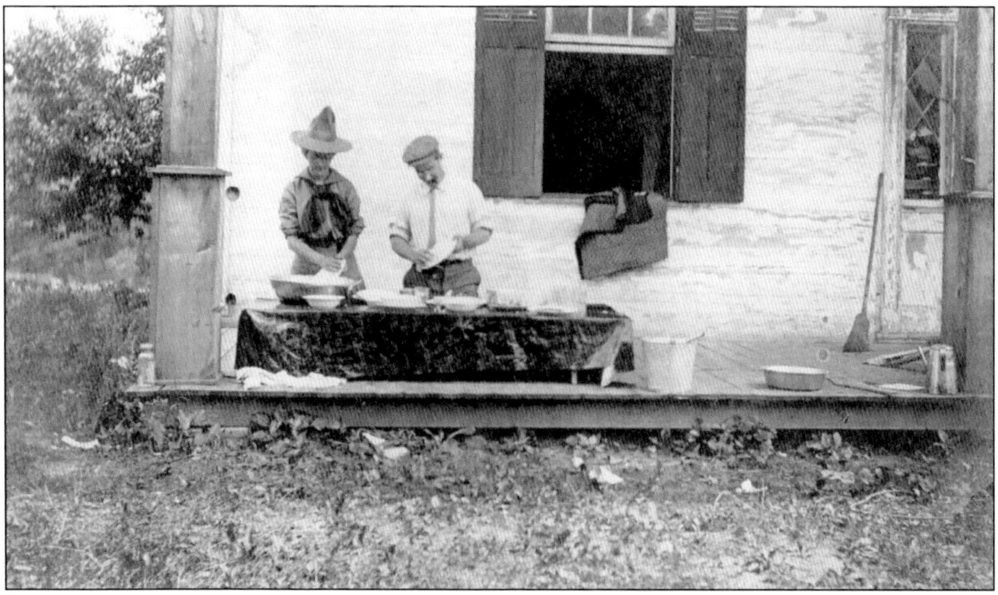

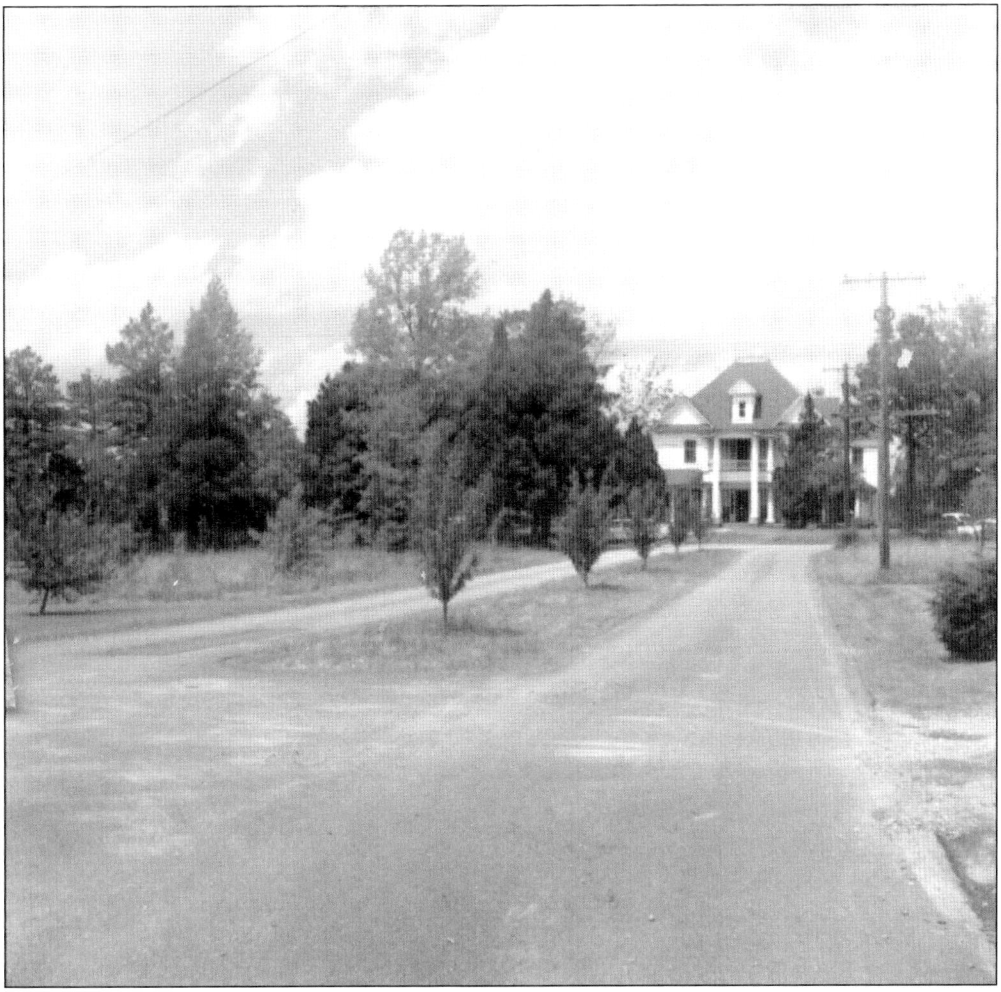

Businessmen interested in having an upscale place to socialize within the city's limits established the Kings Mountain Country Club in 1945. With a golf course designed by Porter Gibson, the club opened to members a year later. The club's first headquarters was inside the home of R.S. Plonk, located off King Street. Soon after organizing, club members constructed a nine-hole golf course on the property. Hunter Neisler designed the tables used in the dining room. He devised a table that could be converted into a bench, which proved useful during the once-monthly dances held at the club. Once the tables were converted into benches, they were pushed against the wall, leaving room for a dance floor. The dances were popular events and often had a focus, the most common being a luau or beach theme. In 1961, the country club erected a new brick structure after a 1958 fire destroyed the Plonk house. The club now offers members an 18-hole golf course, a swimming pool, and tennis courts.

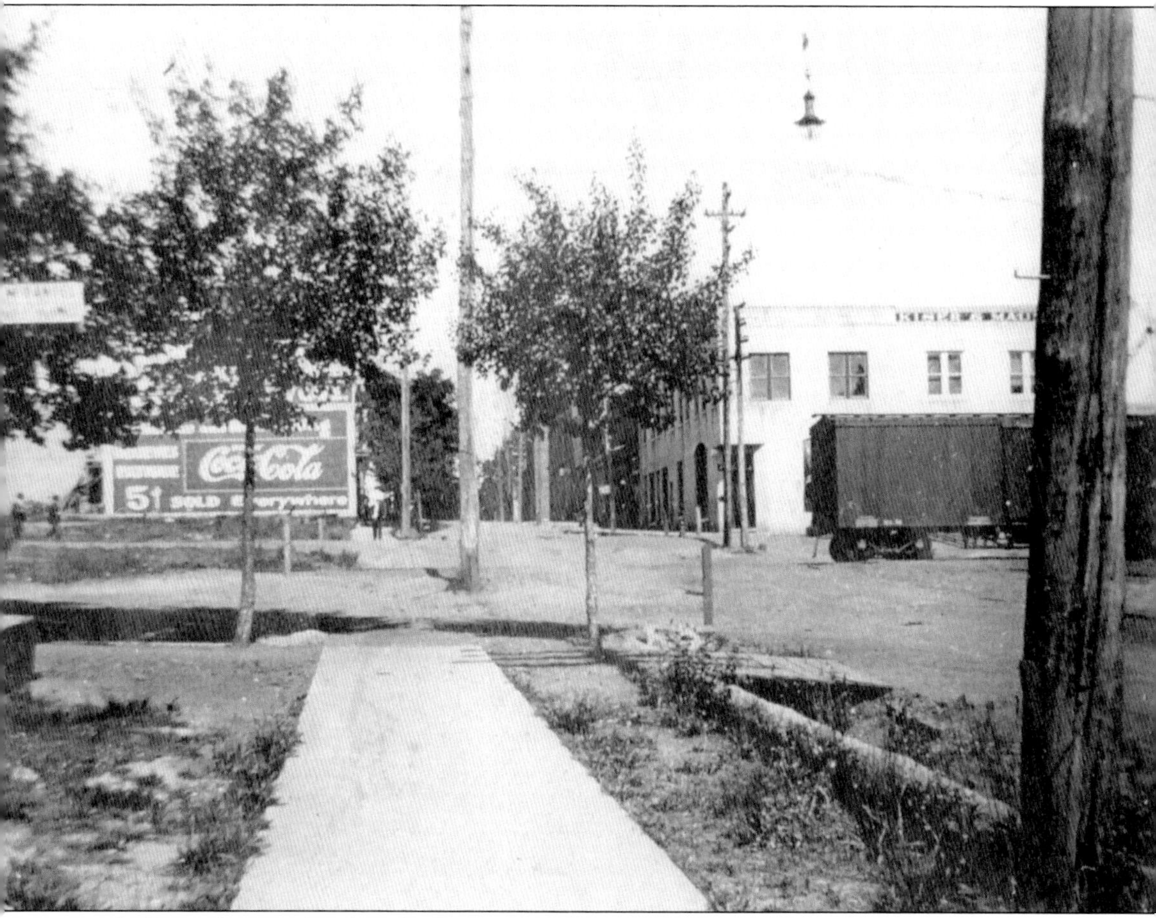

On December 1, 1872, the Charlotte Atlanta Airline Railway, later known as Southern Railway, completed the railroad through Kings Mountain. With it came businesses and opportunities to the rural farming community. The Kiser and Mauney Store, seen in the upper right of the photograph, opened in the late 1800s, just prior to the turn of the century. Larkin A. Kiser, along with his brother-in-law Floyd Mauney, operated the general store. The store was later sold to John Oates Plonk and his family, who eventually renamed the business Plonk Brothers, Inc. Prior to 1911, the roads in Kings Mountain, like those of other cities in the county, were unpaved. With the authority to issue bonds for road improvements, all townships in Cleveland County were building and maintaining their own roads by 1919. (Courtesy of Neisler Brothers, Inc.)

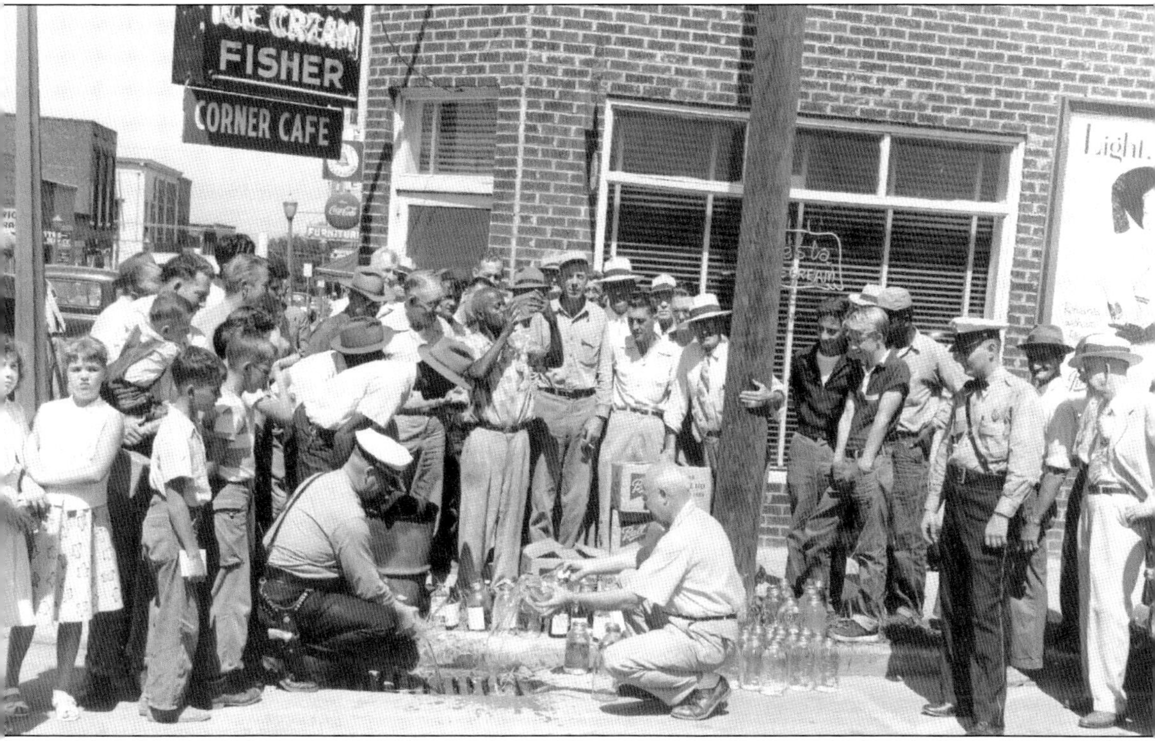

When the city of Kings Mountain was chartered on February 11, 1874, the founding men made spirituous liquids illegal. An election was held soon after regarding the sale of liquor within the city's limits. The result was a unanimous 13-0 vote against permitting liquor sales. Kings Mountain remained a dry city until 2009, when voters approved a liquor-by-the-drink referendum. In this 1950s photograph, then mayor Glee A. Bridges and Cleveland County sheriff Haywood Allen empty jars of confiscated white liquor, or moonshine, down a storm drain at the corner of Gold Street and Battleground Avenue. Moonshine was popular in the Appalachian areas of the country. The illegal clear liquor, similar to whiskey, got its name from the illegal distilleries that would produce and distribute it at night by the light of the moon.

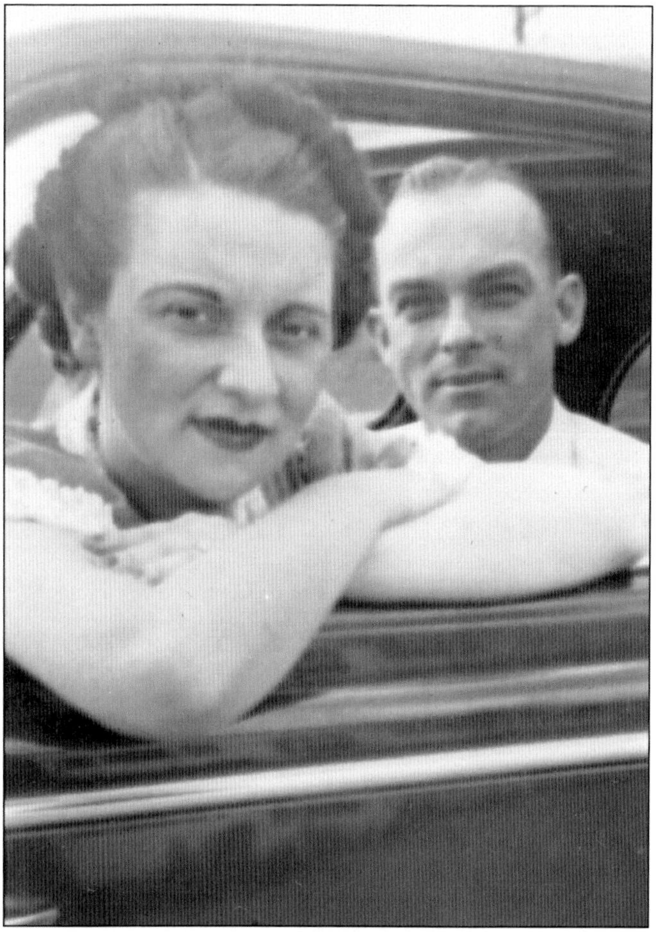

This photograph of Lucille "Ludy" Frances Cansler Falls and Coman Franklin Falls was taken in either the fall of 1940 or the spring of 1941. The Falls were married a few years earlier on November 24, 1937. They lived on West Mountain Street in Kings Mountain. (Courtesy of Mary Lewis Nantz.)

While on leave from World War II, James J. Alexander is shown at his home on Alexander Street in the 1936 Ford convertible he purchased prior to entering the Army Air Corps. During his trip back to Kings Mountain, his brother Charles L. Alexander was also on leave. (Courtesy of Libby Alexander Putnam.)

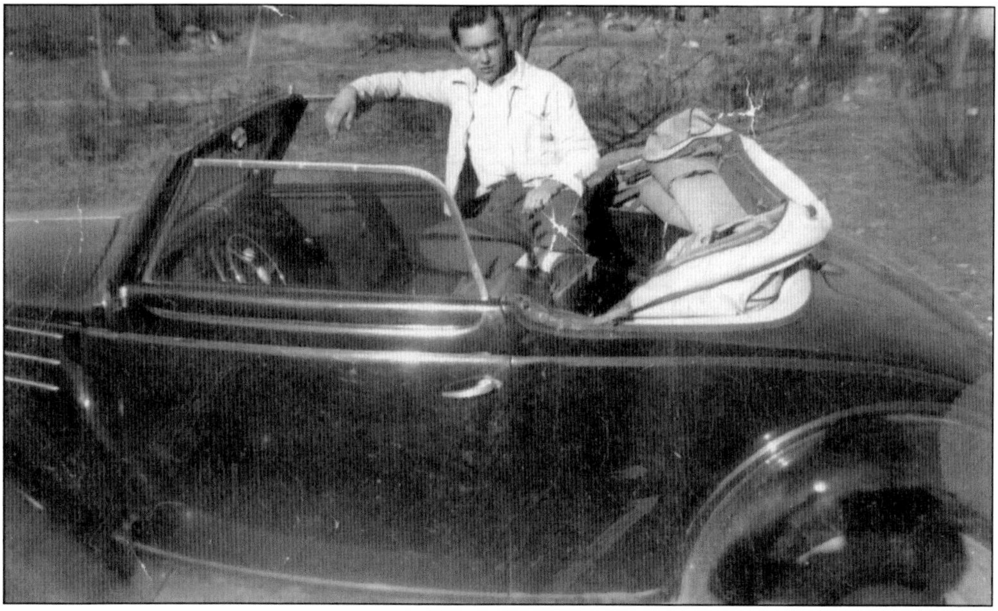

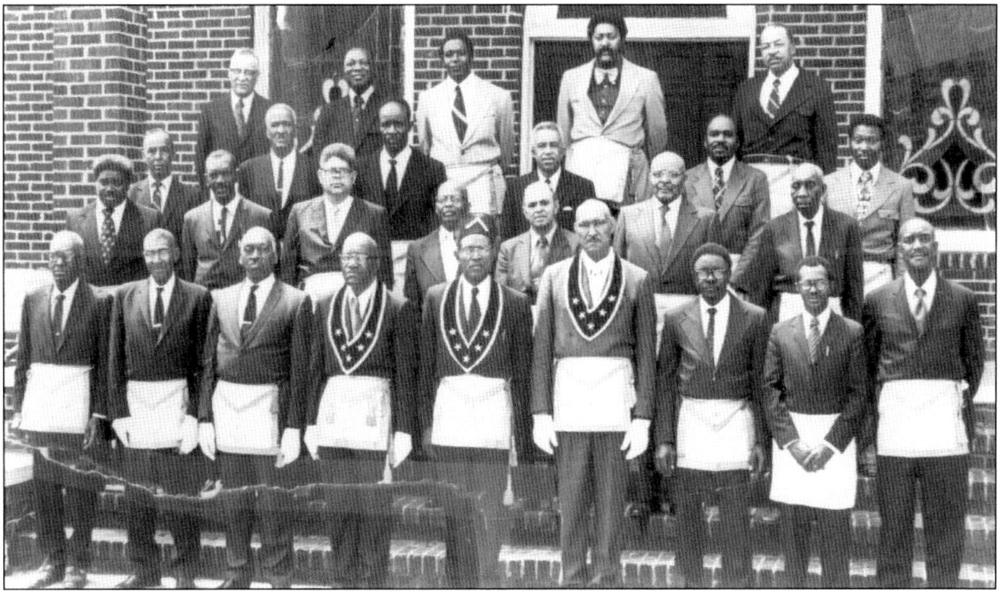

The Mosaic Mason Lodge No. 4 was chartered on June 14, 1946. This photograph was taken in front of the Bynum AME Church in the mid-1970s. The early worshipful masters of the lodge in succession were F. J. Lee, Lewis Curry, Carlee Jenkins, and Benjamin Brown. The civically minded men of the lodge are active in the community, providing assistance to the needy. (Courtesy of Robert Curry.)

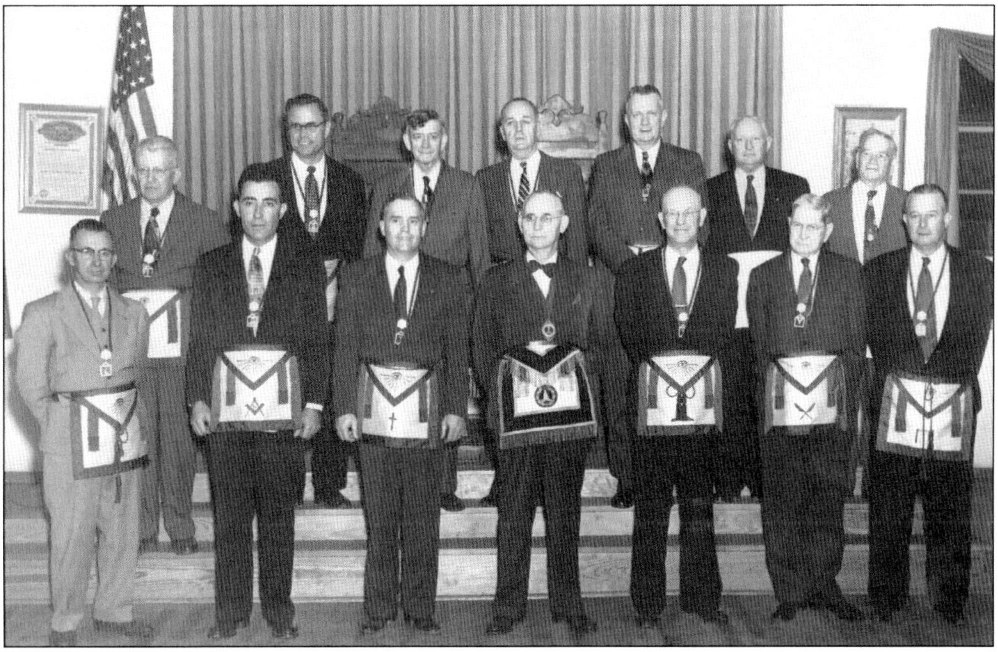

During the 1950s, officers and members of the Fairview Masonic Lodge No. 339 A.F. and A.M. gathered for this photograph, taken by Carlisle Studios. Seen here are, from left to right, (first row) Kenneth Crook, Paul Owens, C.J. Gault, an unidentified visiting Grand Master, O.T. Hayes, Arthur Crouse, and Percy Dilling; (second row) Dr. O.P. Lewis, Arnold Kincaid, Dr. J.E. Anthony, Moffet Ware, John Floyd, Jim Herndon, and Dr. L.P. Baker.

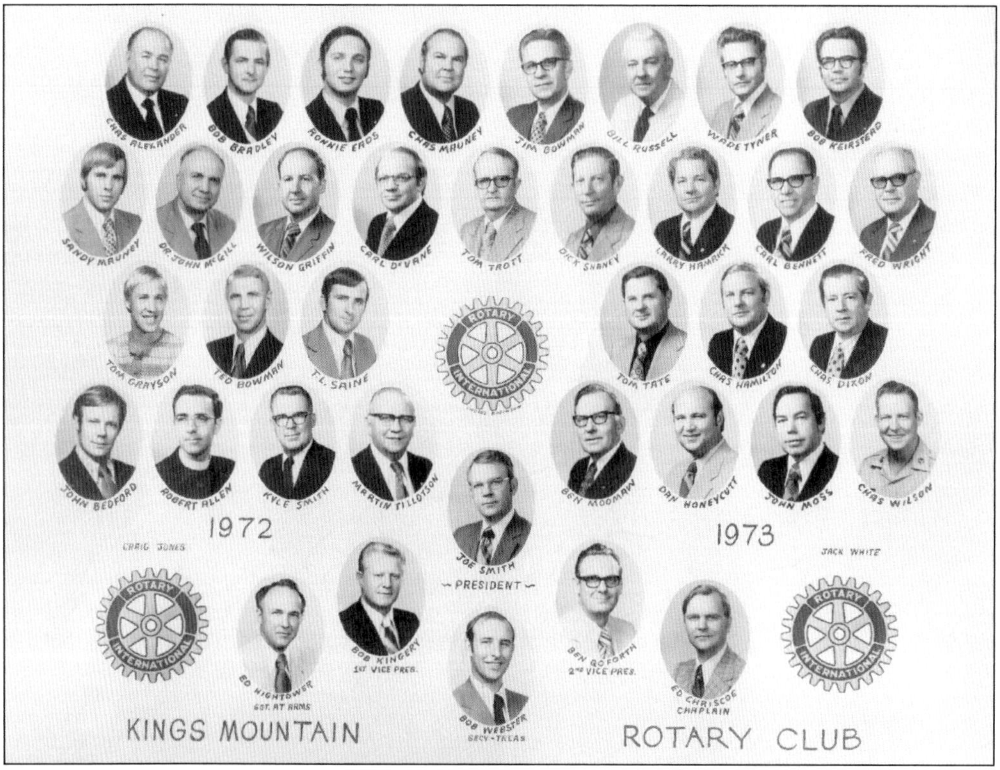

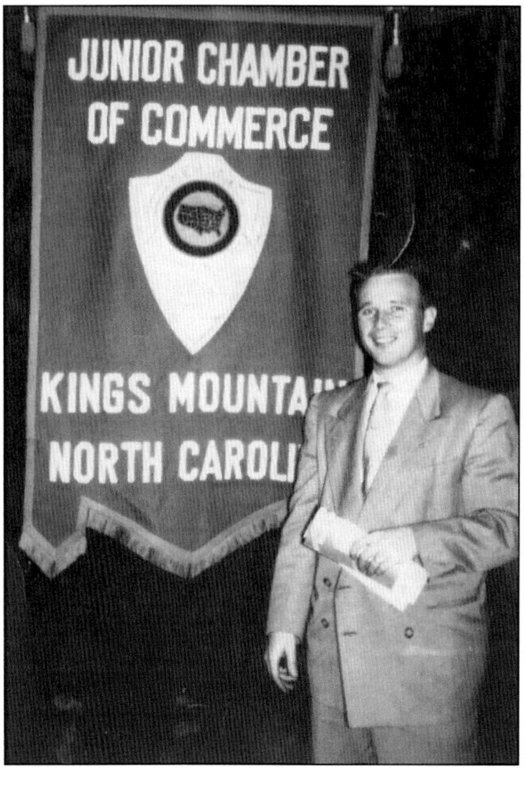

The Kings Mountain Rotary Club was chartered on November 19, 1958, with 20 members. For two years, the civic group met weekly for lunch, programs, and discussion at the Kings Mountain Country Club. After fire destroyed the building in 1960, the club met at various locations until finding a home in the H. Lawrence Patrick Senior Life and Conference Center. Joseph R. Smith, shown in this photograph, served as president of the Kings Mountain Rotary Club from 1972 to 1973. (Courtesy of Sara and Wilson Griffin.)

The Junior Chamber of Commerce, or Jaycees, is a civic organization for young adults. Bill Eldon, president of the Kings Mountain Junior Chamber of Commerce chapter, is shown in this photograph around 1950.

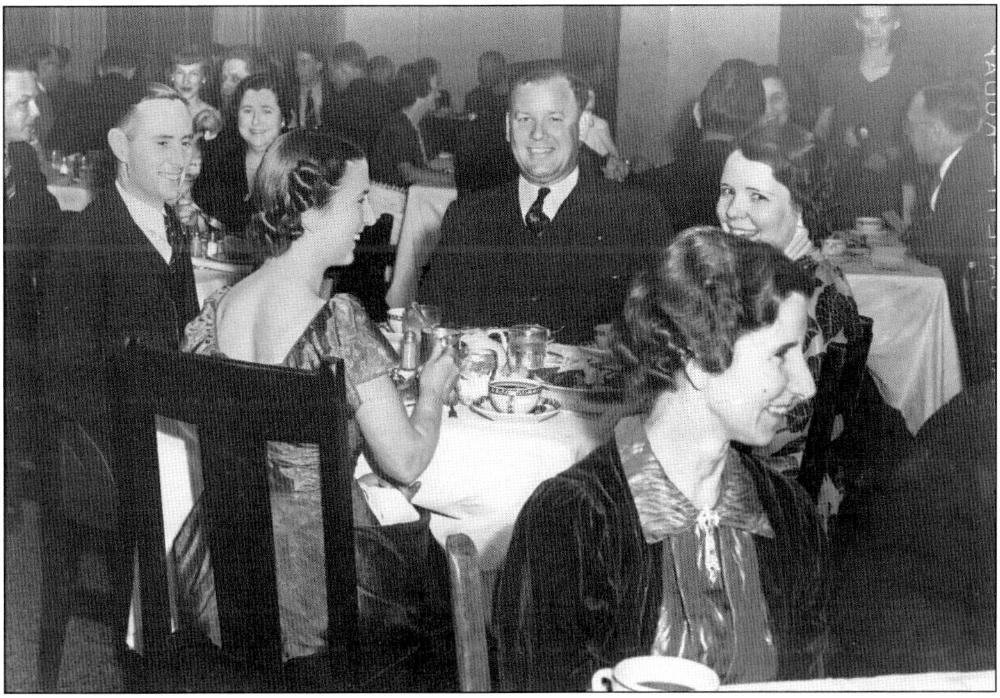

The Kings Mountain Kiwanis Club hosted their charter ceremony and dinner on April 12, 1940. Known as the Kings Mountain Business Men's Club in the 1920s, the club opted to become affiliated with a nationally recognized civic organization in 1940. The club applied for affiliation with Kiwanis International that same year and received its official charter on March 7.

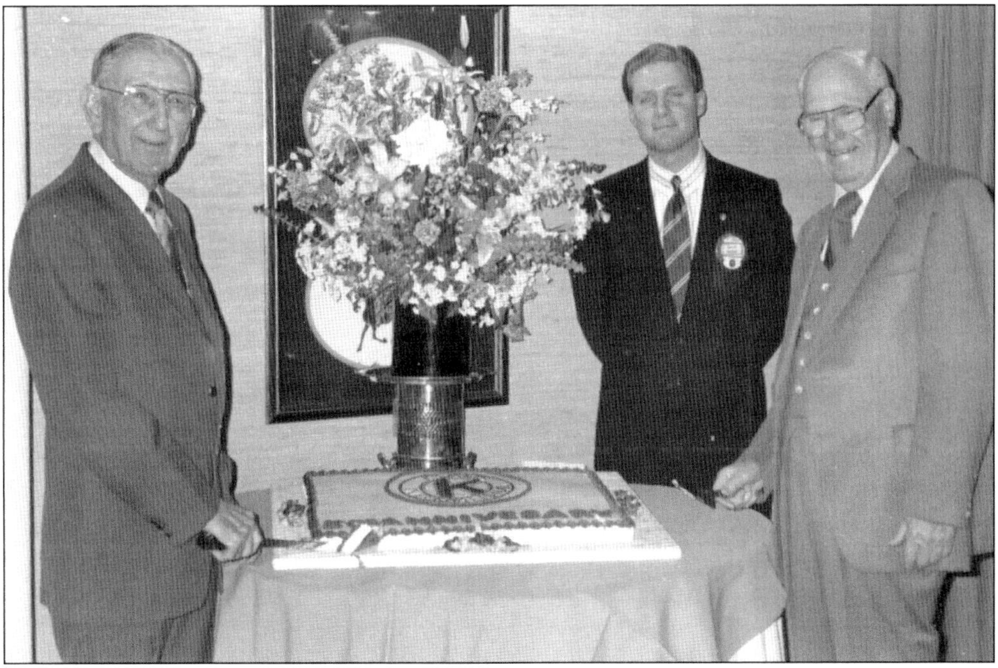

In this photograph, the Kings Mountain Kiwanis Club celebrates their 50th anniversary. Shown in the image from left to right are John McGill, David Neisler, and Bill Craig.

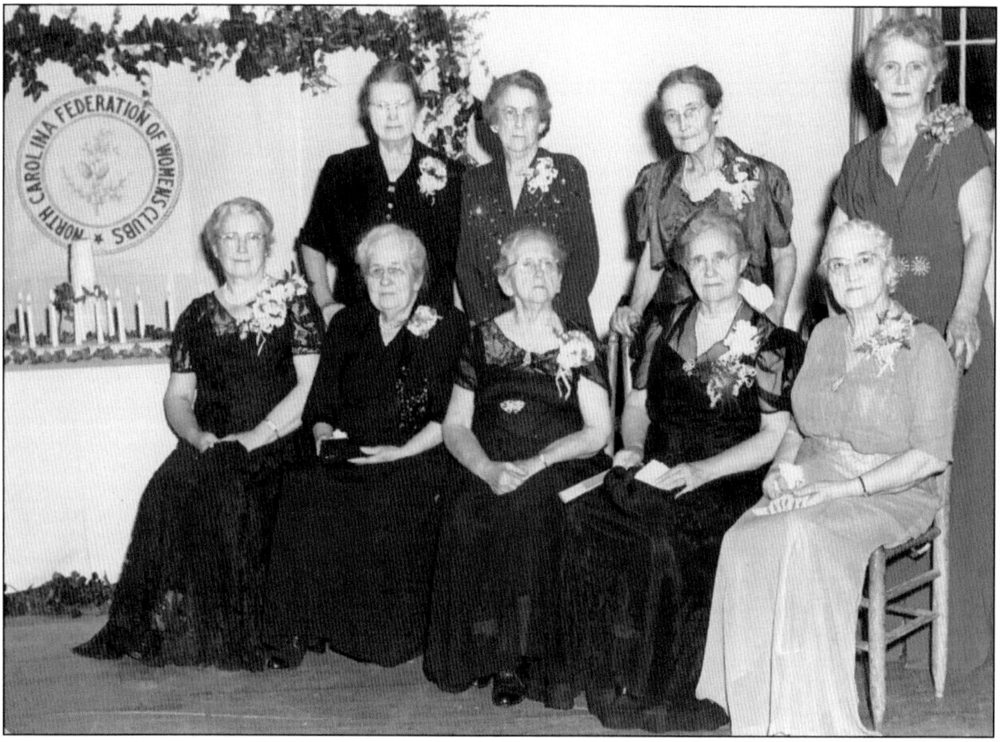

The Kings Mountain Woman's Club was founded in 1902. Pictured from left to right are (first row) Mrs. Geo V. Patterson, Mrs. C.E. Neisler, Mrs. Meek Ormand, Mrs. H.N. Moss, and Mrs. H.L. Fulton; (second row) Mrs. Jimmins Aderholdt, Mrs. D.C. Mauney, Mrs. Ed Campbell, and Mrs. Hunter Patterson.

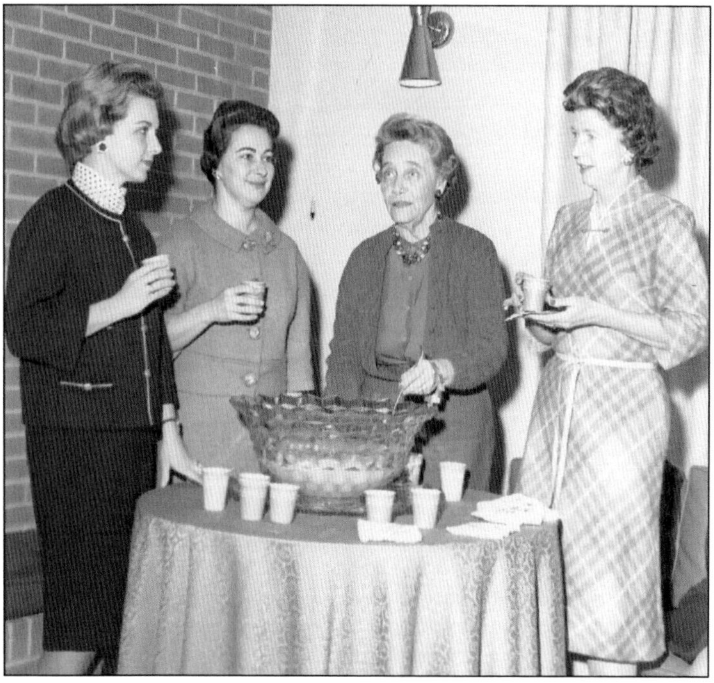

During the early 1970s, the Kings Mountain Ladies' Golf Association met at the Kings Mountain Country Club for a luncheon and fashion show. Pictured from left to right are Marilyn Neisler, Libby Blanton, Katherine Neisler, and Pat Smathers. (Courtesy of Laura Carpenter Bingham.)

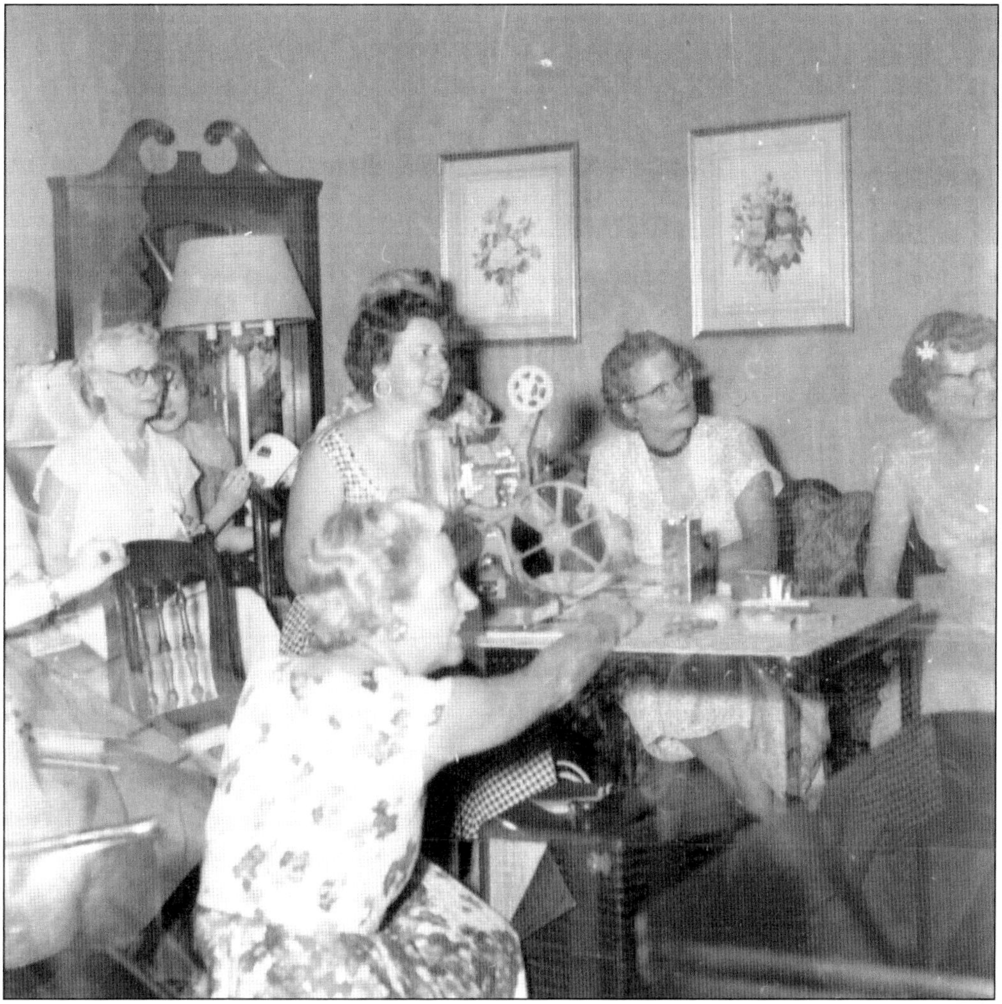

The Kings Mountain Garden Club was founded on March 16, 1949, with eight charter members. In 1950, the members of the club voted to become federated with the North Carolina Garden Club. The role of the Kings Mountain Garden Club is to provide civic experiences for the members. Within its first year of operation, the club voted to assume the responsibility of landscaping the grounds around the newly constructed Kings Mountain Hospital. The club also participated in other events, such as flower shows and community beautification projects, both in Kings Mountain and throughout the state. This photograph shows Ann Lutz Neisler presenting a film at her home during one the club's monthly meetings. Shown in the photograph are, from left to right, Ann Lutz Neisler, Mary Keeter, unidentified, Laura Houser, Catherine Mauney, and Lina McGill.

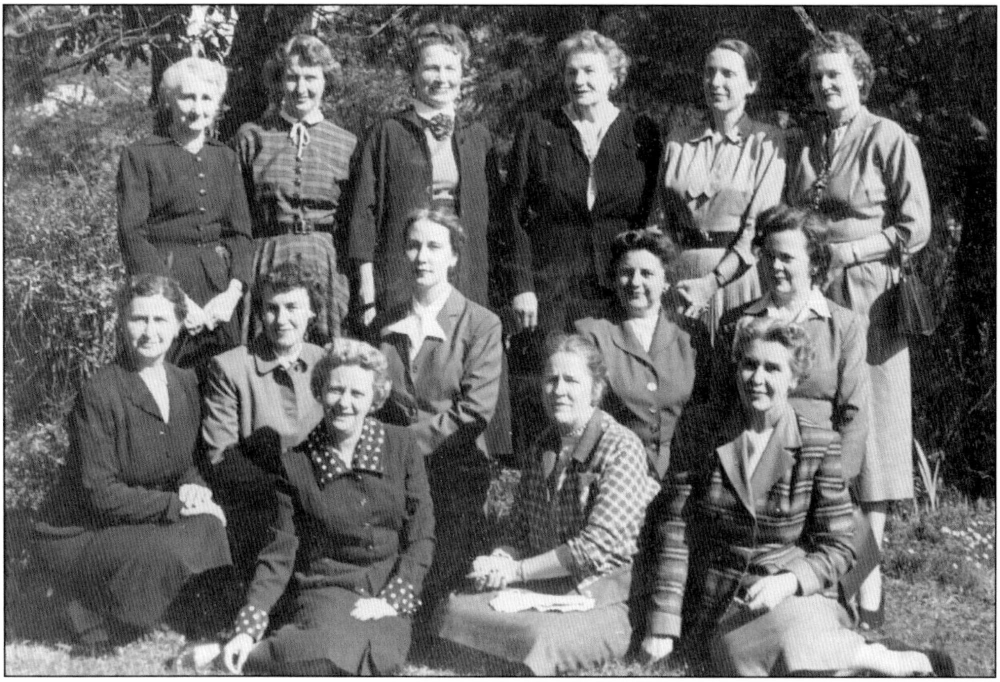

This image shows members of the Kings Mountain Garden Club in the yard of Elizabeth Pressly on March 5, 1955. A month earlier, Pressly traveled to Chicago, Illinois, for the National Garden Club Convention, where she was recognized as the winner of a national horticulture contest. Pictured from left to right are (first row) Ann Neisler, Elizabeth Mayes, and Elizabeth Pressly; (second row) Virginia Herndon, Phylis Cheshire, Dot Finger, Laura Houser, and Babe Ramseur; (third row) Mary Keeter, Barbara Mauney, Hazel Jackson, Johnsie Ware, Charlene Padgett, and Catherine Mauney.

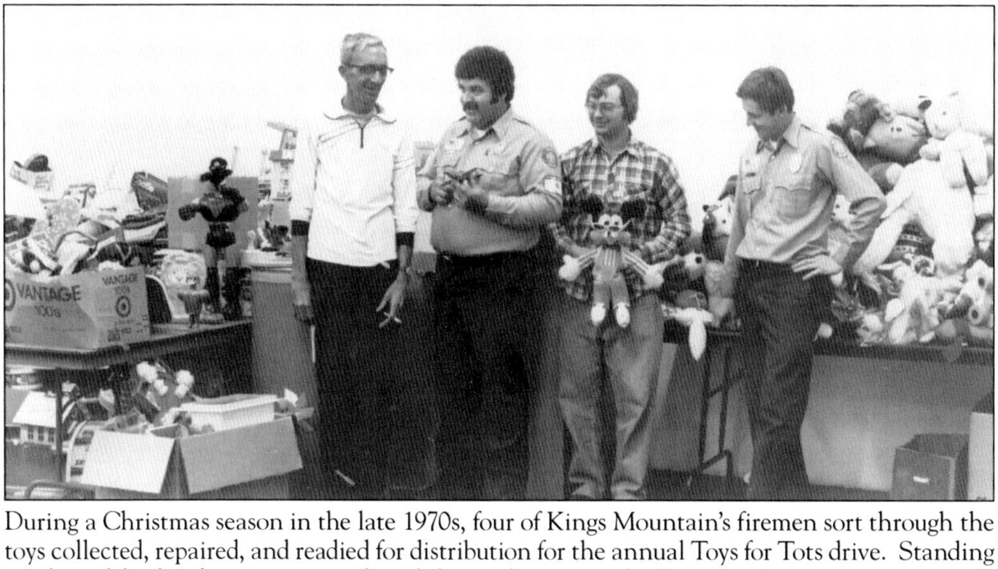

During a Christmas season in the late 1970s, four of Kings Mountain's firemen sort through the toys collected, repaired, and readied for distribution for the annual Toys for Tots drive. Standing in a bay of the fire department are, from left to right, Capt. Charles "Pete" Peterson, Larry Smith, Bruce Canipe, and Lt. Bill Ware. (Courtesy of the Kings Mountain Fire Museum.)

Four

Study

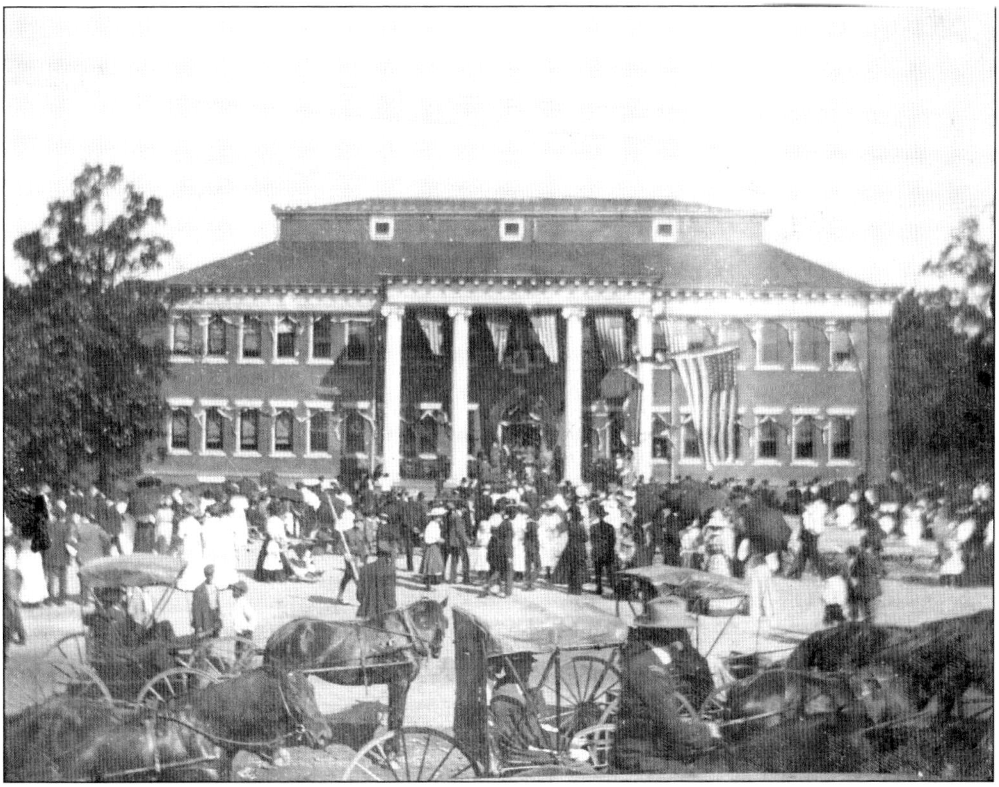

Education in Kings Mountain began with Bell's Military Academy in 1878; it was later known as the Central School. The Central School served as the city's only public school during the early years of education in Kings Mountain. The school is seen here during the October 7, 1911, Battle of Kings Mountain celebration. (Courtesy of the *Kings Mountain Herald*.)

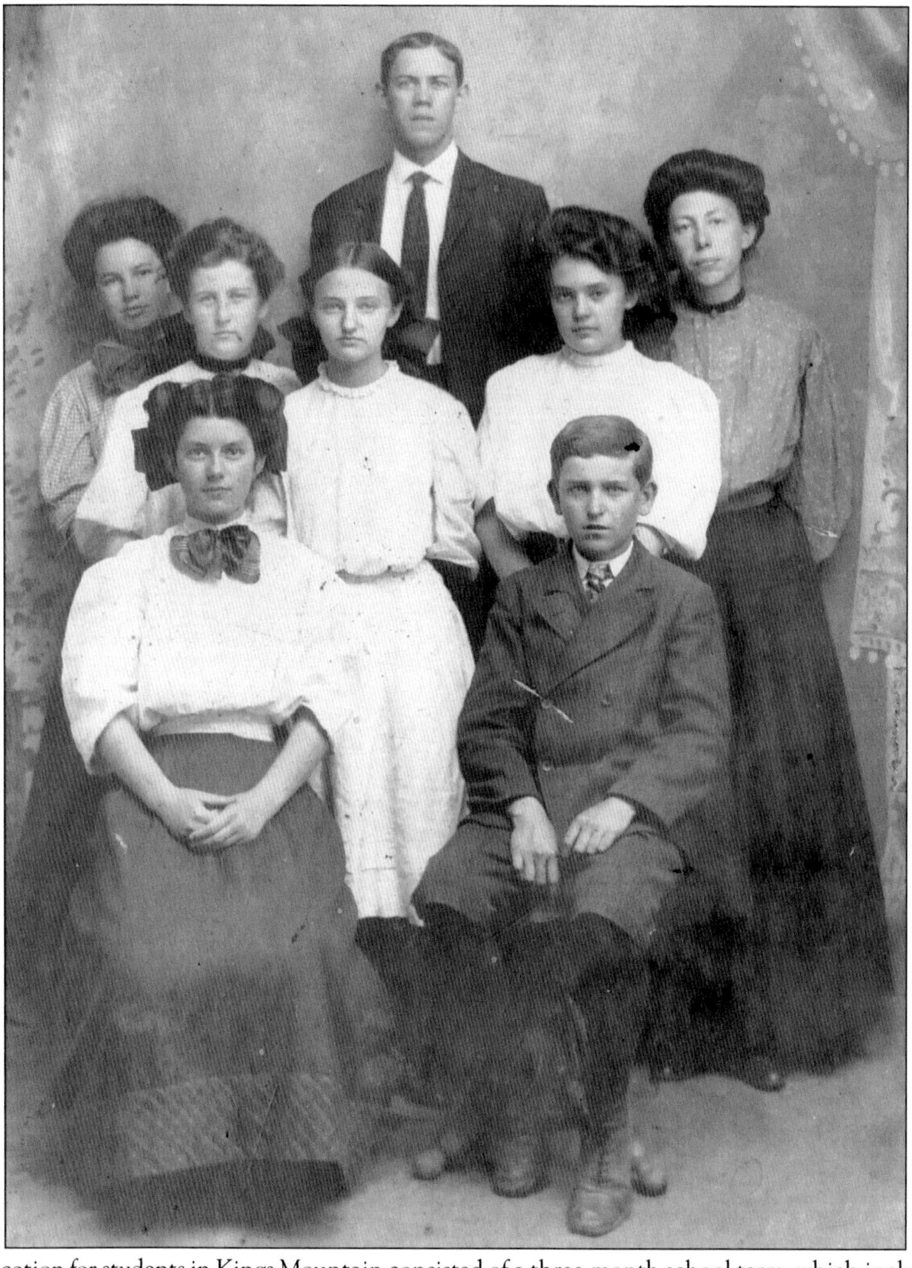

Education for students in Kings Mountain consisted of a three-month school term, which included lessons in mathematics, physics, chemistry, science, English, Latin, French, and German. This photograph shows the Kings Mountain High School class of 1910. From left to right, they are (first row) Kate McKay and Johnny Ramseur; (second row) Lina Allison, Ethel Plonk, and May Plonk; (third row) Estelle W., Theron Allen, and Edith Fulton. Initially the second home of Bell's Military Academy, this property has continued to serve as a place of education until present times. In 1910, a fire destroyed the wooden-frame school building that served the Kings Mountain Central School. The Second Central School, a two-story, redbrick building trimmed with gray granite, was erected in its place. Another fire on November 15, 1932, destroyed both this building and all student records housed there.

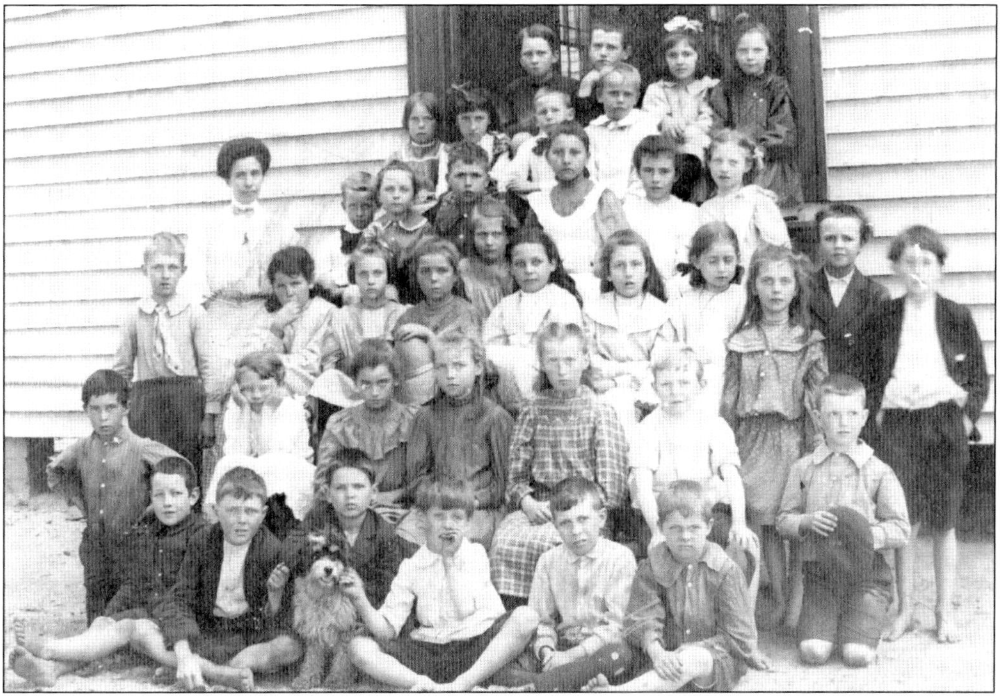

Among the children in this photograph of the 1907–1908 second-grade class at Central Graded School is Ruth Baumgardner (third row, fifth from the left). The one-room classroom brought together older and younger students, seating them alternately to aid the younger ones with their studies.

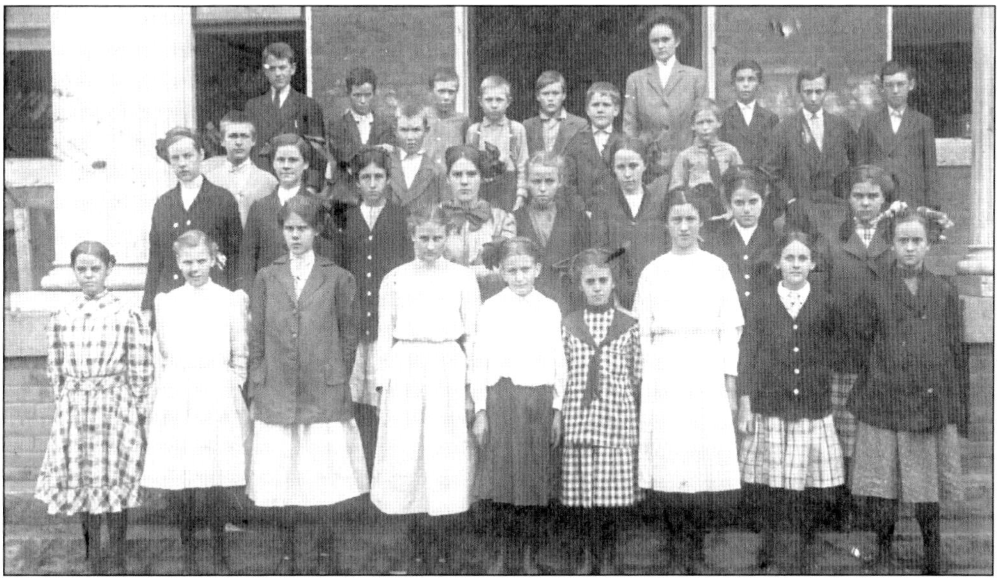

Shown in this image of Miss Frier's 1911 sixth-grade class are Bill Ramseur (left) and Joe Neisler (right) standing next to the teacher in the back row. Also shown in this photograph are Ethel Roberts (first row, seventh from left), Vergie Harmon (second row, second from left), Ruth Baumgardner (second row, third from left), Eula Hayes (second row, fourth from left), and Mary Fulton (second row, eighth from left).

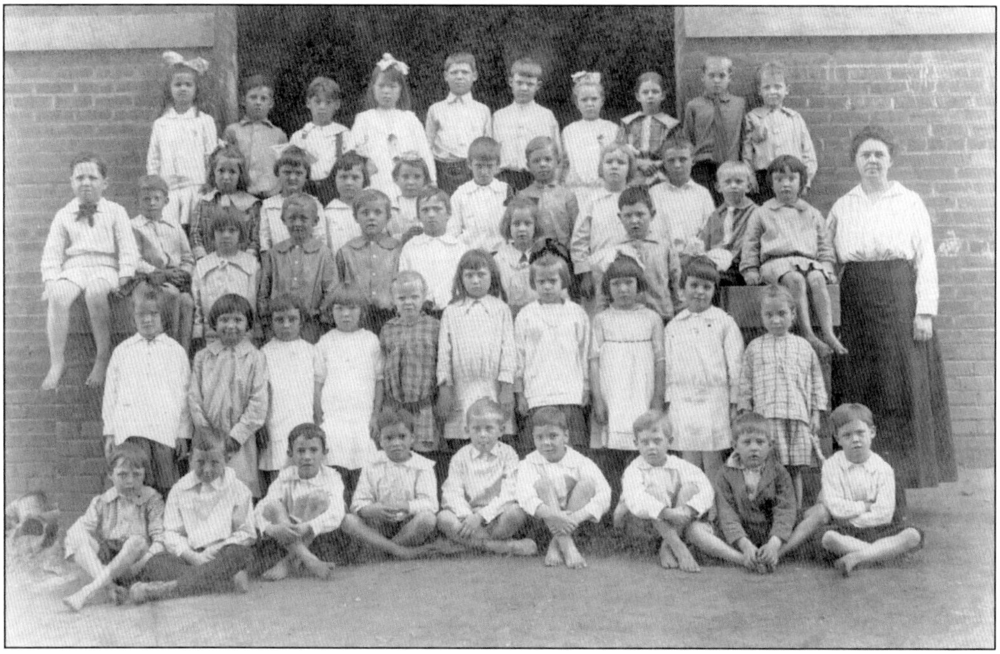

Just prior to the American entry into World War I in 1914, the Central School was organized into nine grades with eight teachers. In addition, the school's trustees extended the school term from three to eight months. At this time, athletics and other extracurricular activities were not part of school life. In the photograph above, Daisy Lovelace (far right) stands with her first-grade class in 1915 outside of the Central School building. The class photograph below was taken on May 3, 1917. Emelyn Dilling and Robert Dilling are among those seated with the class in this image.

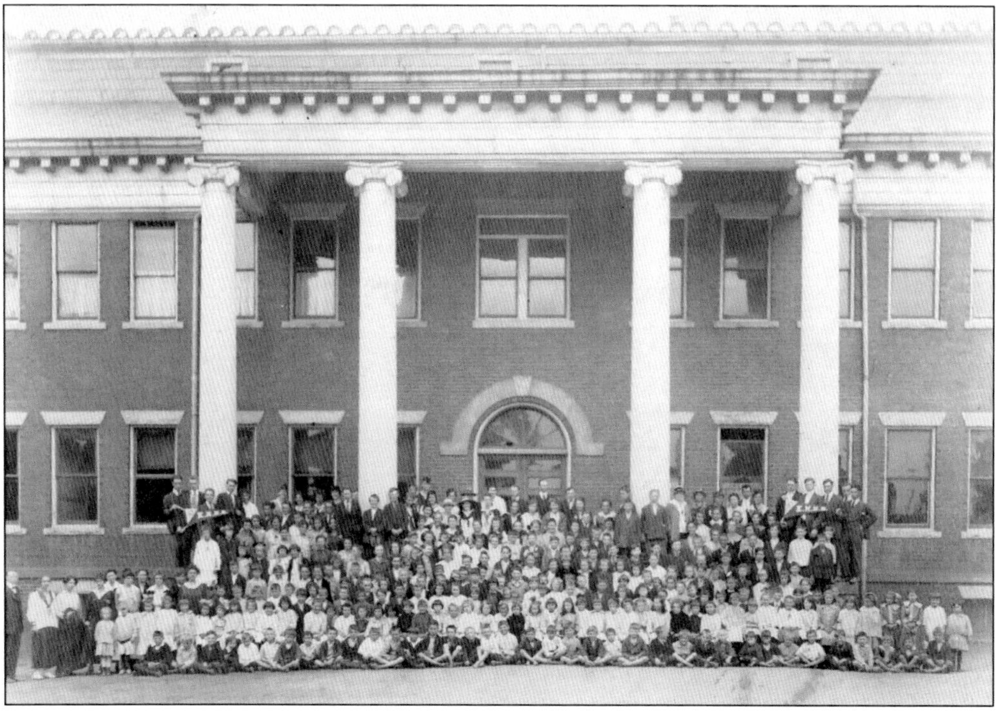

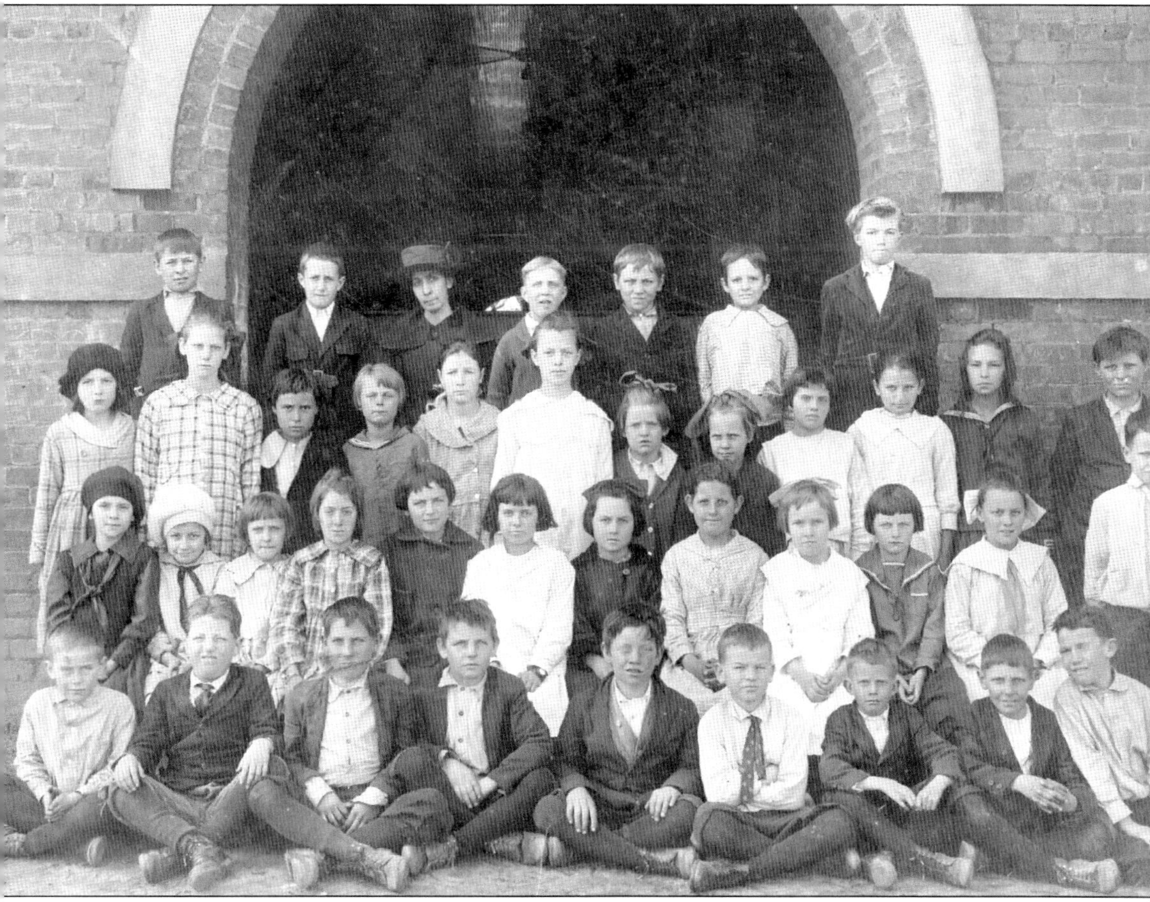

In 1919, Bessie Simonton taught the Central School third-grade class. In this photograph, from left to right, are (first row) George Moss, Harold Crawford, G.L. Wright, Everett Cashion, Clyde Jolly, Arthur Sanders, Hubert Davidson, Hubert McGinnis, and Glenn Wilson; (second row) Lucille Cansler Falls, Helen Ridenhour Ferguson, Elizabeth Ware Leslie, Ivy Falls Weaver, Aileen Cobb, Louise Carpenter, Ruth McGinnis Caveny, unidentified, Helen Logan, Mable Regan, Carrie Huffstetler, and Eugene Roberts; (third row) Beatrice Hord, Willie Morris, Maude Williams McGill, Thelma Huffstetler, Nellie Jackson, Lucy Haynes, Grace Neisler Page, Mary Elizabeth Elam Vance, Ruth Lindsay, Nellie Detmar, Vera Cole Cash, and Robert Barber; (fourth row) Lumuel Ware, Buck Dilling, Bessie Simonton, LeRhyne Houser, Floyd Jenkins, Clyde Detmar, and Curtis Falls.

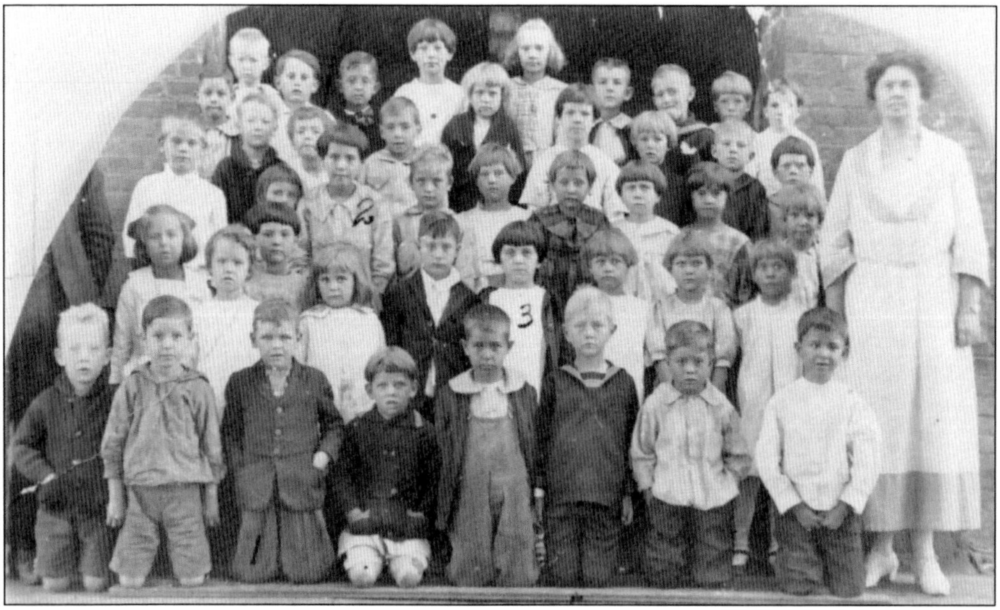

This image of the Central School 1921–1922 first-grade class shows, from left to right, (first row) Allen Herndon, Jack Ormand, Jake Earley, Bill Jolly, unidentified, Clarence Lovell, Howard Huffstetler, and unidentified; (second row) Edith Ledford, Jessie Falls, Bernice Ware, two unidentified children, Mary Frances McGinnis, two unidentified children, Lucille McGinnis, and Daisy Lovelace (teacher); (third row) Charlie Sims, Lillian Lackey, Ruth Jenkins, unidentified, Hilda Barber, unidentified, Juanita Costner, unidentified, and Estelle Barrett; (fourth row) George Houser, Arnold Jackson, Sarah Finger, Jim Anthony, unidentified, Martha Frances McGill, unidentified, Hubert Aderholt, and Bill Black; (fifth row) Thomas Styers, unidentified, Jack Parsons, Guynell Gladden, unidentified, Wendell Phifer, Enos Huffstetler, Vida Wright, and Elizabeth Arnette.

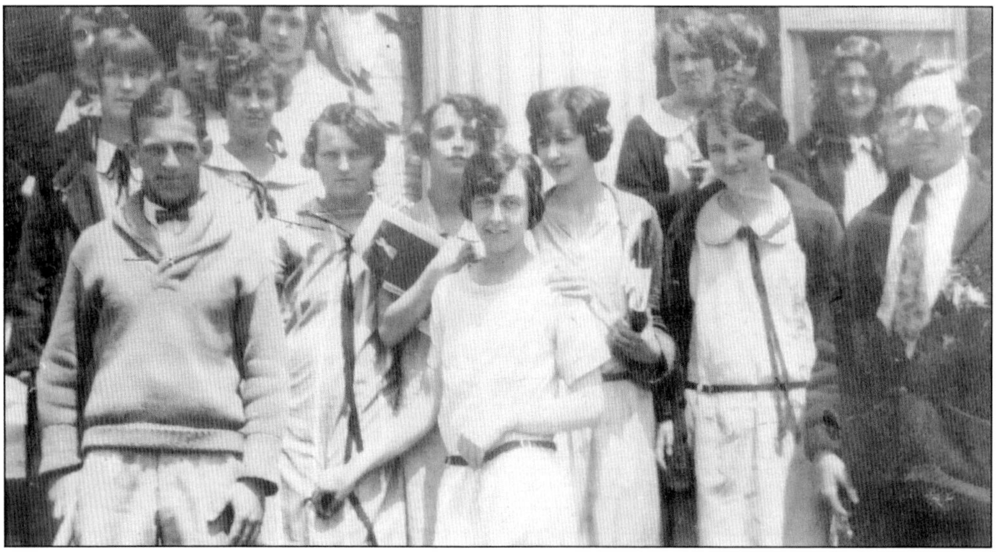

This photograph of the Kings Mountain High School junior class of 1925 came from a scrapbook belonging to Helen Hay. A note in the scrapbook next to the photograph lists the junior class officers: Nannie Plonk as president, Madge Patterson as vice president, Nell Hord as secretary, and Roy Hord as treasurer. (Courtesy of the *Kings Mountain Herald.*)

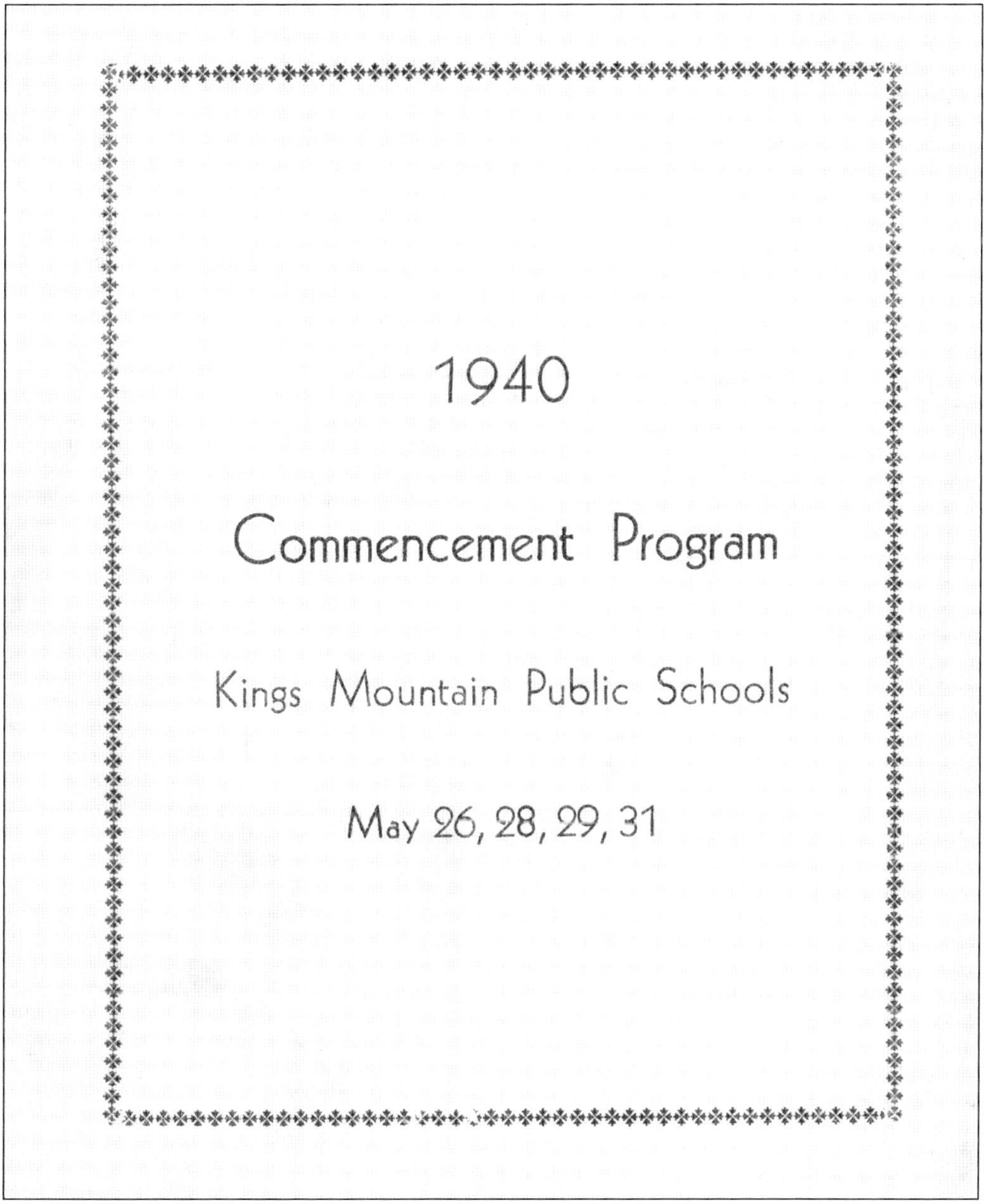

1940

Commencement Program

Kings Mountain Public Schools

May 26, 28, 29, 31

Commencement for the Kings Mountain Public Schools took place over a period of several days, starting each evening at 8:00 p.m. One evening was dedicated for a sermon, another for the grammar school, and another for the high school's program. In this 1940 commencement program, the occasion begins with a sermon on Tuesday, May 26. While there are no commencement activities on Wednesday, most likely to avoid interfering with religious services, the program resumed on Thursday, May 28 with the grammar school graduating exercises. The high school graduating exercises were then held that Friday evening with the awarding of the diplomas. On Saturday, May 31, the festivities concluded with the senior class play *China Boy*. The girls', boys', and grammar school glee clubs all performed throughout the event. In addition to the class roster and list of class officers, the program also contains additional information about the class (their motto was "to be, rather than to seem" and their colors were orchid and pink).

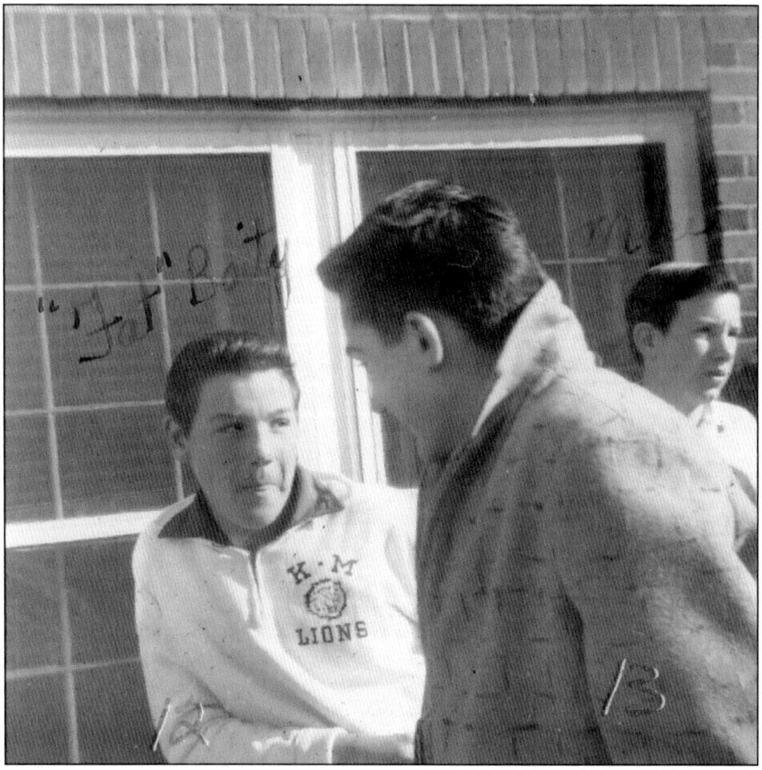

This photograph, taken near the back of the Kings Mountain High School during the 1956–1957 school year, shows, from left to right, eighth-graders James Baity, Arthur Allen, and Mike McSwain. During that school year, the high school consisted of grades 8 through 12. Eighth-grade classes were held on the first floor, while the high school was on the upper and basement floors. (Courtesy of Mary Lewis Nantz.)

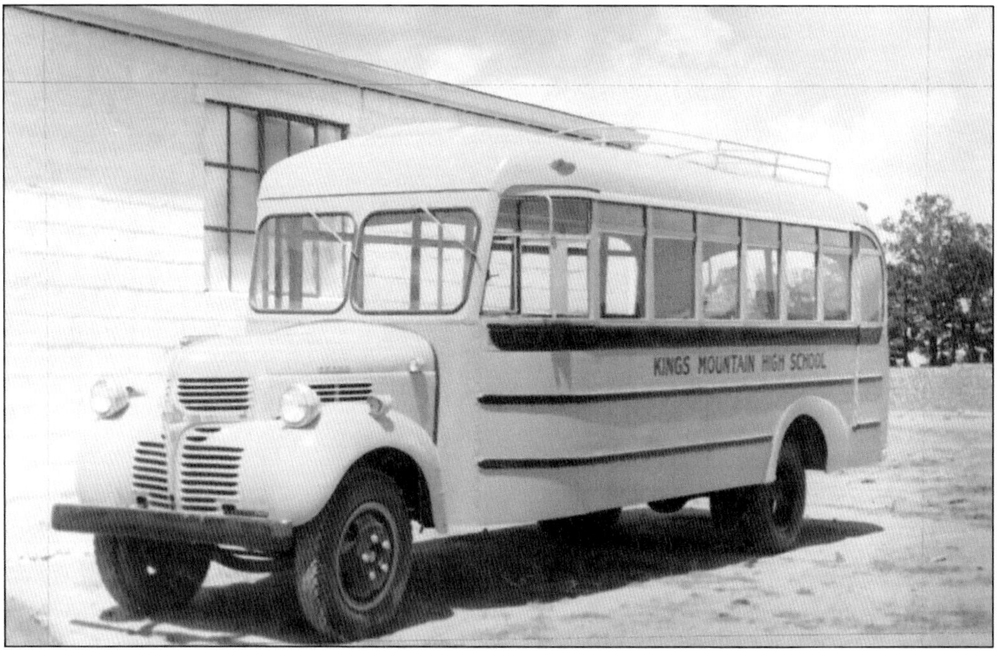

The Kings Mountain High School bus shown in this photograph dates to the 1950s. School buses became popular after World War II; as suburban areas grew, the distance children needed to travel to reach the school increased. This led to an increase in the demand for school buses in cities, suburbs, and rural areas.

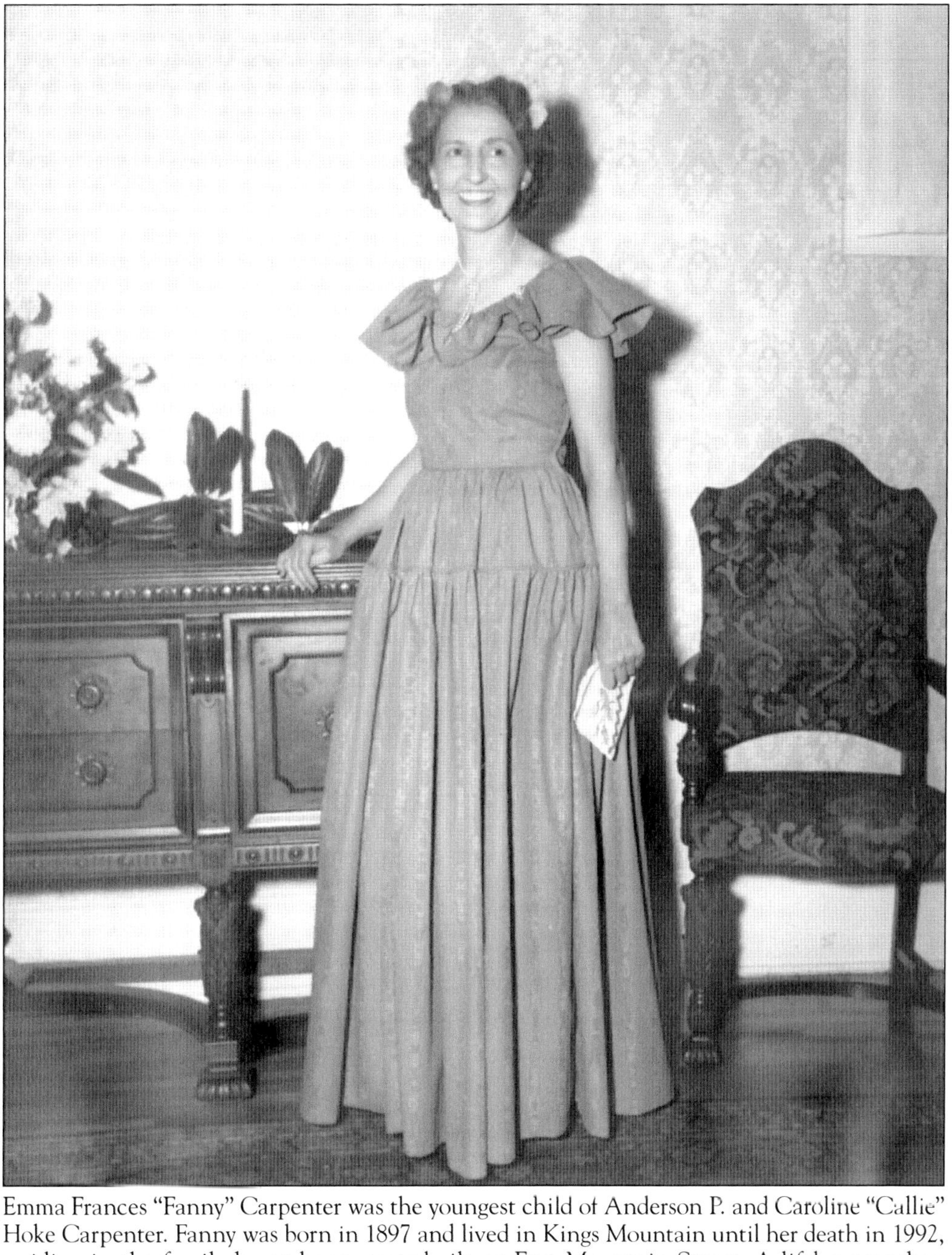

Emma Frances "Fanny" Carpenter was the youngest child of Anderson P. and Caroline "Callie" Hoke Carpenter. Fanny was born in 1897 and lived in Kings Mountain until her death in 1992, residing in the family home her parents built on East Mountain Street. A lifelong teacher, Fanny taught third grade for several schools, primarily in the Kings Mountain School District, for decades. Fanny went away to college at Georgia Normal, now the University of Georgia. At that time, it was uncommon for women to continue their education past high school. (Courtesy of Laura Carpenter Bingham.)

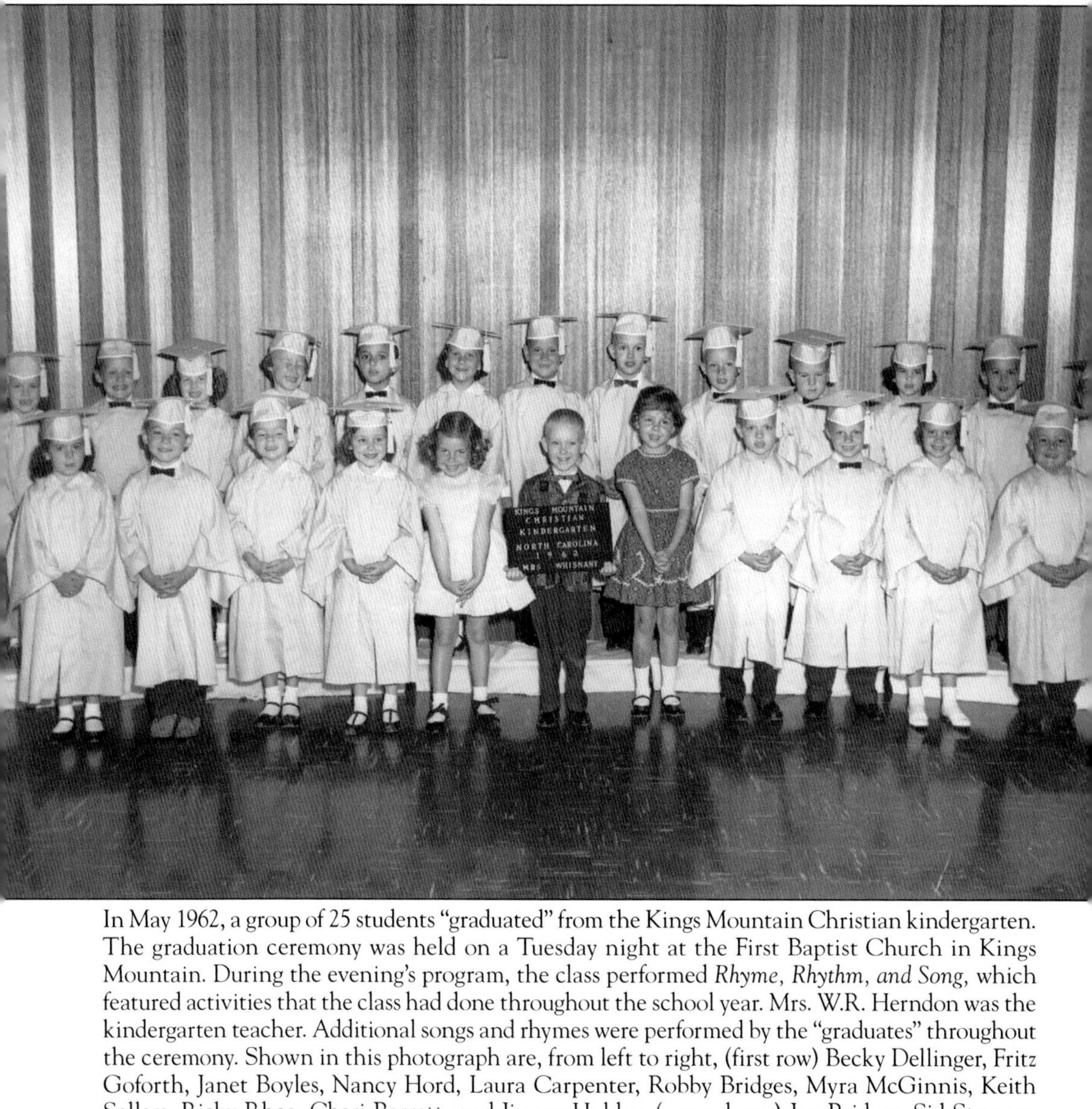

In May 1962, a group of 25 students "graduated" from the Kings Mountain Christian kindergarten. The graduation ceremony was held on a Tuesday night at the First Baptist Church in Kings Mountain. During the evening's program, the class performed *Rhyme, Rhythm, and Song,* which featured activities that the class had done throughout the school year. Mrs. W.R. Herndon was the kindergarten teacher. Additional songs and rhymes were performed by the "graduates" throughout the ceremony. Shown in this photograph are, from left to right, (first row) Becky Dellinger, Fritz Goforth, Janet Boyles, Nancy Hord, Laura Carpenter, Robby Bridges, Myra McGinnis, Keith Sellers, Ricky Rhea, Cheri Barrett, and Jimmy Holder; (second row) Joy Bridges, Sid Stroupe, Patricia McKee, Jane Tate, Mike Hardin, Johnanna Phifer, Marty Phifer, Billy Talbert, Monty Wilson, Mark Withers, Sharon Timms, John Knox McGill, and Keith Dillingham. (Courtesy of Laura Carpenter Bingham.)

Josephine Ellerbe Weir is shown at work in the Kings Mountain High School Library. Weir worked in the Kings Mountain schools for over 40 years. She was civically active and cochaired the Kings Mountain centennial celebration in 1974 as well as the beautification committee for the new city hall. The Weir Auditorium was dedicated in her honor as part of the 1988 renovation of the Mauney Memorial Library.

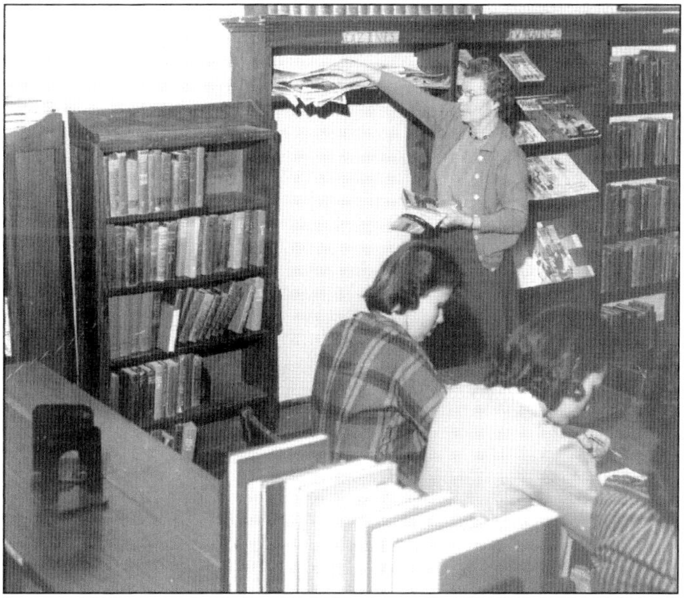

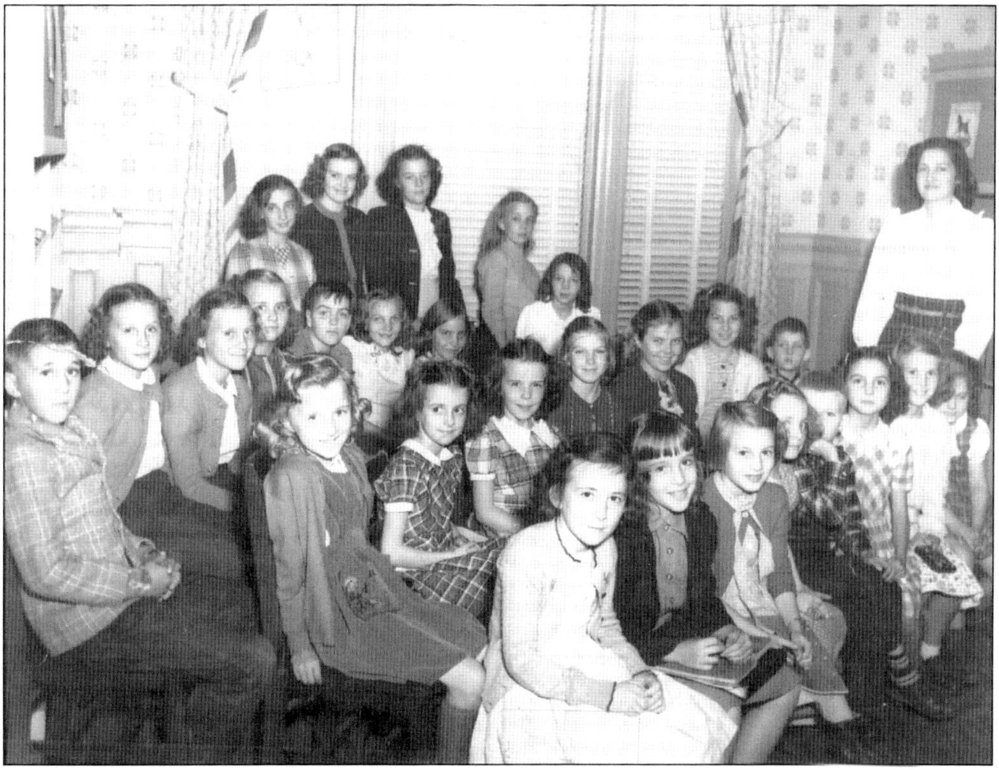

Children's services are an important part of library services. Among those attending a library program, as identified by names written on the back of this photograph, are Ronnie Ledford, Evelyn Hullender, Mearl Valentine, Pat Edwards, Louise Hullender, Ruth McCurdy Matthews, Peggy Black, Sue Barrett, Frank Hoyle, Jackie Dixon, Dianne Henderson, Judy Cooper, Kathy Hoyle, Patti Ledford, Anne Dillany, Lee Jackson, Dixie Blanton, and Peggy Cline Wells. (Courtesy of the Jacob S. Mauney Memorial Library.)

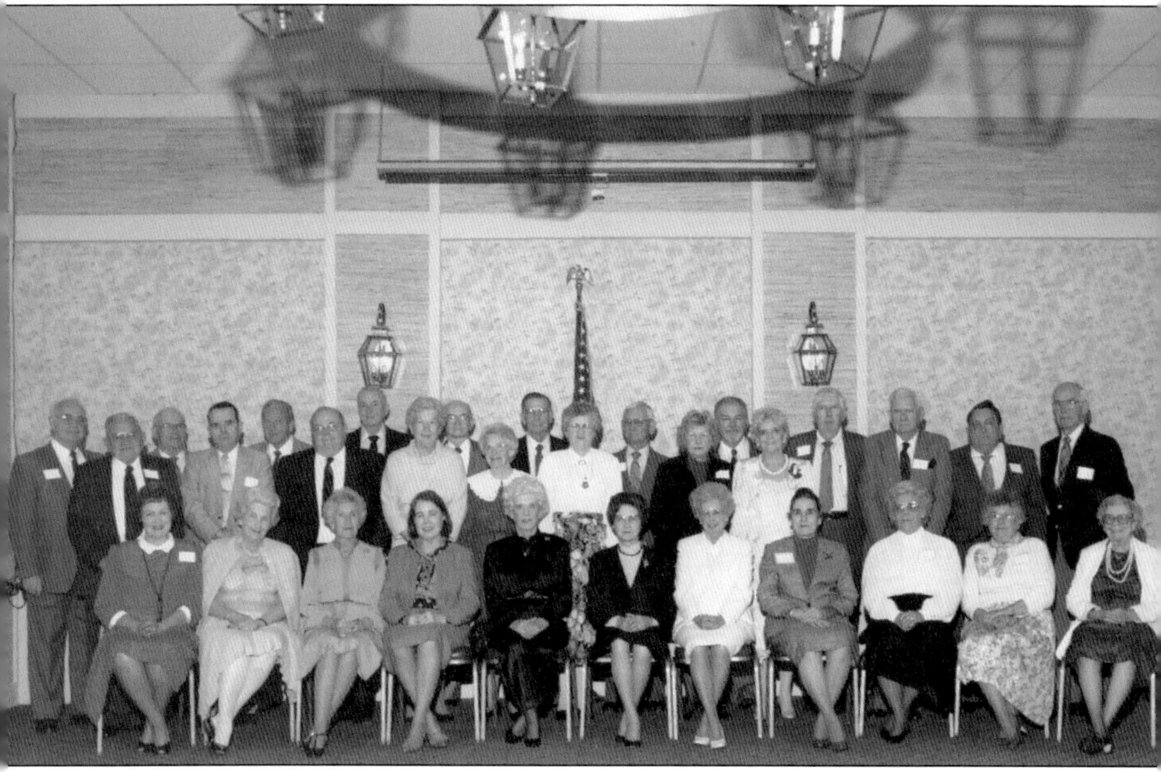

When the 1938 Kings Mountain High School class graduated, 48 students received diplomas. On October 8, 1988, thirty of those members met at the Holiday Inn for their 50th class reunion. Through the late 1930s, the Kings Mountain school system required 11 grades for graduation. The class of 1938 was one of the final graduating classes to stop at 11th grade. Pictured are Aileen (Black) Gibson, Lois (Baity) Guyton, Jewell (Brackett) Grigg, C.T. Carpenter Jr., Betty (Cloninger) Smith, Marion Everette Cloninger, William L. Davis, Charles A. Earp, Irene (Gladden) McAbee, Ned Hayes, Mildred (Jolly) English, John D. Jones, Virginia (Logan) Sams, George H. Mauney, Lillian (Moss) Wright, Buren S. Neill Jr., Phyllis (Patterson) Cheshire, Faye (Penland) Cowan, Elizabeth (Plonk) Mercer, J. Harold Plonk, Nina (Putman) Nebel, Nell (Sherrer) Brafford, Sarah Henry (Summitt) Randall, Paul Stewart, Paul W. Walker, Lloyd Excell Welch, Marriott D. Phifer, Charles B. Campbell Jr., Robert Cecil Crook, and Norma (Mayhew) Guyton. (Courtesy of Laura Carpenter Bingham.)

Five

Play

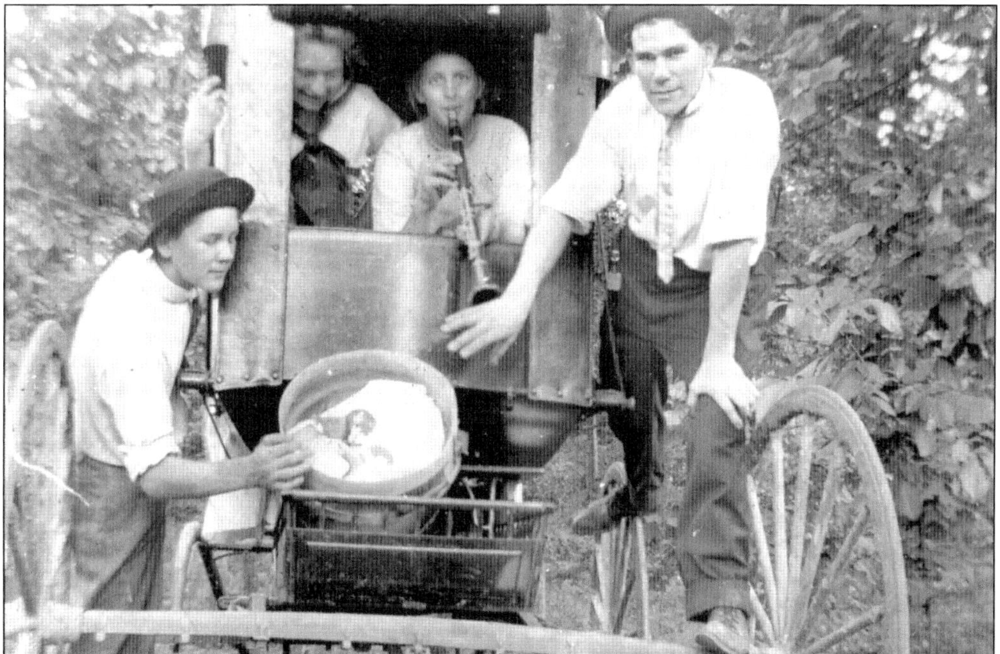

Music was an important part of Southern life during the early 20th century. Many people played an instrument, and impromptu bands would form in mill villages and at community and social events. Those that were unable to play an instrument often accompanied the group by singing. Shown in this c. 1910 photograph are members of the Neisler family. (Courtesy of Neisler Brothers, Inc.)

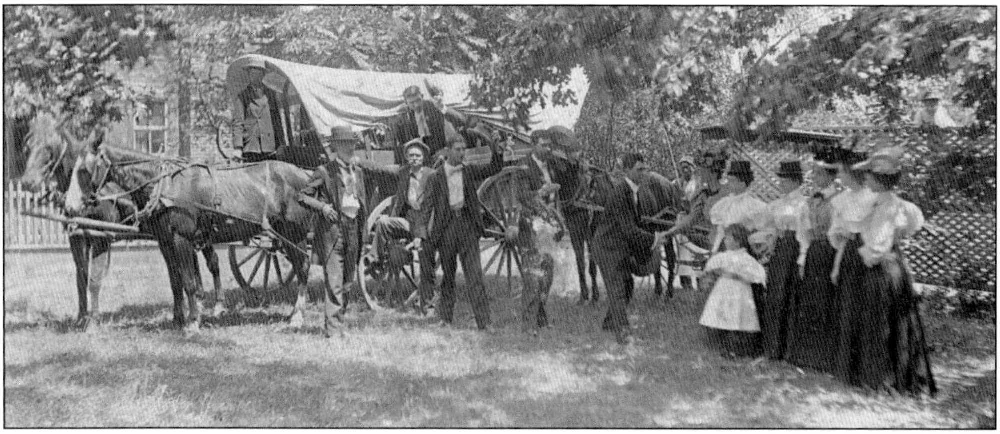

During the 19th century, residents of the area would travel on short trips to the mountains for rest and recreation. This photograph from the scrapbook of Helen Hay shows the members of the Hay family preparing for a trip. On the back of the photograph, a handwritten note explains, saying "Hay men bidding goodbye starting on a trip to the mountains. Circa mid-nineteenth century." (Courtesy of the *Kings Mountain Herald*.)

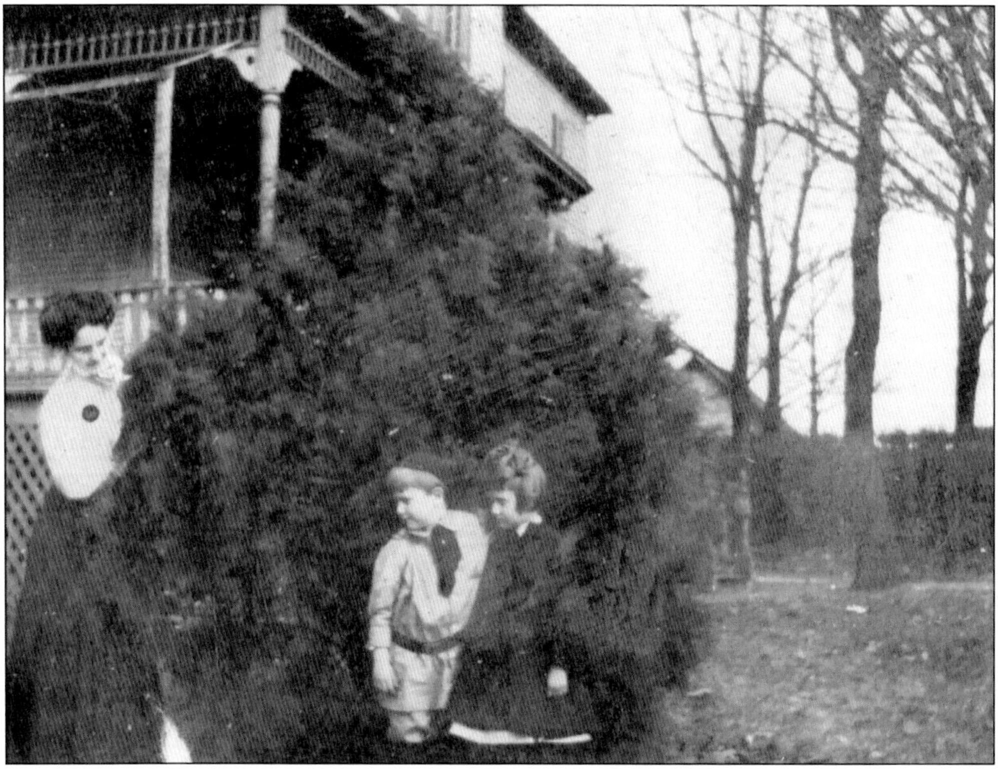

This photograph, taken at the home of Ida Pauline Mauney Neisler on Piedmont Avenue, shows mother and children engaged in a game of hide-and-seek. Hide-and-seek was a popular form of entertainment for children during the 1900s, as were card games, marbles, handmade dolls, and other wooden toys. (Courtesy of Neisler Brothers, Inc.)

Picnics were a popular recreational activity for families during the late 19th and early 20th centuries. These social occasions were often held at locations with visual appeal. Members of the Neisler family are seen in this c. 1910 photograph near Kings Mountain. (Courtesy of Neisler Brothers, Inc.)

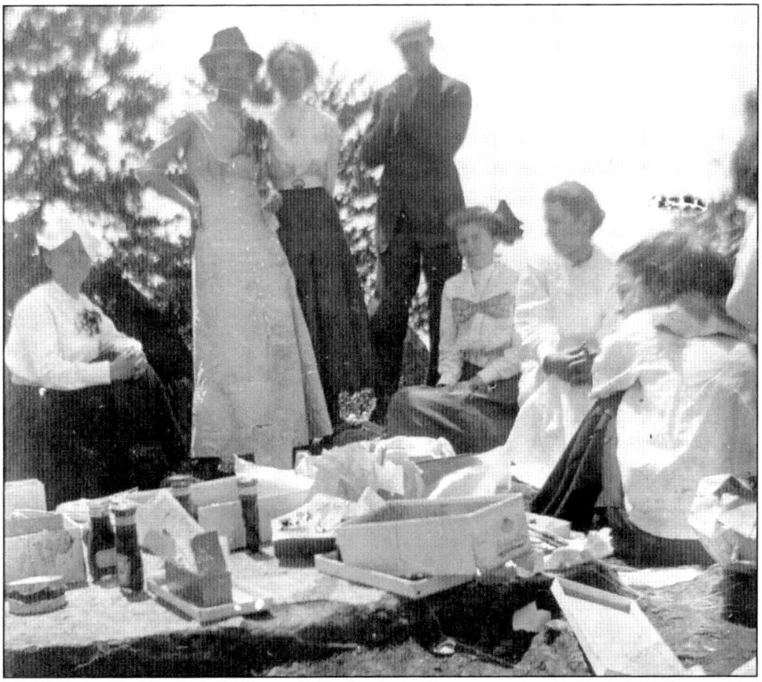

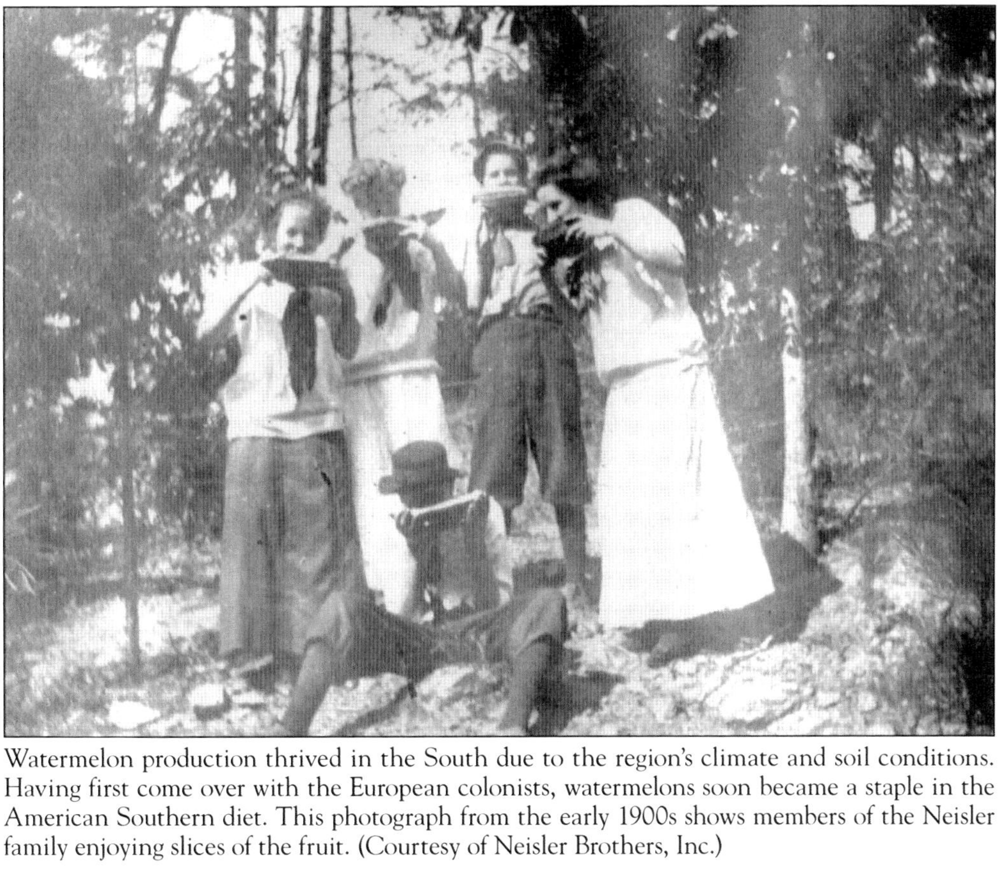

Watermelon production thrived in the South due to the region's climate and soil conditions. Having first come over with the European colonists, watermelons soon became a staple in the American Southern diet. This photograph from the early 1900s shows members of the Neisler family enjoying slices of the fruit. (Courtesy of Neisler Brothers, Inc.)

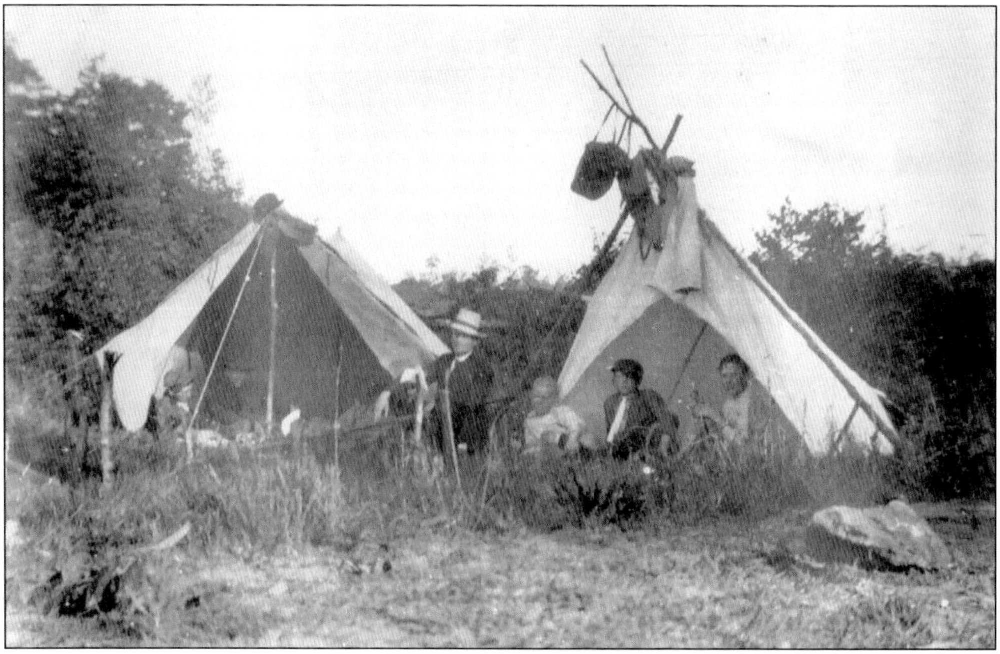

The Boy Scouts of America developed from a British version founded by Lord Robert Baden-Powell in London, England. Popular programs for the young men who participated in the program, usually between the ages of 11 and 18, involved outdoor activities, such as camping and hiking. In 1910, Kings Mountain was the first city in North Carolina to institute its own Boy Scout troop. The group met in the evenings at St. Matthew's Lutheran Church. Although it is not certain whether these young men were Boy Scouts, they are shown doing the activities that would have taken place during a scouting program. (Courtesy of Neisler Brothers, Inc.)

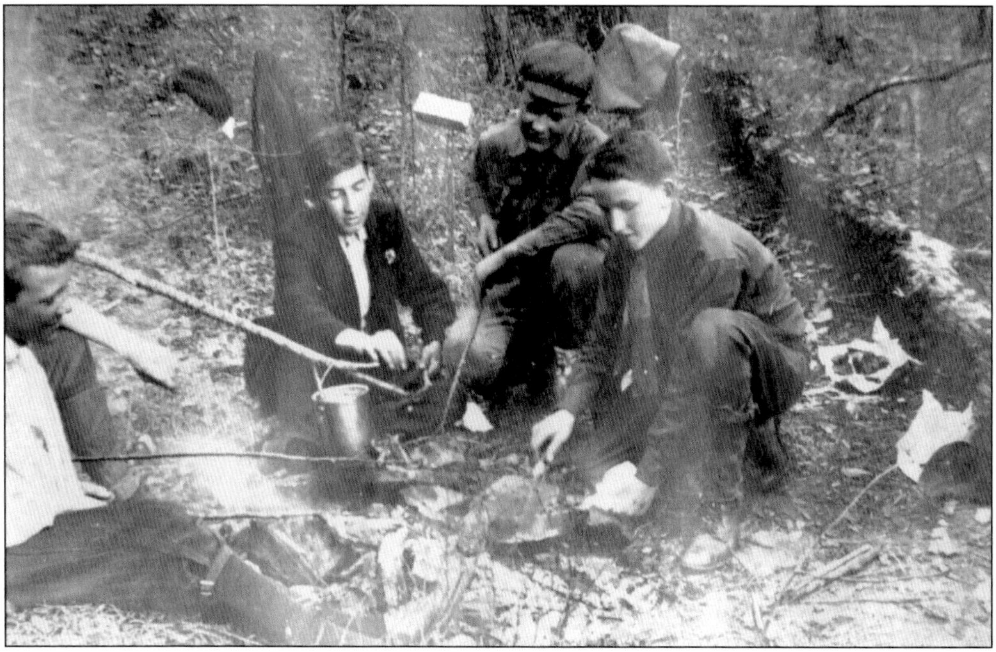

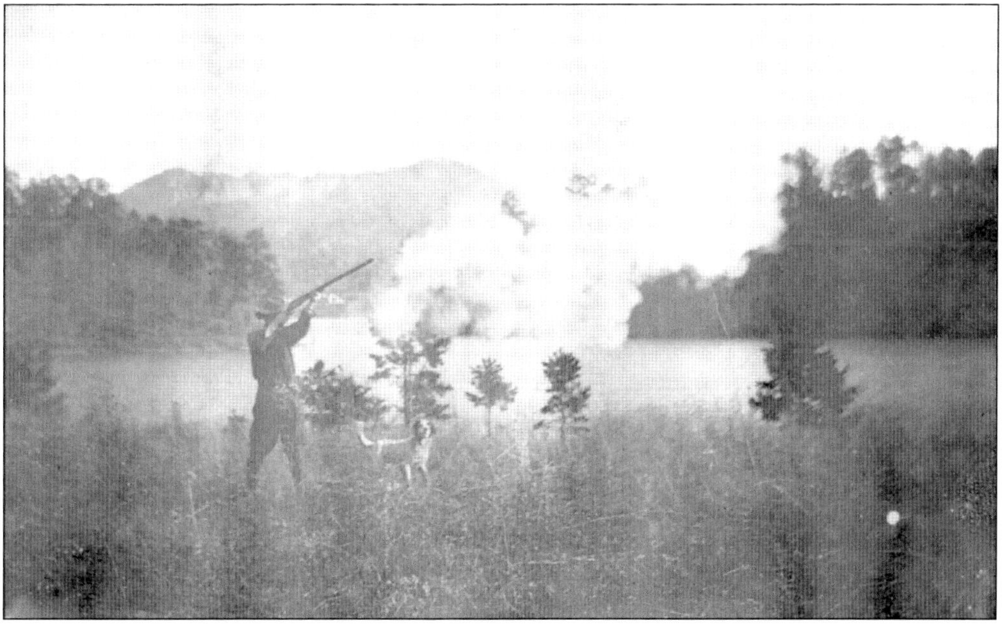

This photograph of a young man and dog was taken from the Neisler family scrapbooks. It is hard to determine whether the man is hunting or partaking in the recreational activity of skeet shooting. In the background is Kings Mountain. The origin of the mountain's name is unknown, but tradition suggests that it came not from an individual man, but is a reference to an English king. (Courtesy of Neisler Brothers, Inc.)

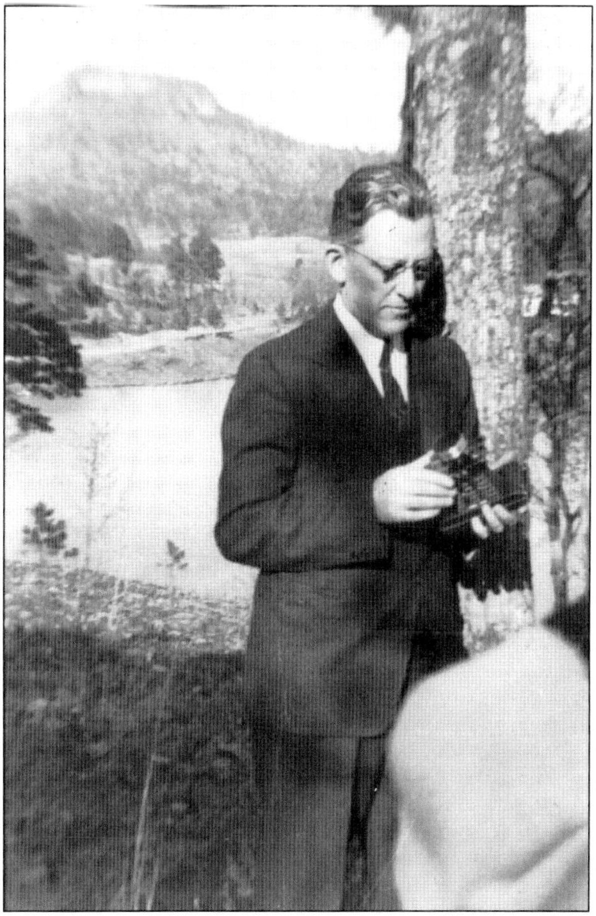

Dr. O.P. Lewis is shown resting next to a tree with his camera while out at his cabin at Lake Montonia during the spring of 1940. In the background is Kings Pinnacle, part of the Kings Mountain Range, famous for the Revolutionary War battle that raged there on October 7, 1780. (Courtesy of Mary Lewis Nantz.)

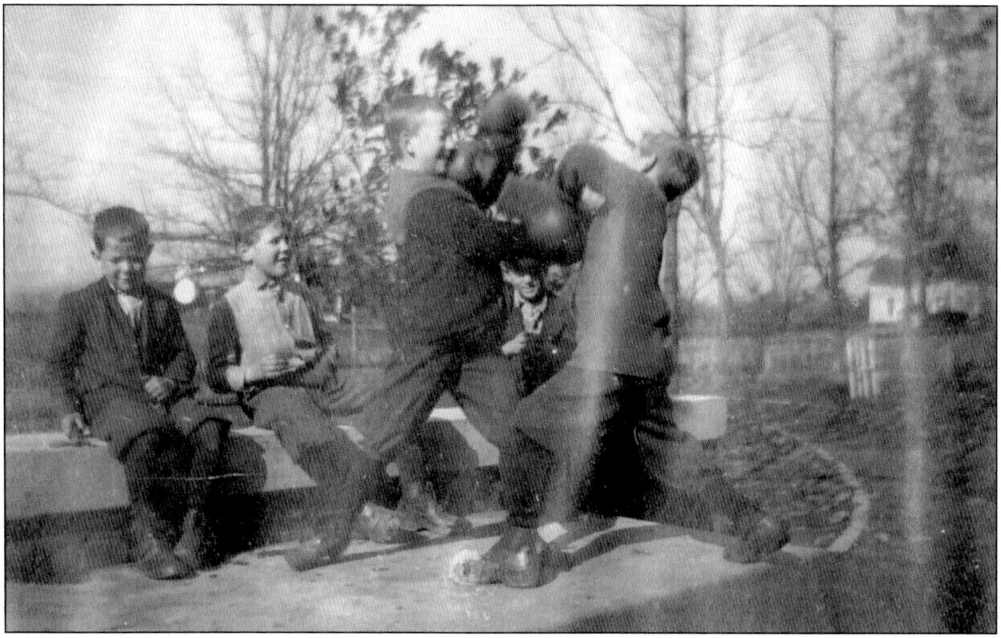

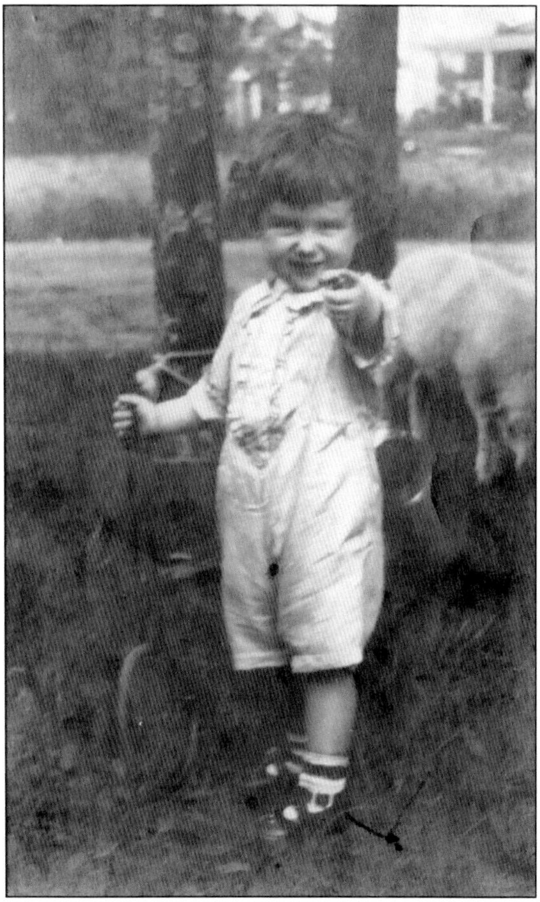

Hunter and Joe Neisler are seen boxing in this early-20th-century photograph. The sons of Charles Eugene and Ida Pauline Neisler, both Hunter and Joe went on to work for Neisler Mills, Inc.; Hunter as the chief designer, and Joe as the company's secretary. (Courtesy of Neisler Brothers, Inc.)

Charles T. Carpenter Jr. is shown in this photograph at age three or four with his pet lamb at the family's home on Gold Street. Troy and Aileen Ormand Carpenter built the family's house in 1923. Charles Carpenter went on to serve in Europe during World War II. Before leaving the military in 1946, he was awarded many medals, including Silver and Bronze Stars. (Courtesy of Laura Carpenter Bingham.)

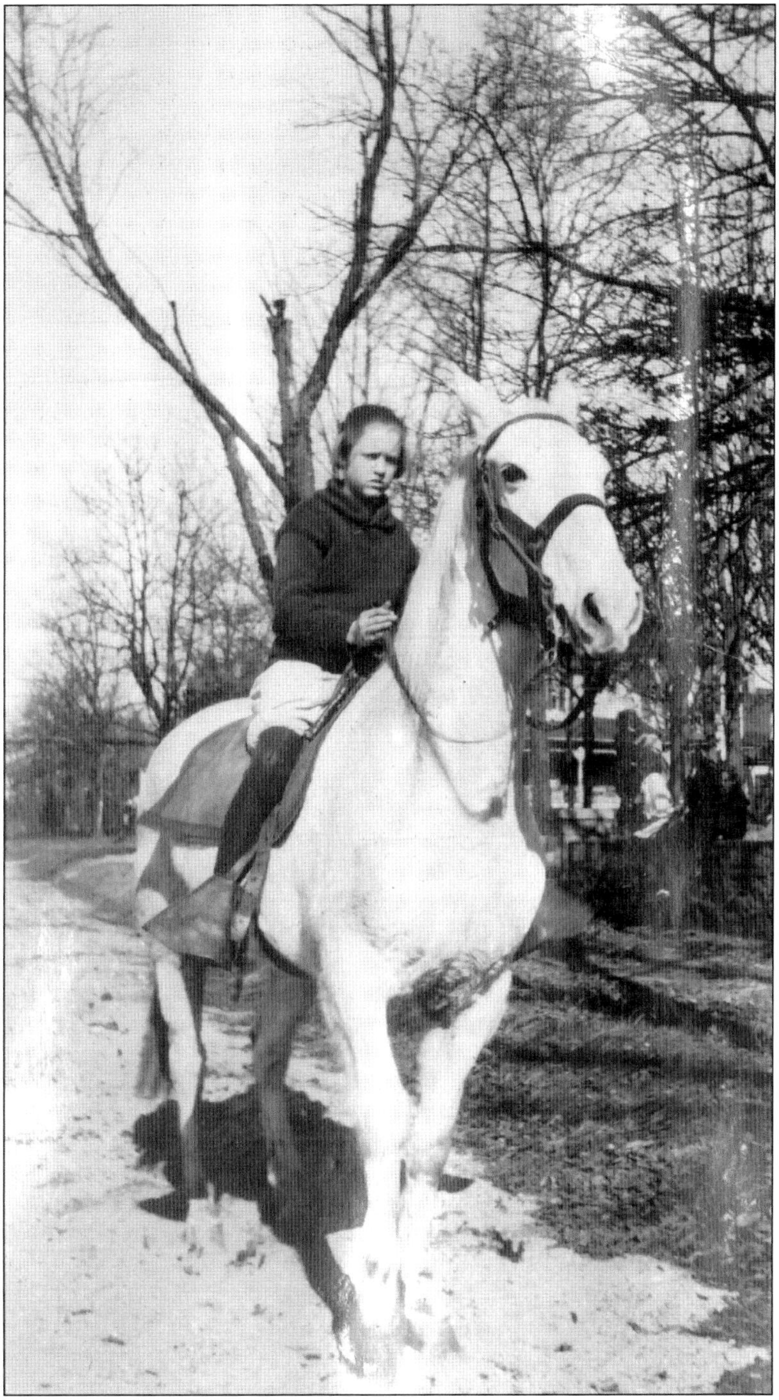

Grace Neisler Page was the daughter of Charles Eugene and Ida Pauline Mauney Neisler. In high school, Grace participated on the Kings Mountain High School women's basketball team from 1923 to 1927. In 1935, she won the North Carolina Women's Skeet Shooting Championship. The following year, she was a runner-up at the North-South Women's Skeet Shooting Championship. In 1937, Grace Neisler married Harry Ephraim Page. (Courtesy of Neisler Brothers, Inc.)

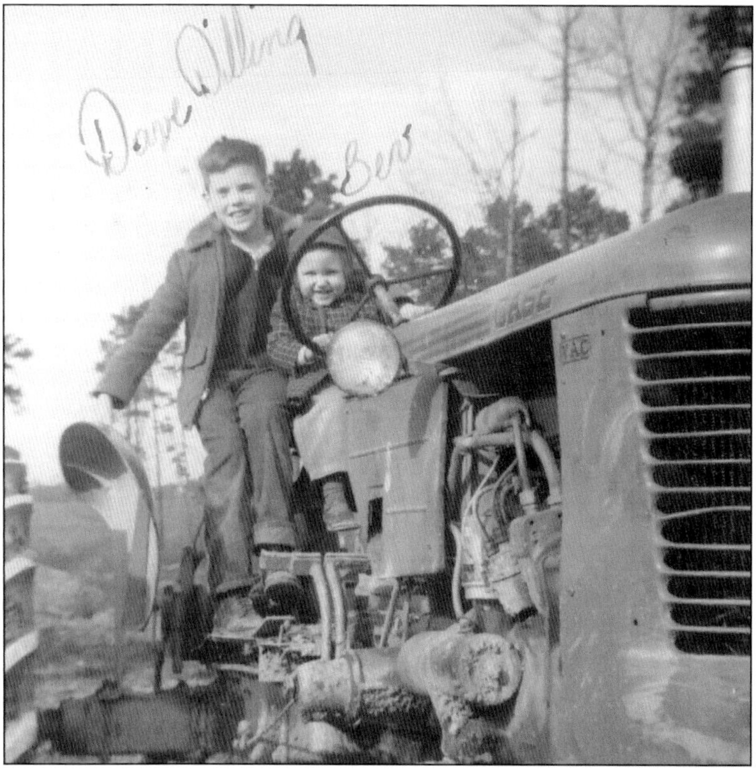

In 1957, David Thomas Dilling and Beverly Dorcas Plonk posed on this Case tractor at the farm of John Butler Plonk. John Plonk and his wife, Dorcas Carpenter Plonk, operated a dairy farm on County Line Road in Kings Mountain. The milk produced at the farm was shipped to Coble Dairy. (Courtesy of Mary Lewis Nantz.)

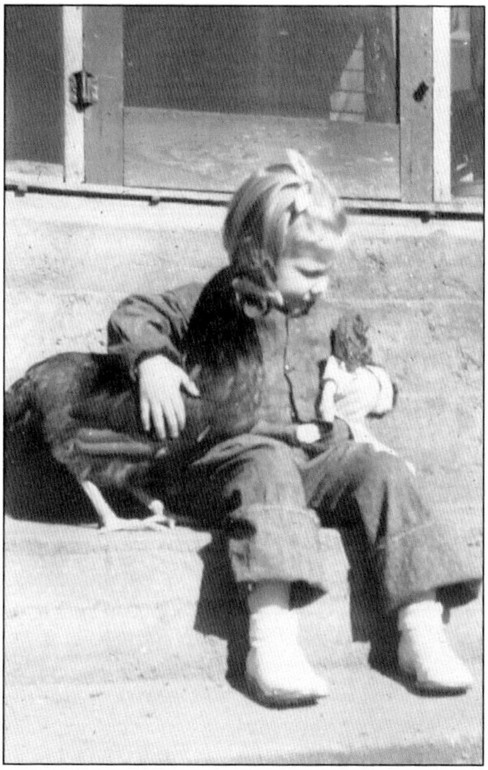

During her early childhood, Mary Lillian "Pucky" Lewis's playmates were the chickens in the backyard of her grandparents' house. This photograph from February 3, 1946, was just one of many taken by Sara Kate Ormand Lewis to send to her husband overseas during World War II. (Courtesy of Mary Lewis Nantz.)

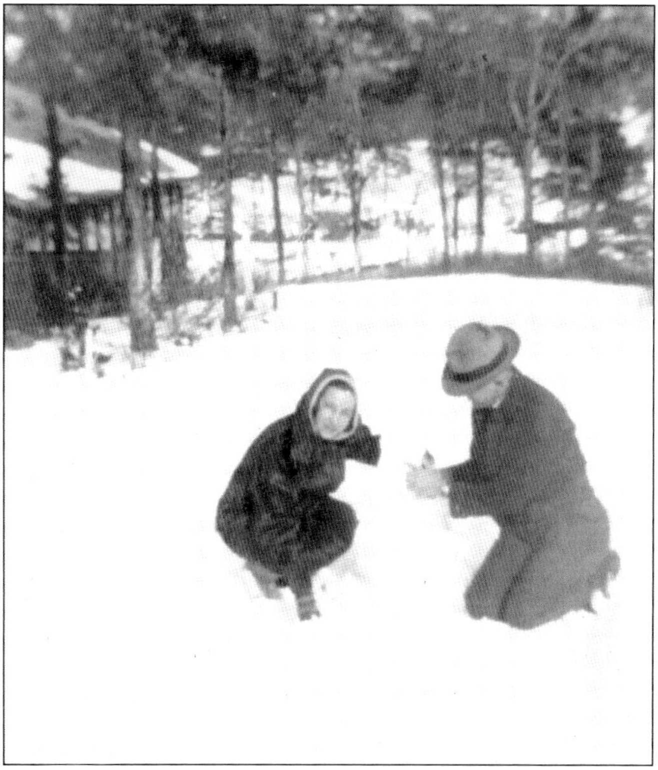

During the winter of 1939–1940, Sara Kate Ormand Lewis was able to take a photograph of Mary Mitchell and Dr. O.P. Lewis playing outside in front of the Lewises' cabin at Lake Montonia. The cabin shown in the background belonged to their neighbor J.C. Wilson of Gastonia. Dr. Lewis was a dentist, and Mary Mitchell taught eighth grade in Kings Mountain. (Courtesy of Mary Lewis Nantz.)

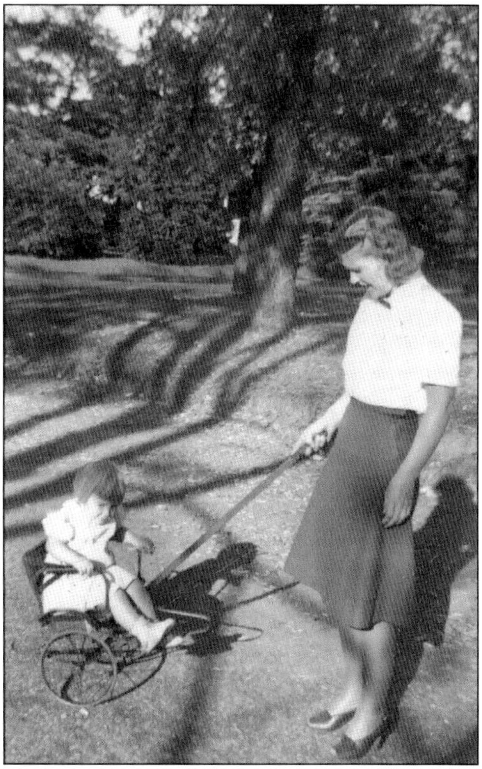

While her father was overseas during World War II, Mary Lillian "Pucky" Lewis and her mother, Sara Kate Ormand Lewis, lived with her grandparents, Lillian and B.M. Ormand, at the corner of West Mountain and Tracy Streets. This photograph shows Mary Lewis and her mother near the house in October 1944. (Courtesy of Mary Lewis Nantz.)

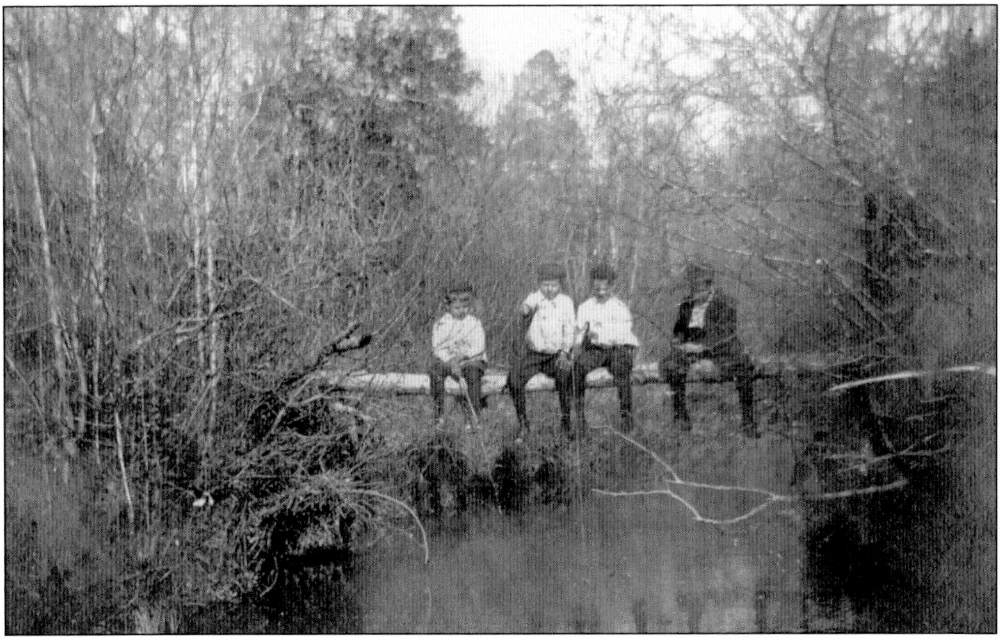

This photograph, taken during the early 1900s, shows four boys (most likely the sons of C.E. Neisler) fishing in a local river. Fishing was a popular and inexpensive pastime for young boys. Although the first commercially produced fishing rod was manufactured by the 1900s, many in rural communities continued to fish by tying twine to one end of a found stick. (Courtesy of Neisler Brothers, Inc.)

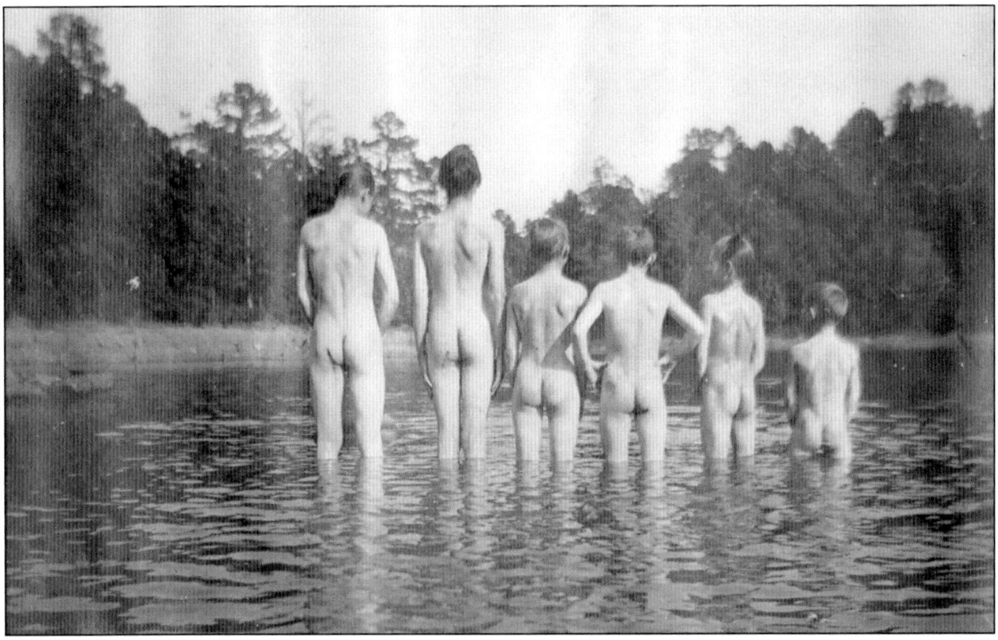

Businessmen from both Kings Mountain and Gastonia, combining the names of both places, created Lake Montonia in the early 1920s. The man-made lake and private recreational club offered a place where the men and their families could get away from the city to relax, hunt, fish, and, as shown in this photograph, swim. (Courtesy of Neisler Brothers, Inc.)

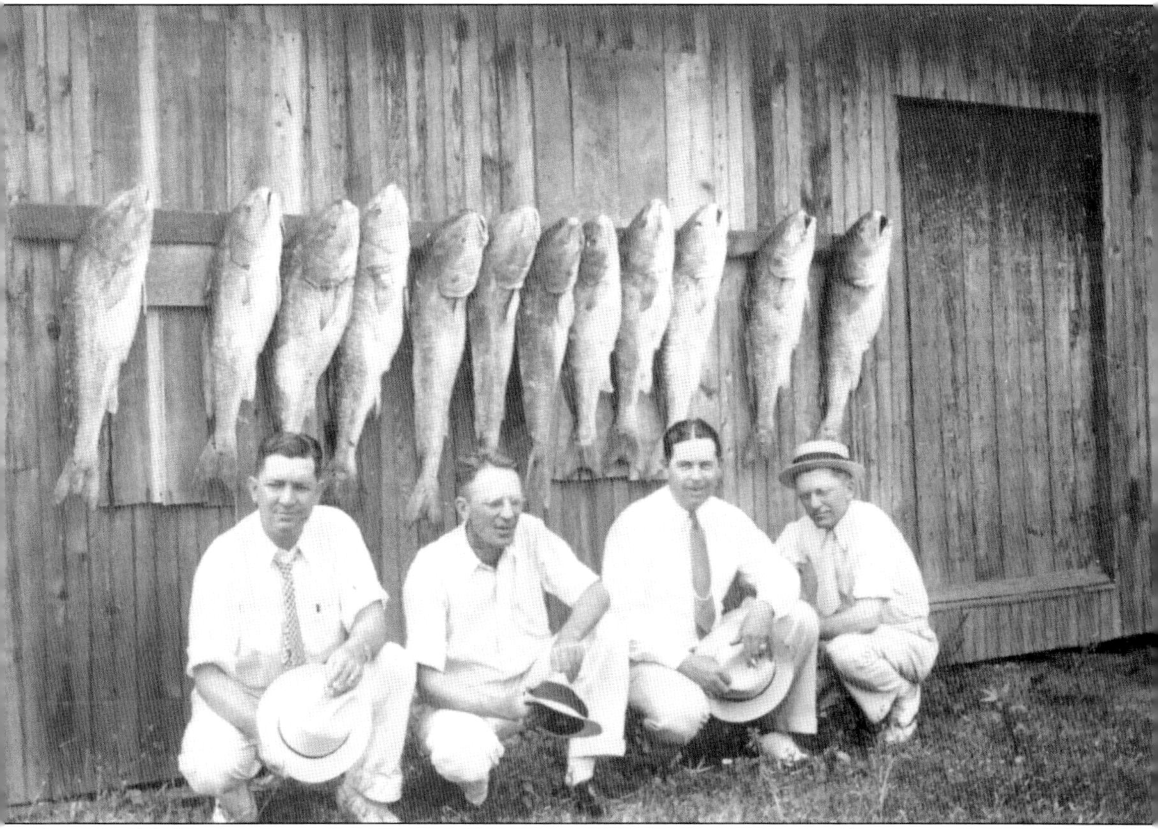

Fishing and hunting were sports enjoyed by many of the residents of Kings Mountain. Men from the Mauney and Neisler families often went on these sporting excursions together. Over time, they began including business associates on their trips. In this photograph, several members of the Kings Mountain business community are shown at "the old house, Catawba River," according to writing on the photograph, sometime between 1930 and 1932. Shown from left to right are Hunt Ramseur Neisler, Paul Mauney, Dr. William Lee Ramseur, and Dr. O.P. Lewis. The Catawba River is located not far from Kings Mountain and is still a popular fishing spot for residents. In addition to fishing, the men would spend time at Oakland Plantation in eastern North Carolina for an annual deer hunt. Oakland Plantation was purchased by Joseph A. Neisler Sr. in 1941 and is still owned by the Neisler family. (Courtesy of Mary Lewis Nantz.)

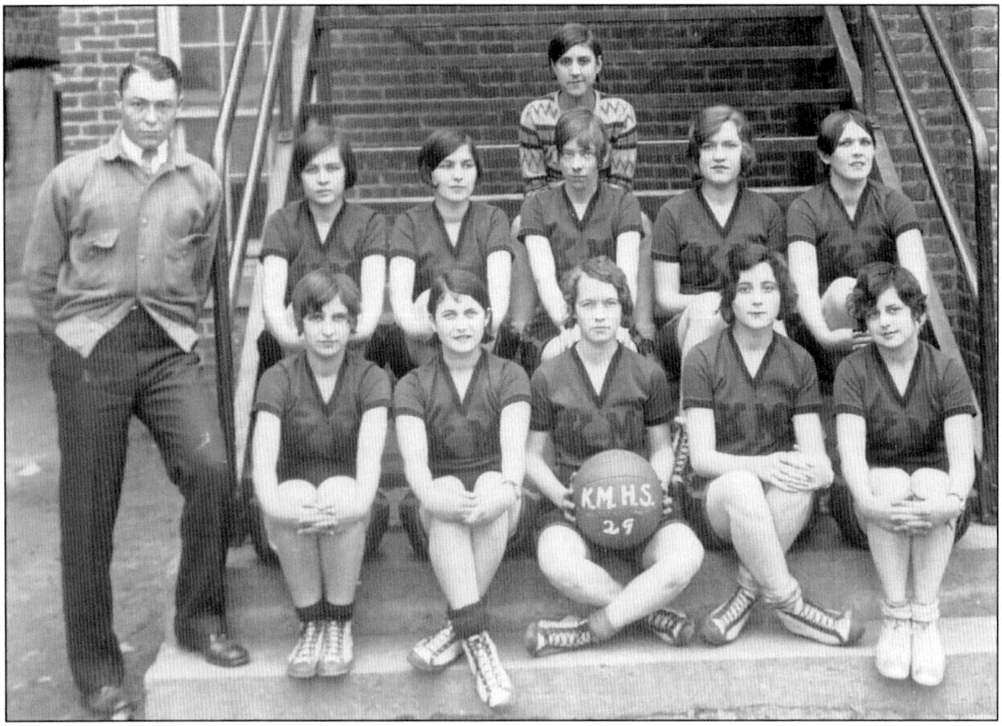

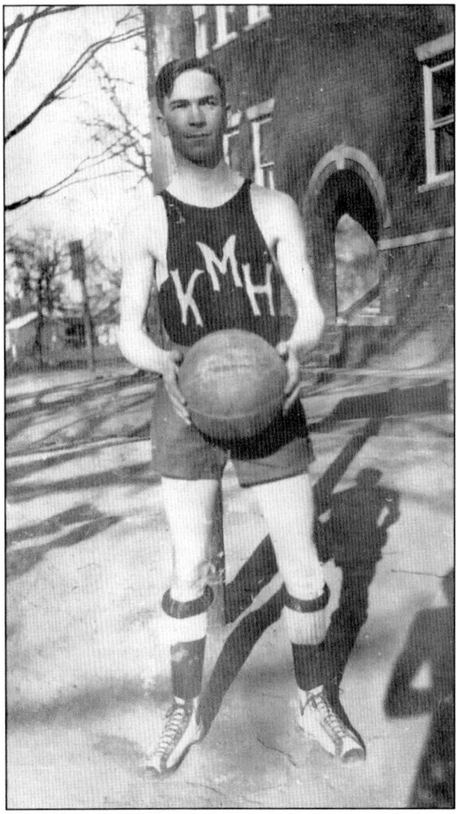

In this photograph of the 1929 Kings Mountain High School women's basketball team are, from left to right, (first row) coach E.A. Christenberry, Sara Hambright, Katherine O'Farrell, Bertie Wright, ? Hendrick, and Laura Mauney; (second row) Octavia Crawford, unidentified, Nancy Hord, Pauline Neisler, and Sara Ormand; (third row) Ruth Jenkins.

This unidentified basketball player was a member of the Kings Mountain High School basketball team around the 1920s. During the early 20th century, players were required to purchase their own equipment. The rules of the game at that time permitted only the center to stand at center court for the jump ball, while the other players waited for the ball to be tipped to them. (Courtesy of Neisler Brothers, Inc.)

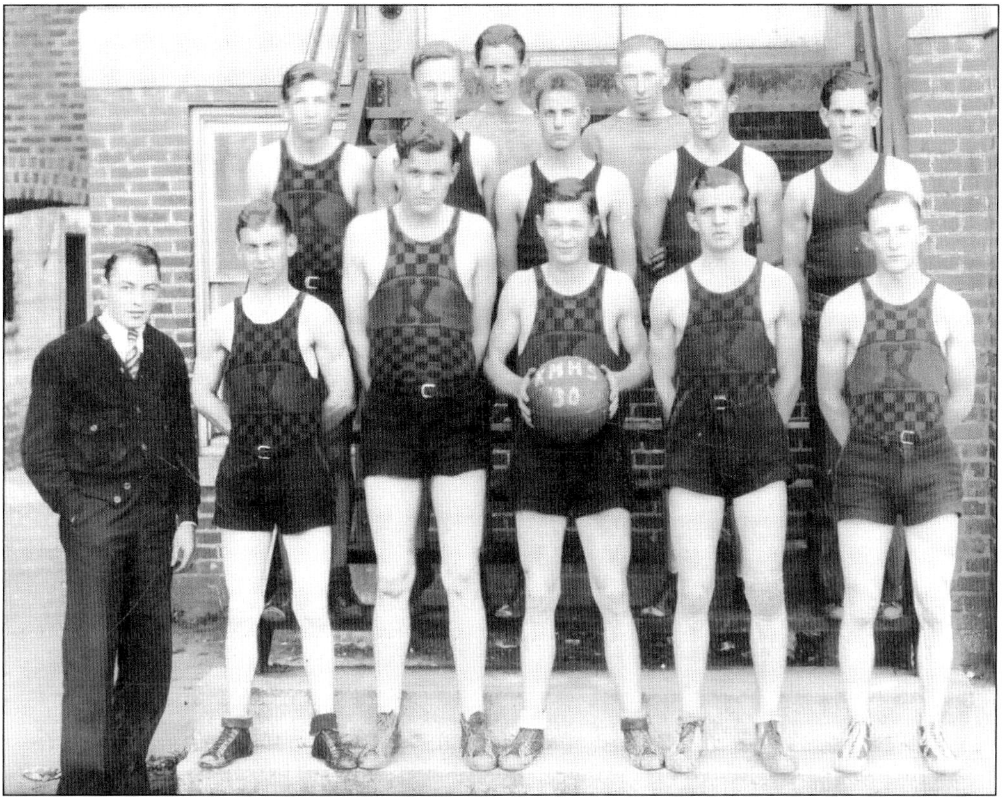

The 1930 Kings Mountain High School men's basketball team are, from left to right, (first row) coach E.A. Christenberry, Joe Mauney, unidentified, Bus Oates, Jacob Mauney, and unidentified; (second row) unidentified, Otto Williams, Bruce McDaniel, Wilson Crawford, unidentified, Red Layton, and Hilliard Black.

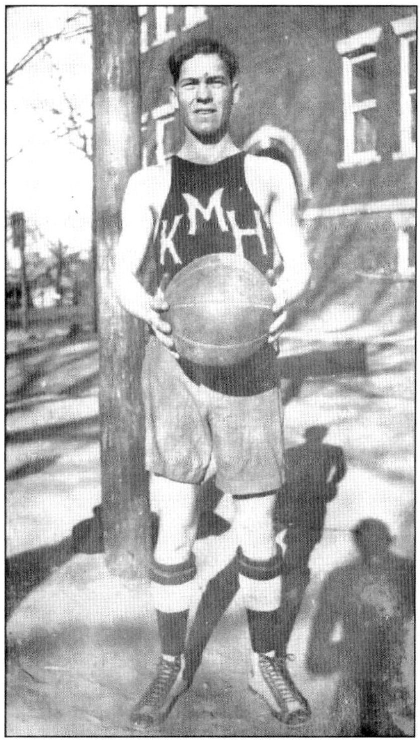

In 1922, the Kings Mountain High School basketball team played on a dirt court behind St. Matthew's Lutheran Church on the Central School grounds. During the early 1920s, uniforms were not available to the team, so players wore clothes they already owned. This player, possibly Tom Saunders, is wearing a uniform with the initials for the school clearly marked on his jersey, suggesting that this photograph dates to the late 1920s. (Courtesy of Neisler Brothers, Inc.)

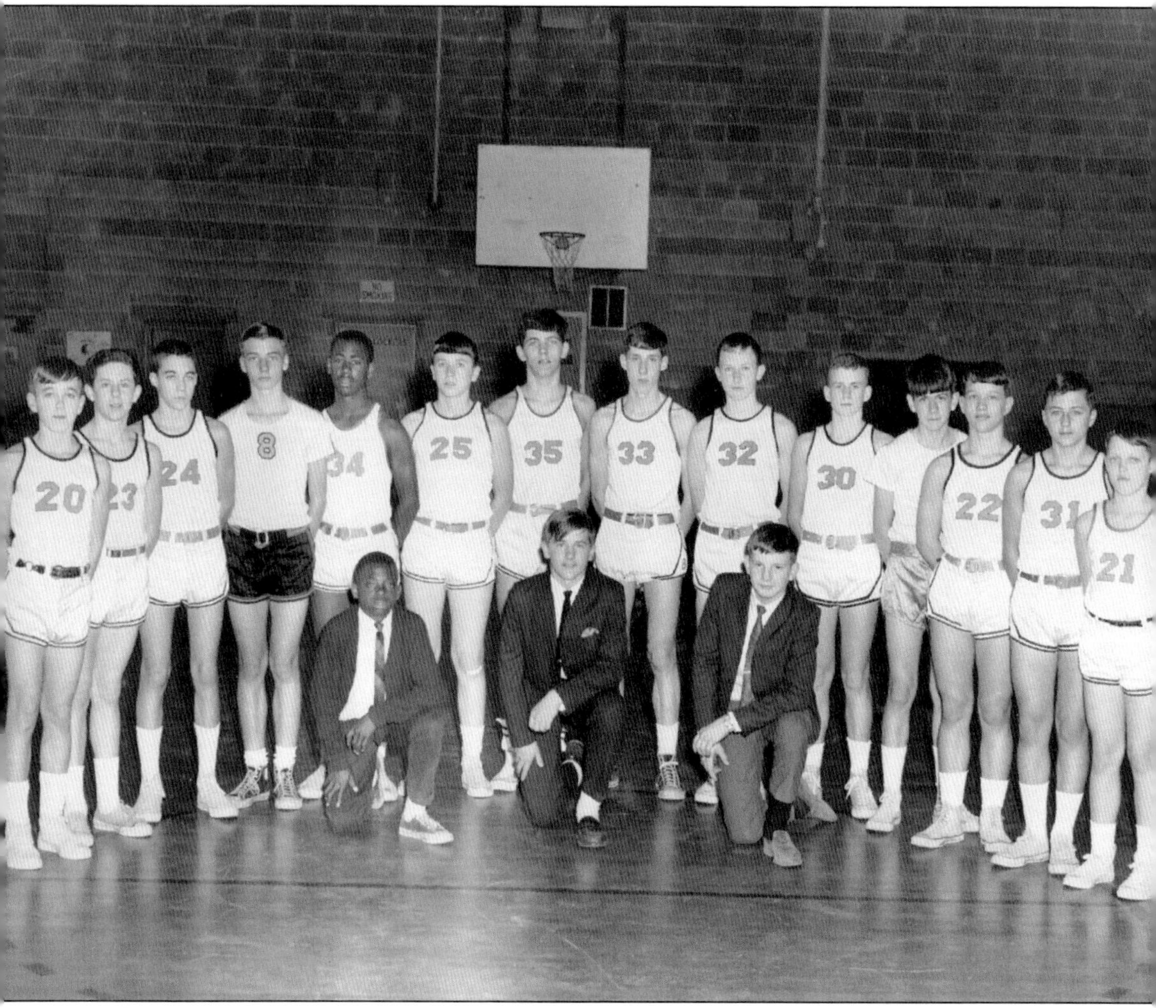

This early-1970s Kings Mountain High School basketball team was coached by Porter Odell Griggs. Pictured are, from left to right, (kneeling) Todd Rhodes, Arthur Carroll, and Marty Burton; (standing) Ricky Hord, Billy Parker, Steve Powell, Bobby Phillips, Mike Spencer, Barry Willis, Wilson Ledford, Ray Hughes, Geeper Howard, Chuck Carpenter, David Randall, Ronnie Payne, David Bolin, and Dana Franklin. (Courtesy of Laura Carpenter Bingham.)

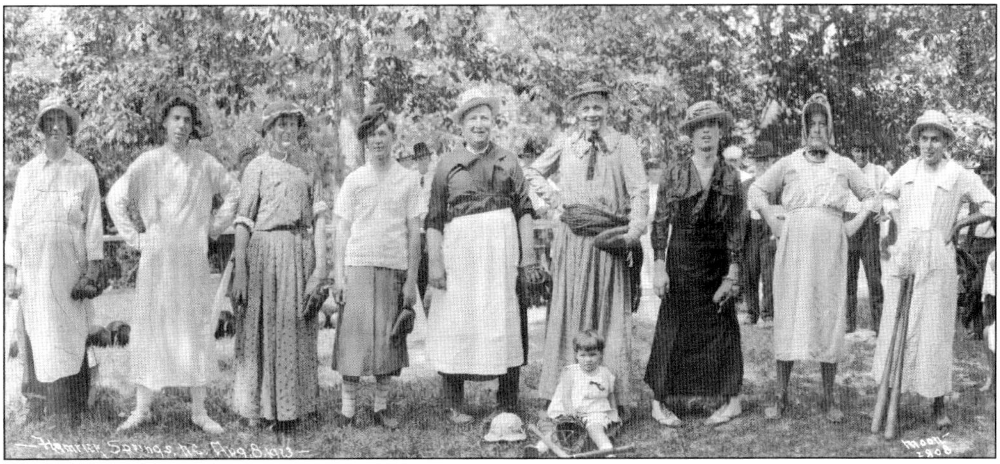

In the past, the residents of Kings Mountain would gather for an annual town picnic. On August 8, 1923, community members met at Hamrick Springs. No one is sure why the men in this photograph are dressed as women. They are, from left to right, two unidentified people, O.P. Lewis, Gene Neisler, Floyd, Paul Mauney, Bill Saunders, and two more unidentified people. The child sitting in front is also unidentified.

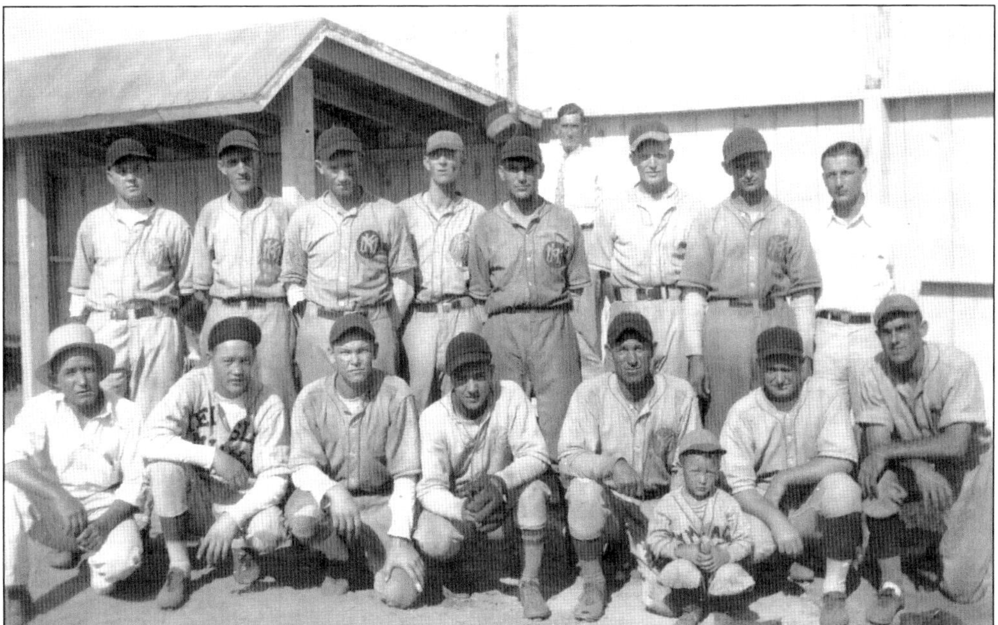

Hugh "Red" Ormand kneels in the front row, second from the right in this 1920s photograph of the Kings Mountain High School baseball team. Ormand went on the play baseball at Trinity College (now Duke University) from 1921 to 1923, playing on the all-state team his final year. Before returning to Kings Mountain, Ormand played with the Reading Keystones from 1923 to 1924. During the 1930s, Ormand played for the Margrace Mill baseball team, after which he went on to coach baseball in the American Legion.

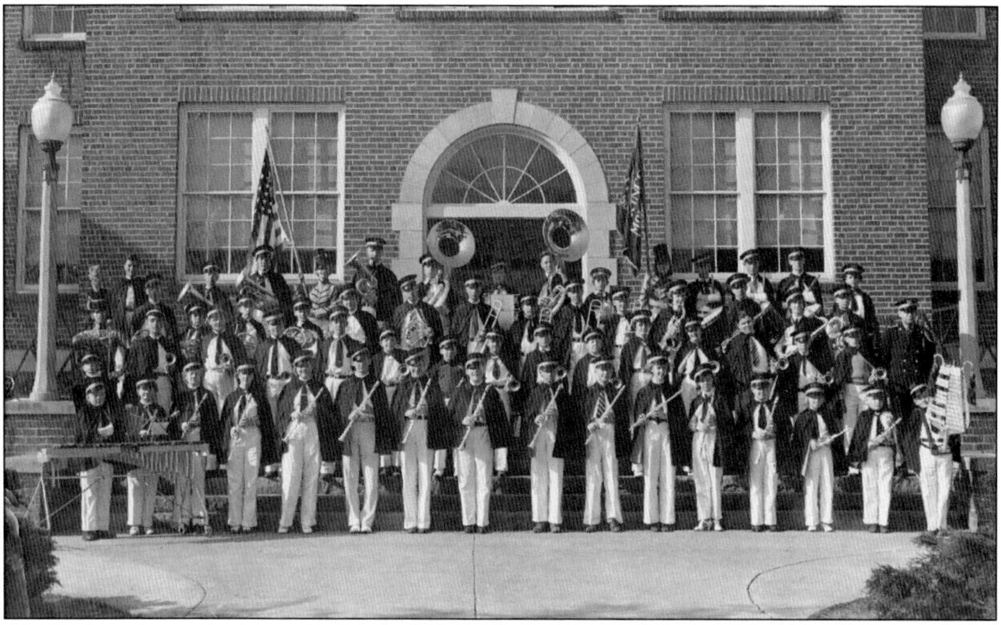

With 15 students, Paul Hendricks Sr. formally organized the Central High School Marching Band in 1935. Hendricks directed the band until he entered the military prior to World War II. The marching band went on to represent the State of North Carolina, playing for Pres. Franklin Delano Roosevelt at the opening of the Great Smoky Mountain National Park.

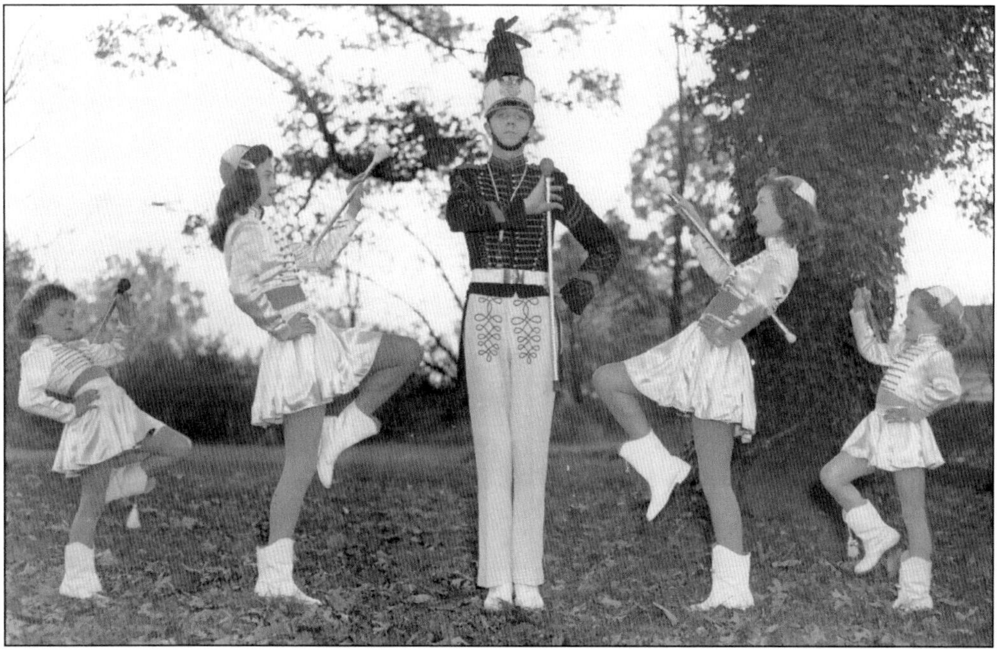

Prior to 1940, band members wore matching shirts, pants, and ties, as well as a black cape. The capes were homemade, having been sewn by several of the band members' mothers. By 1939, the Kings Mountain Band Association had raised enough money to purchase uniforms, such as those seen in this photograph. At the time, it cost the Kings Mountain Band Association $2,000 to purchase uniforms for all of the band members.

This 1958 photograph shows the Kings Mountain Marching Band and fans sitting in the city stadium. When the high school on Phifer Road was built, the football stadium was dedicated in honor of John Gamble, who coached football at the high school from 1957 to 1961. The stadium was dedicated on Friday, September 9, 1967.

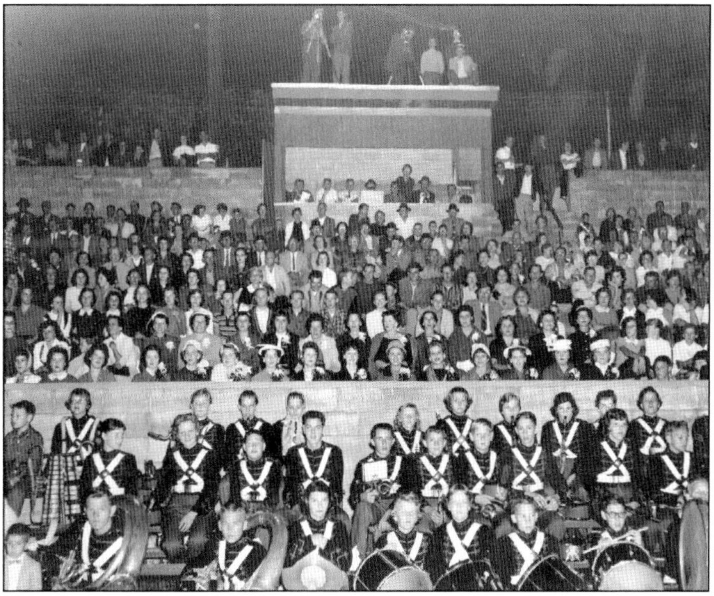

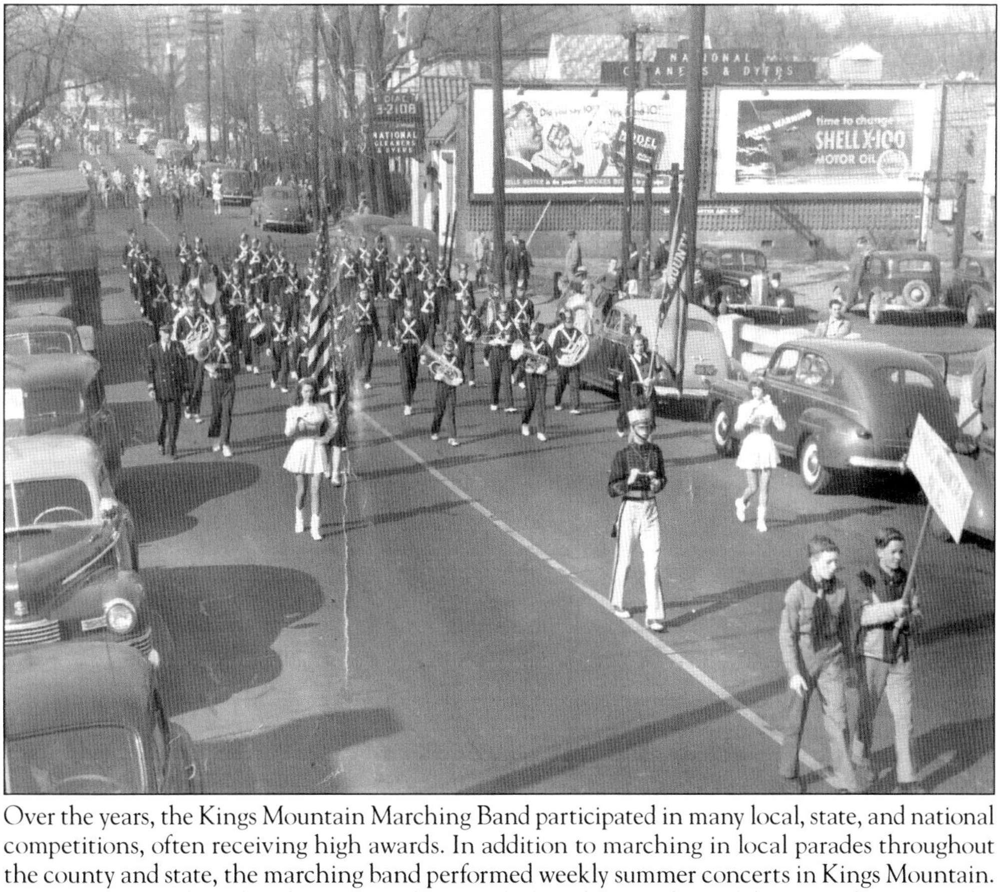

Over the years, the Kings Mountain Marching Band participated in many local, state, and national competitions, often receiving high awards. In addition to marching in local parades throughout the county and state, the marching band performed weekly summer concerts in Kings Mountain. In 1939, the marching band was invited to play before the president of the United States at the dedication of the Great Smoky Mountain National Park.

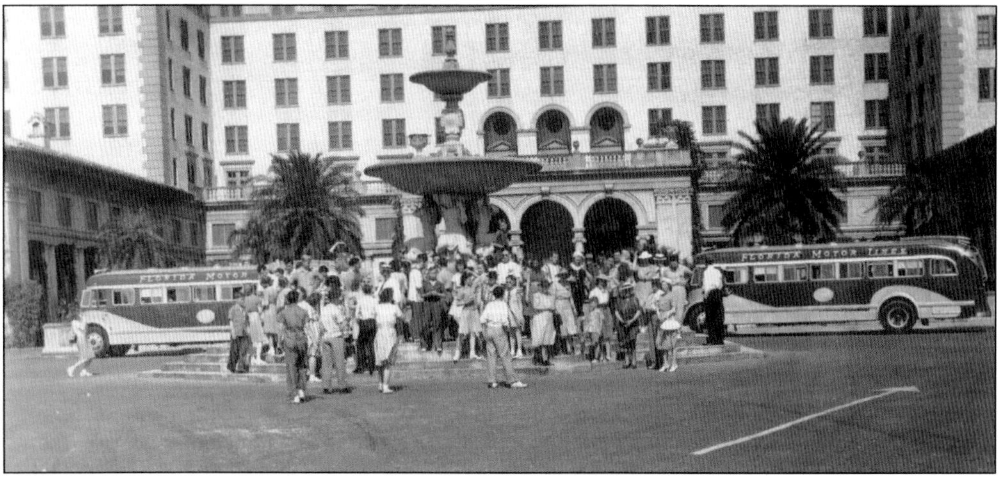

In May 1940, Paul E. Hendricks (director of the Kings Mountain High School Band) took 45 boys, 29 girls, and eight chaperones via the Southern Railway from Kings Mountain, North Carolina, to West Palm Beach, Florida. There, the band participated in the Fourth Annual Eighth Region National School Music Competition–Festival, which took place over three days. During their time in Florida, the band competed against five other bands and marched in the festival's parade. These photographs show the group getting ready for the final portrait of the marching band members in front of the festival's headquarters at the Hotel Royal Worth.

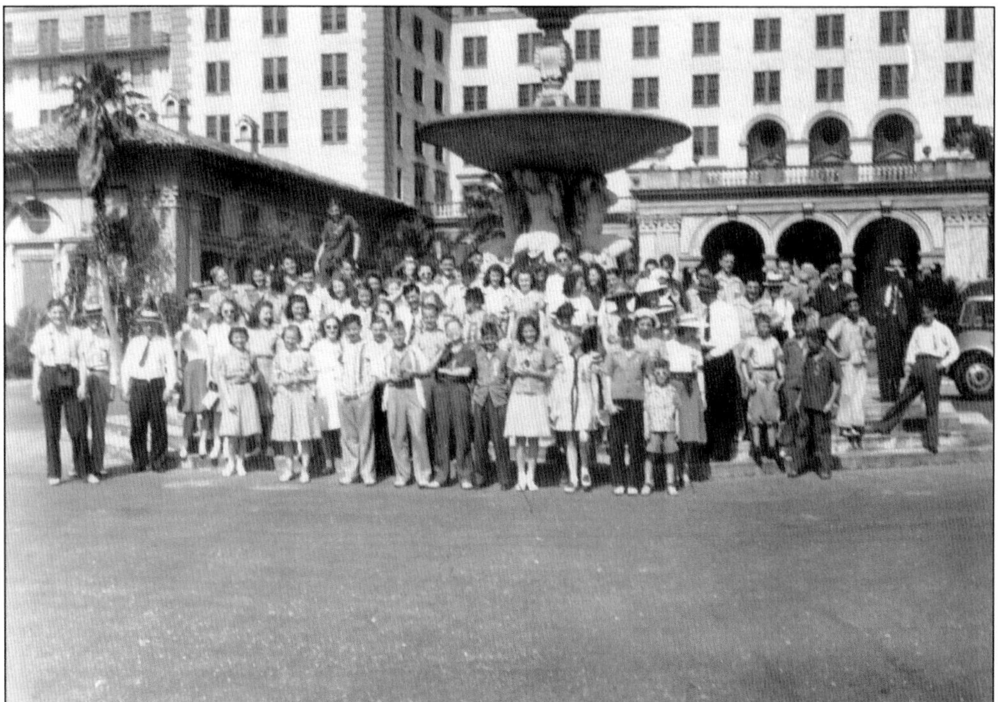

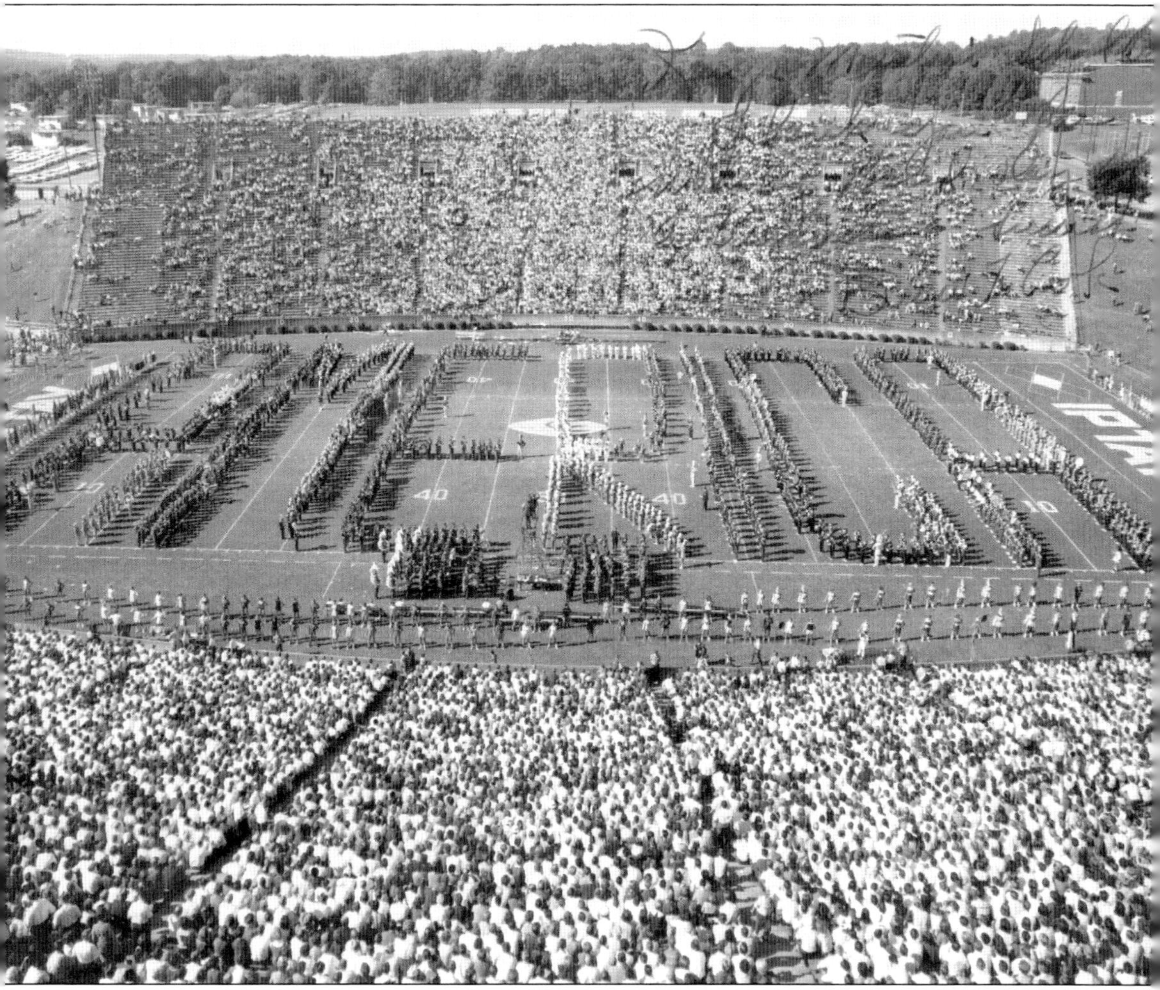

Band Day was an important experience for Kings Mountain High School students. High school marching bands were invited to play on the football field as part of the games' halftime activities at regional college campuses; this gave students the opportunity to see a university in action and to develop ideas of going to college. Arriving in Kings Mountain in 1945, Joe Hedden, band director, worked with the Kings Mountain schools for over 20 years as a band director and principal. The band is shown spelling out *AMERICA* at "Death Valley" Stadium in Clemson, South Carolina, nearly two hours away. In the upper right-hand corner of the photograph, a handwritten note is addressed to the band, thanking them for making the 1961 School Band Day "a tremendous success" It is signed by Brett F. Cook.

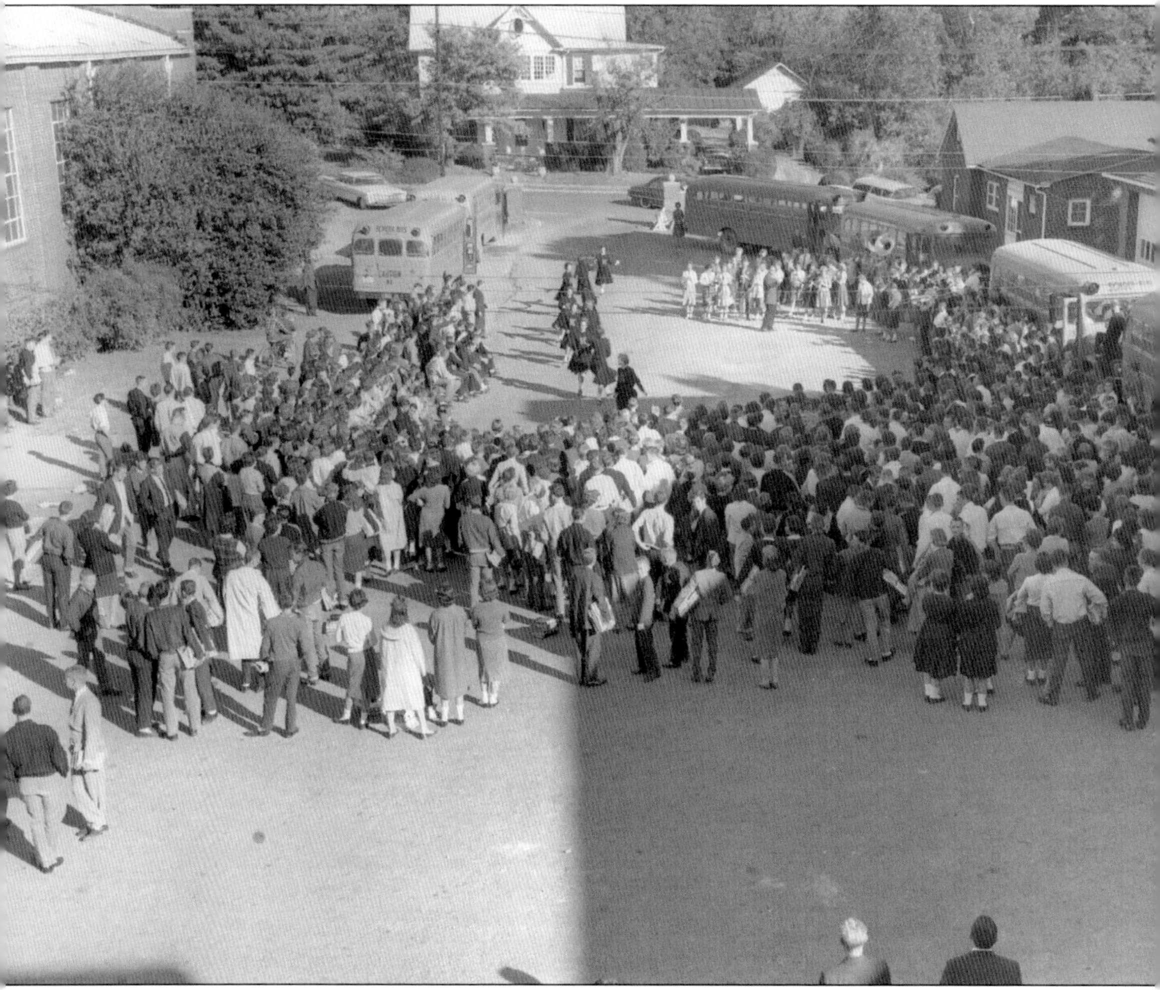

This 1960 photograph shows a pep rally taking place behind the Kings Mountain High School in the paved area between the school and the gymnasium. Several students, in addition to the cheerleaders, marching band members, and athletes, have come out to support the school's team. In the center of the photograph, the cheerleaders are performing a cheer for the crowd. The six buses on the far right of the photograph suggest that the team is preparing for an away game. A closer look reveals that, while they members have their instruments, they have not yet changed into their uniforms.

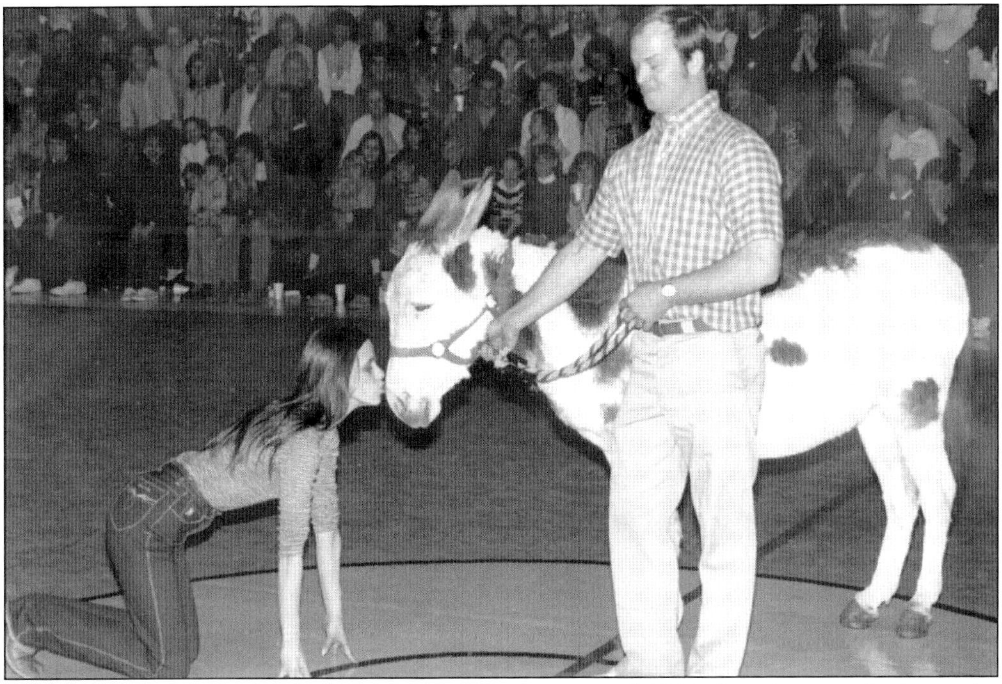

Taken at the Kings Mountain Community Center around 1974, this photograph shows the "Queen of the Ball" kissing a donkey while Frank Burns holds its leash. The Donkey Ball game was a fundraiser by the fire department for the creation of the Kings Mountain Fire Museum. (Courtesy of the *Kings Mountain Herald*.)

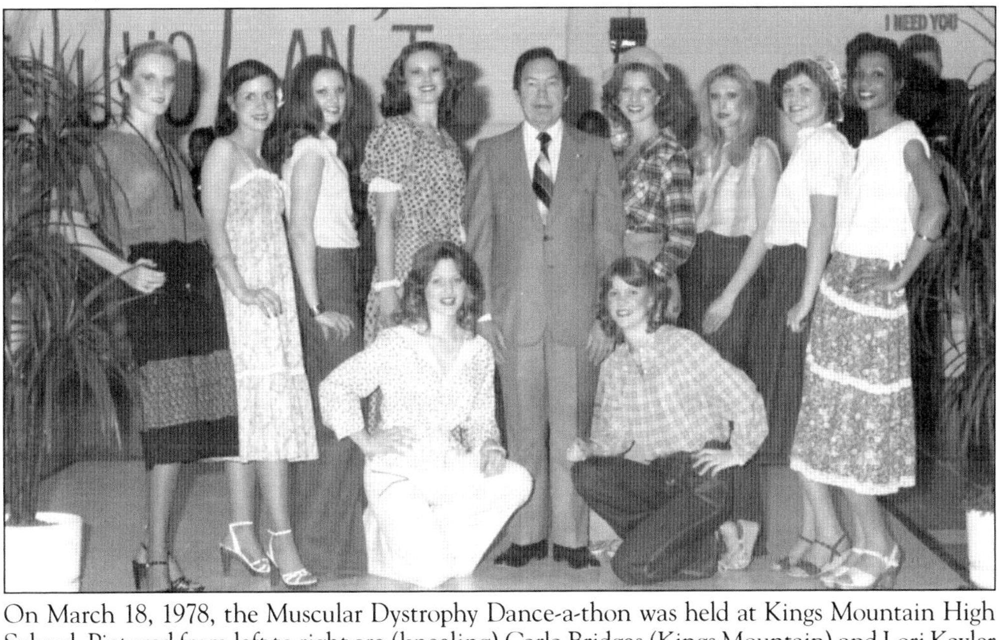

On March 18, 1978, the Muscular Dystrophy Dance-a-thon was held at Kings Mountain High School. Pictured from left to right are (kneeling) Carla Bridges (Kings Mountain) and Lori Kayler (Gastonia); (standing) Tonyia Camp (Shelby), Sadie Bromome (Cherryville), Angelia Connor (Gastonia), Nola Holt (Gastonia), then mayor John Henry Moss, Linda Williams (Shelby), Patti Tolbert (Belmont), Janice Bolin (Kings Mountain), and Gale Bess (Lincolnton).

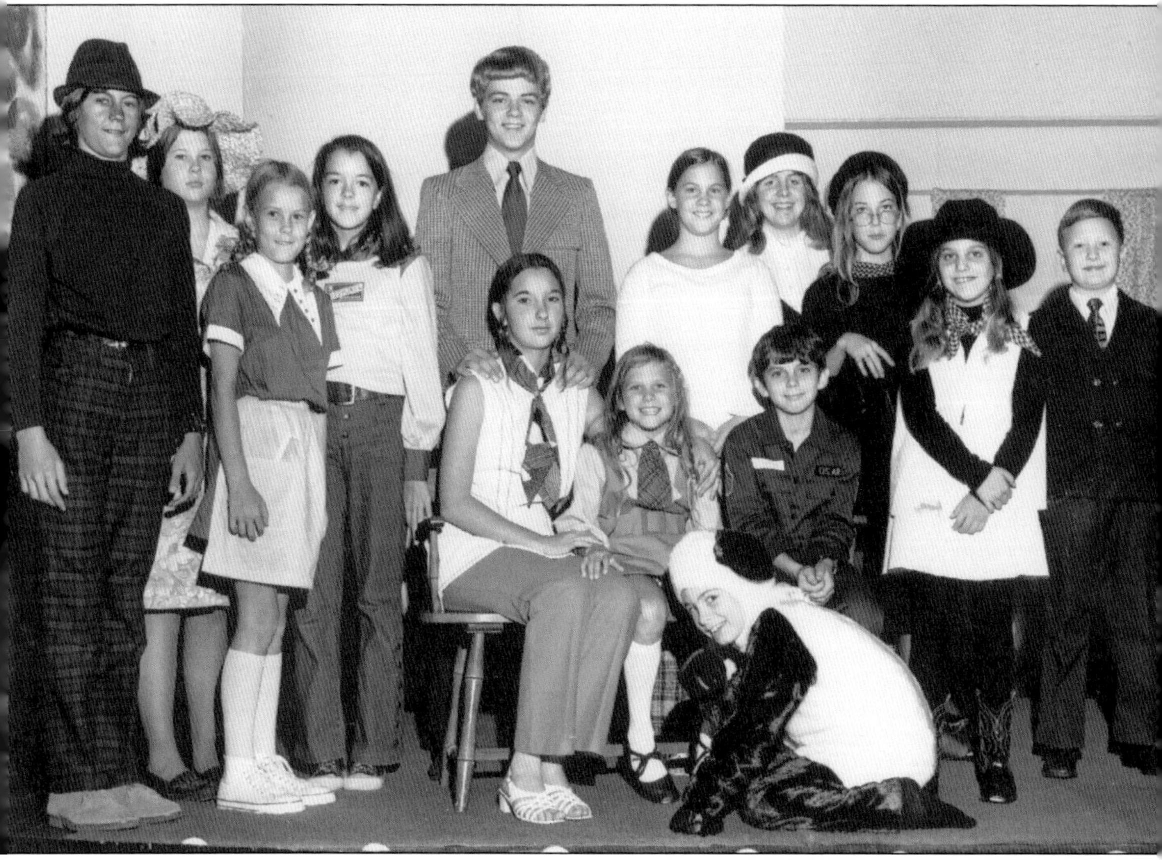

In November 1972, the Kings Mountain Little Theater put on the children's production *The Panda and the Spy* under the direction of Sylvia Holmes. The play was written in 1954 by Mary Virginia Heinlein of New York. The Kings Mountain Little Theater opened in the 1950s and, for many years, borrowed space from schools, churches, and civic organizations for their performances. Early in 2000, the Kings Mountain Little Theater moved into the vacated Joy Theater at the corner of South Railroad Avenue and West Gold Street. Pictured from left to right are (kneeling) Scott Laughridge (dressed as the panda); (seated) Cyndi Robinson, Becky Bates, and David Barrett; (standing) Chris Holmes, Ann Rowell, Lindsay Holmes, Sara Maner, Ronnie Morrison, Laura McGinnis, Laura Carpenter, Kim Gladden, Carol Bennett, and unidentified. (Courtesy of Laura Carpenter Bingham.)

Six

CELEBRATE

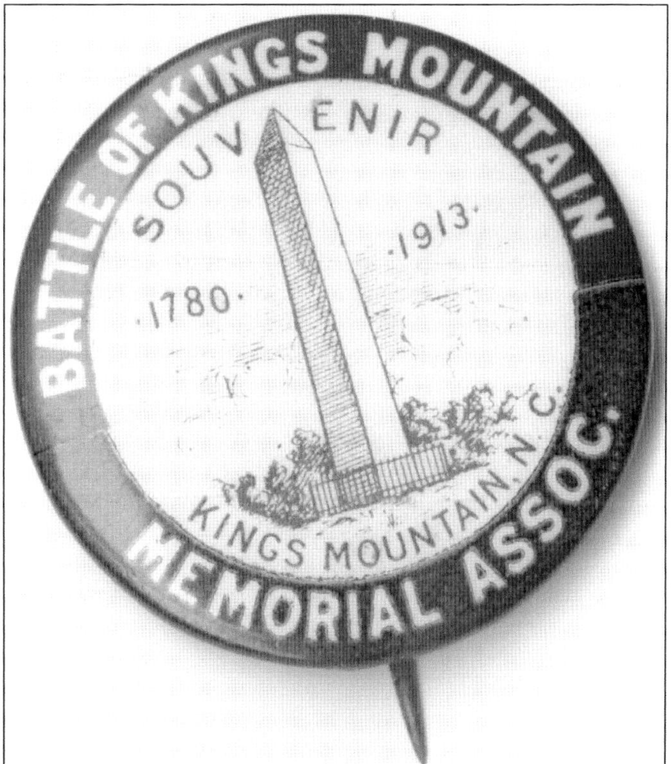

This commemorative pin was made by the Torsch & Franz Badge Co. in Baltimore, Maryland, for the 133rd anniversary celebration of the Battle of Kings Mountain in 1913. Annual celebrations were held both in the city of Kings Mountain and at the nearby military park to celebrate the historic 1780 battle.

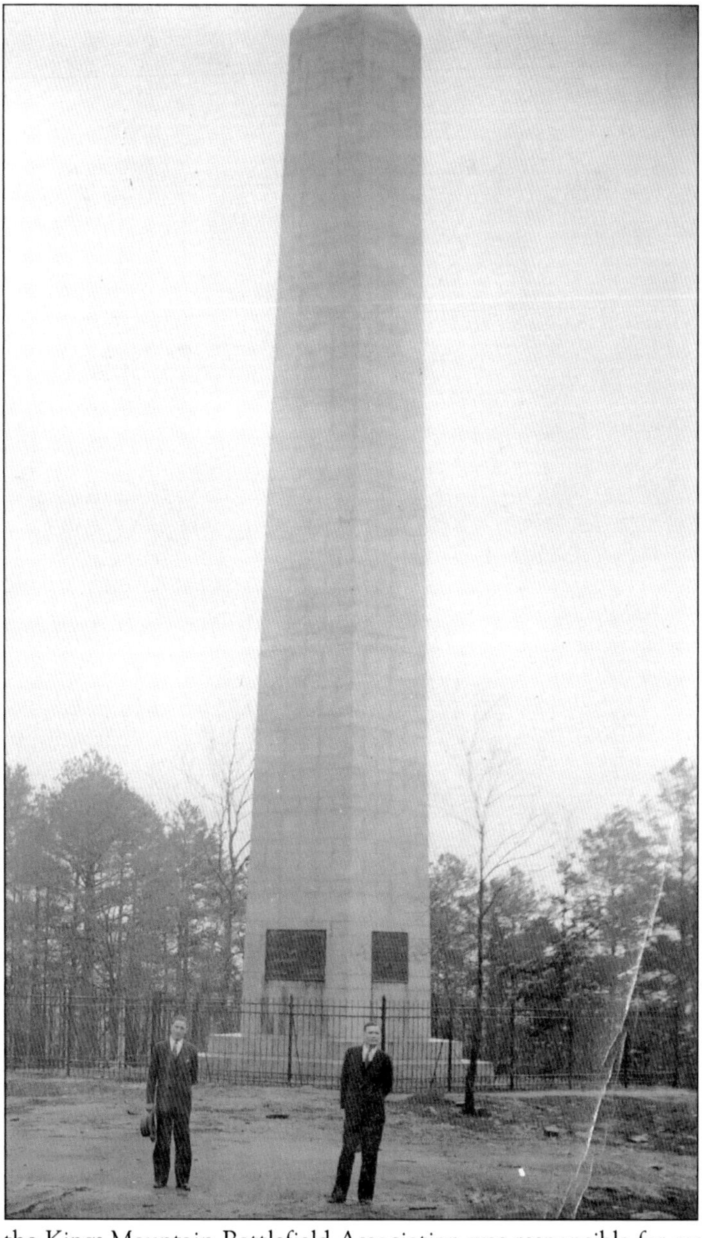

Prior to 1909, the Kings Mountain Battlefield Association was responsible for maintaining the battlefield. They had the original, smaller monument placed there in 1880. When it was unveiled, standing just around 28 feet high, over 12,000 people visited the battlefield. The festivities lasted for over a week as people pitched tents and camped on the site. Over time, the association disbanded, and the battlefield was left neglected. North Carolina congressman E.Y. Webb and South Carolina congressman D.E. Finley took an interest in the historic location and were instrumental in getting the area designated as a United States National Park and in having a new monument constructed. Due to their requests, Congress appropriated $30,000 to erect a larger, more modern monument at the site. On October 7, 1909, in commemoration of the Revolutionary War battle at Kings Mountain, the federal government unveiled a 90-foot-high obelisk on the site. People gathered for the two-day event, including dignitaries from the surrounding states.

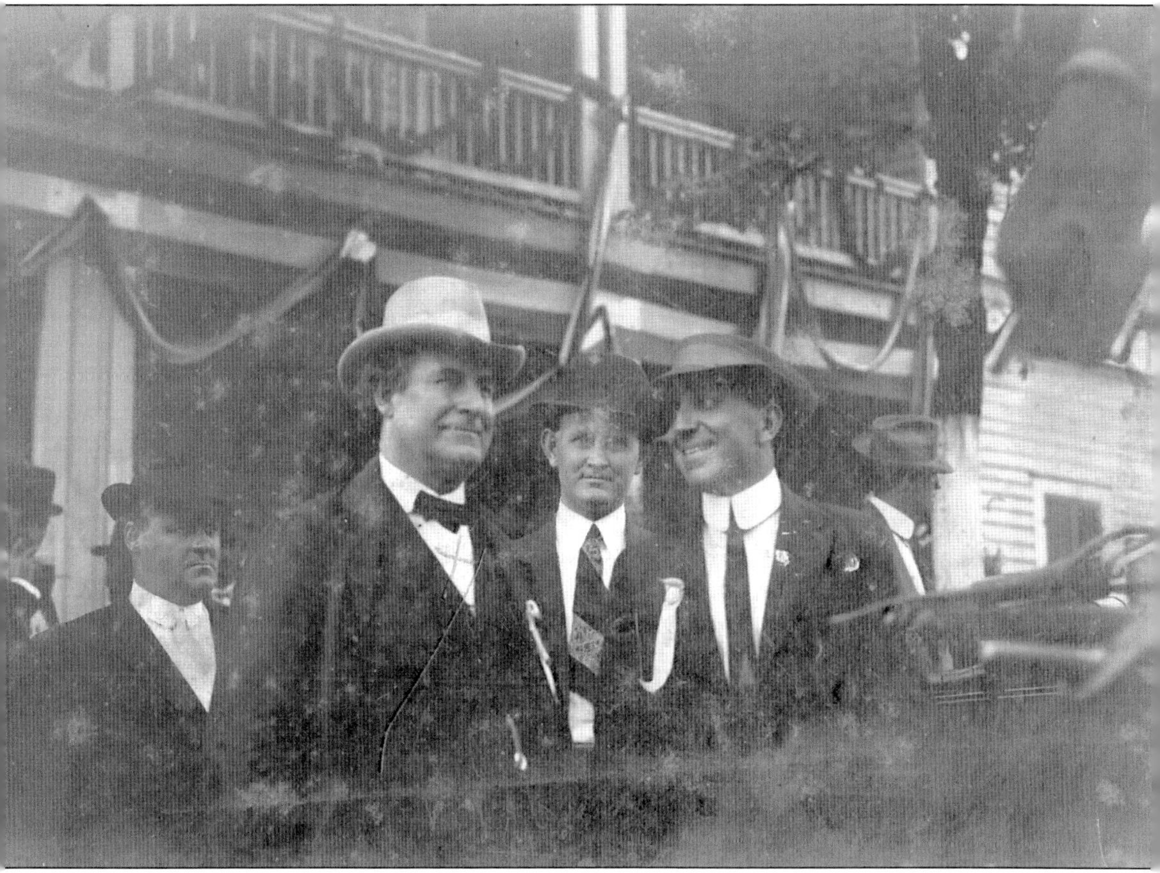

In 1912, William Jennings Bryan made a visit to Kings Mountain. Bryan spoke at the Kings Mountain battleground for the 132nd anniversary celebration. A lawyer and three-time Democratic presidential candidate, Bryan became best known for his role as the prosecutor in the 1925 Scopes Trial. The trial, which Byran won, found John Thomas Scopes guilty of teaching evolution to his students, therefore violating Tennessee's Butler Act. Seen in the background of this photograph is the Mountain View Hotel, which was located down the street from the passenger train depot on the corner of Railroad Avenue and Gold Street. It operated in Kings Mountain from 1876 until it was demolished in 1948. For many years, the John Ferguson family managed the hotel. Sisters Emma and Agnes Norris operated the hotel prior to its razing. The block where the hotel once stood was later occupied by a movie theater and is now home to the Joy Performance Center. (Courtesy of the Cleveland County Historical Collection and the Earl Scruggs Center.)

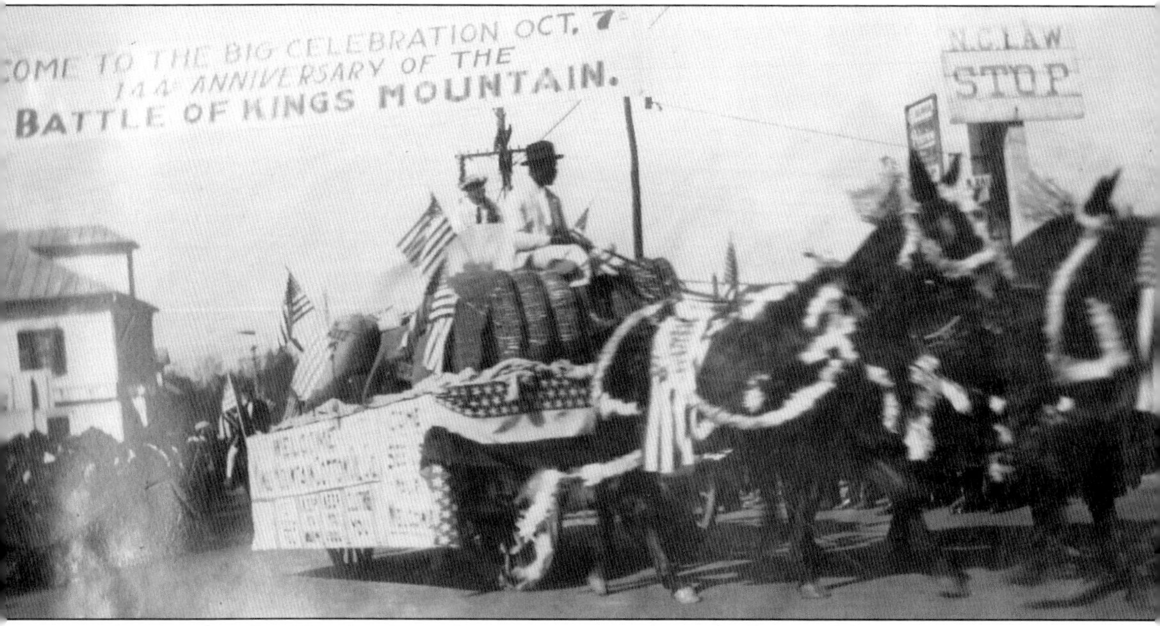

On October, 7, 1924, the City of Kings Mountain hosted a large celebration in town for the 144th anniversary of the Battle of Kings Mountain. Hanging above North Railroad Street was a large banner advertising the event. On the float, a welcoming message greeted the spectators. Sponsored by the American Legion, the float consisted of a wagon pulled by mules and decorated in a patriotic theme. The American Legion had other floats in the parade. They were decorated in the same theme and carried individuals dressed in uniforms, such as a soldier, a sailor, and a Red Cross nurse. (Courtesy of Mary Lewis Nantz.)

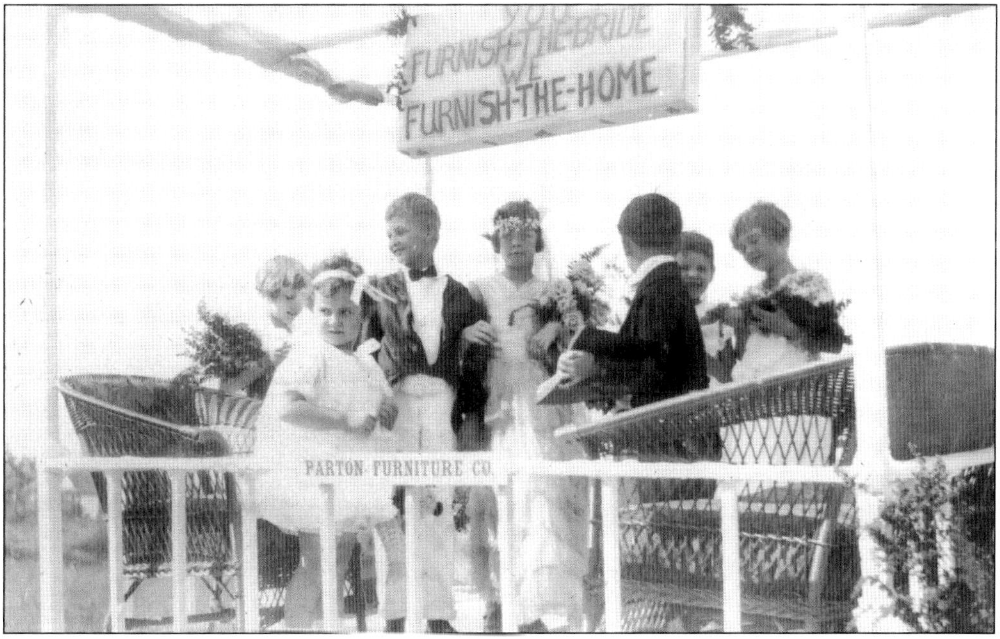

Floats in parades were used to add revelry to a celebration, although they were expensive to manufacture. As a way to offset the expense of constructing the float, the Parton Furniture Company in Kings Mountain used their float to advertise their business during the 1927 anniversary celebration. The sign on the float read, "You furnish the bride[,] we furnish the home." (Courtesy of Mary Lewis Nantz.)

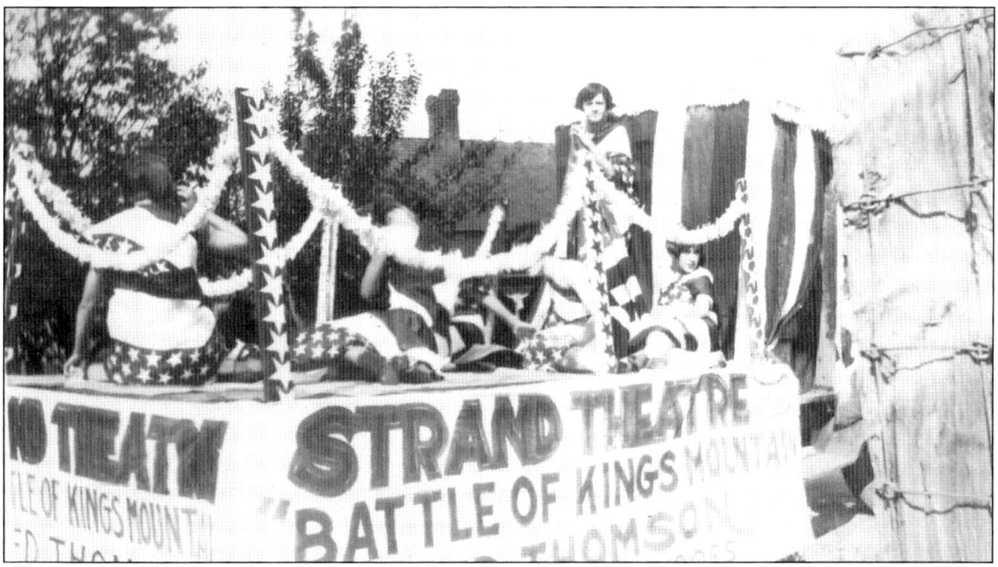

This photograph, taken by Dr. O.P. Lewis on October 7, 1924, shows a float used in a parade during a Battle of Kings Mountain anniversary celebration. Written on all four sides of the float is an advertisement for the Strand Theater production of *Thunder Hoofs*. (Courtesy of Mary Lewis Nantz.)

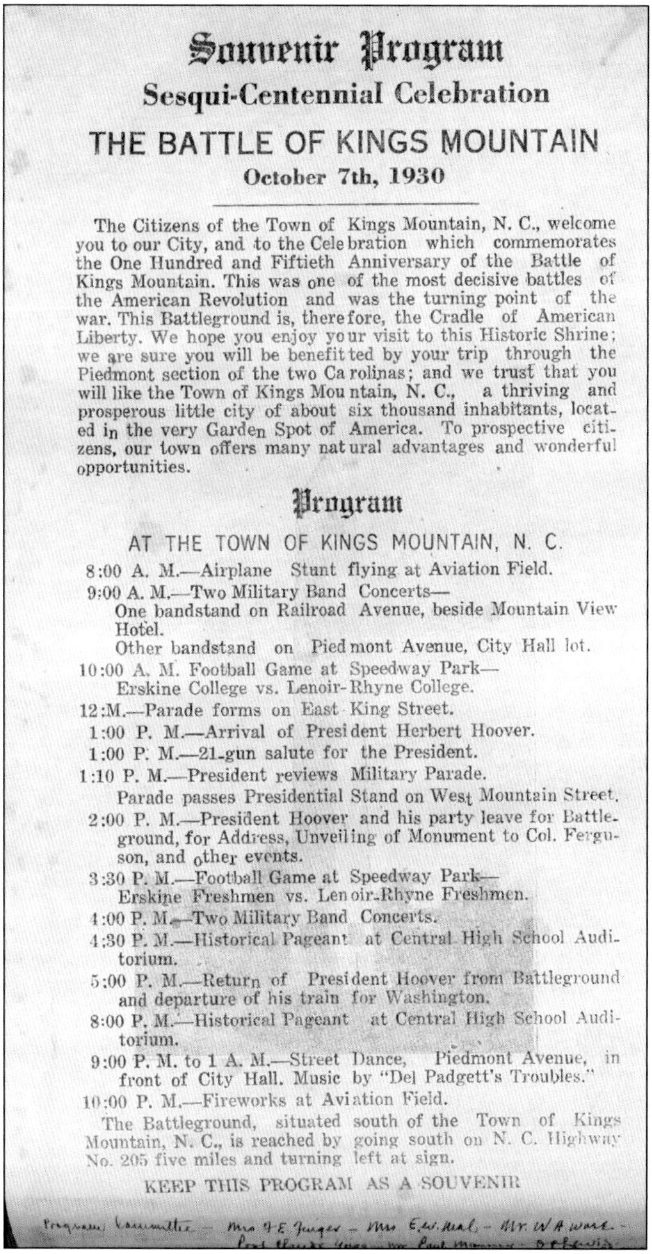

Souvenir Program

Sesqui-Centennial Celebration

THE BATTLE OF KINGS MOUNTAIN

October 7th, 1930

The Citizens of the Town of Kings Mountain, N. C., welcome you to our City, and to the Celebration which commemorates the One Hundred and Fiftieth Anniversary of the Battle of Kings Mountain. This was one of the most decisive battles of the American Revolution and was the turning point of the war. This Battleground is, therefore, the Cradle of American Liberty. We hope you enjoy your visit to this Historic Shrine; we are sure you will be benefitted by your trip through the Piedmont section of the two Carolinas; and we trust that you will like the Town of Kings Mountain, N. C., a thriving and prosperous little city of about six thousand inhabitants, located in the very Garden Spot of America. To prospective citizens, our town offers many natural advantages and wonderful opportunities.

Program

AT THE TOWN OF KINGS MOUNTAIN, N. C.

8:00 A. M.—Airplane Stunt flying at Aviation Field.

9:00 A. M.—Two Military Band Concerts—
One bandstand on Railroad Avenue, beside Mountain View Hotel.
Other bandstand on Piedmont Avenue, City Hall lot.

10:00 A. M. Football Game at Speedway Park—
Erskine College vs. Lenoir-Rhyne College.

12:M.—Parade forms on East King Street.

1:00 P. M.—Arrival of President Herbert Hoover.

1:00 P. M.—21-gun salute for the President.

1:10 P. M.—President reviews Military Parade.
Parade passes Presidential Stand on West Mountain Street.

2:00 P. M.—President Hoover and his party leave for Battleground, for Address, Unveiling of Monument to Col. Ferguson, and other events.

3:30 P. M.—Football Game at Speedway Park—
Erskine Freshmen vs. Lenoir-Rhyne Freshmen.

4:00 P. M.—Two Military Band Concerts.

4:30 P. M.—Historical Pageant at Central High School Auditorium.

5:00 P. M.—Return of President Hoover from Battleground and departure of his train for Washington.

8:00 P. M.—Historical Pageant at Central High School Auditorium.

9:00 P. M. to 1 A. M.—Street Dance, Piedmont Avenue, in front of City Hall. Music by "Del Padgett's Troubles."

10:00 P. M.—Fireworks at Aviation Field.

The Battleground, situated south of the Town of Kings Mountain, N. C., is reached by going south on N. C. Highway No. 205 five miles and turning left at sign.

KEEP THIS PROGRAM AS A SOUVENIR

On October 7, 1930, the City of Kings Mountain hosted a sesquicentennial celebration honoring the anniversary of the Battle of Kings Mountain. This program details the events occurring around town. Handwritten on the bottom of the souvenir program is a list of the program committee members. They were Mrs. F.E. Finger, Mrs. E.W. Neal, Mrs. W.A. Ware, Prof. Claude Grigg, Paul Mauney, and Dr. O.P. Lewis, who served as chairman. One event, the historical pageant, was held at the Central High School auditorium. The three-hour production consisted of a cast of over 300 members depicting various scenes from the battle, in addition to other allegorical themes relating to battle. The festivities also included several football games and military band concerts throughout the day. The event concluded with a street dance on Piedmont Avenue and fireworks at Aviation Field. (Courtesy of Mary Lewis Nantz.)

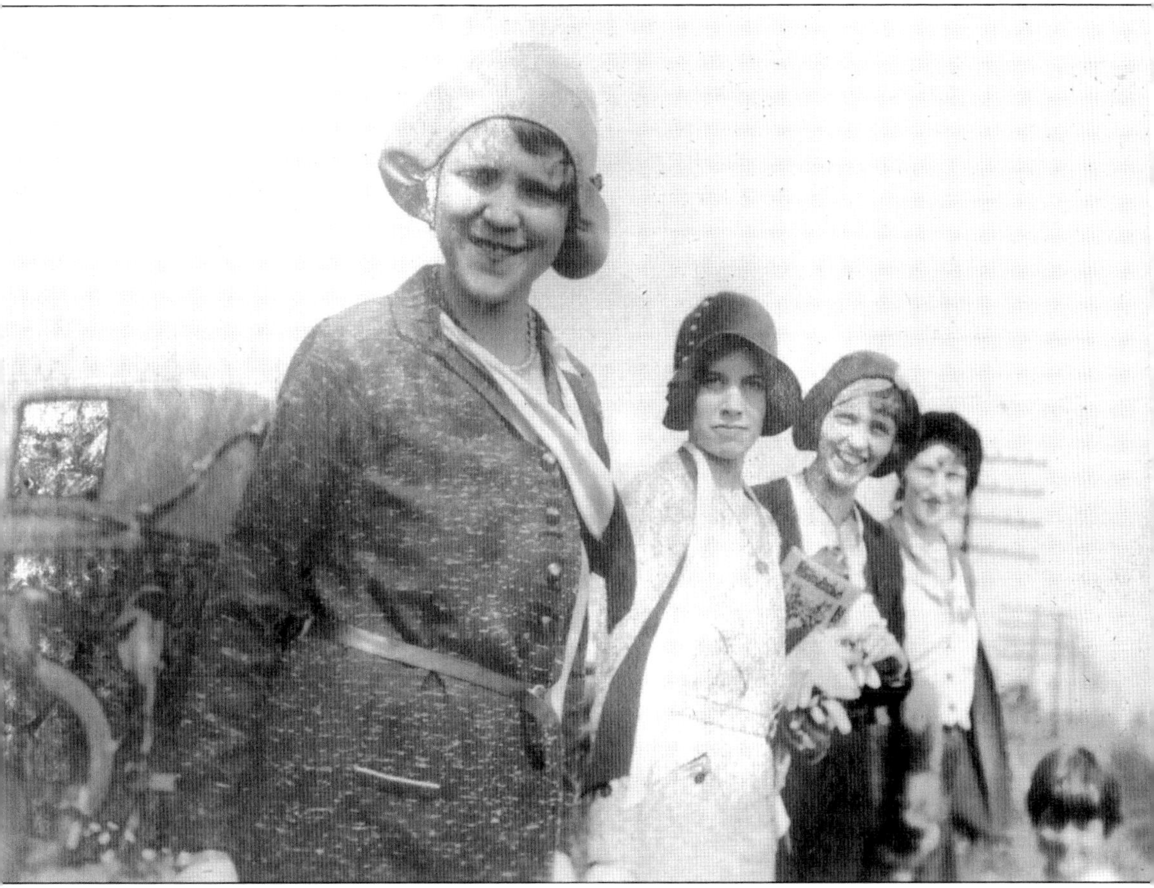

Pres. Herbert Hoover visited the Kings Mountain Military Park on October 7, 1930, to commemorate the 150th anniversary of the battle. He arrived in Kings Mountain by train and was greeted by a 21-gun salute. The president spoke at 2:30 p.m. to an estimated crowd of 30,000 assembled at the battlefield site eight miles south of the city. After a review of military troops on Mountain Street, the president was driven to the battlefield in a convertible roadster. This image shows, from left to right, Margaret Neisler, an unidentified woman, Annie Lee Neisler, and Betty Neisler as they wait on the road behind the Margrace Mill to watch the motorcade passing through town. (Courtesy of Neisler Brothers, Inc.)

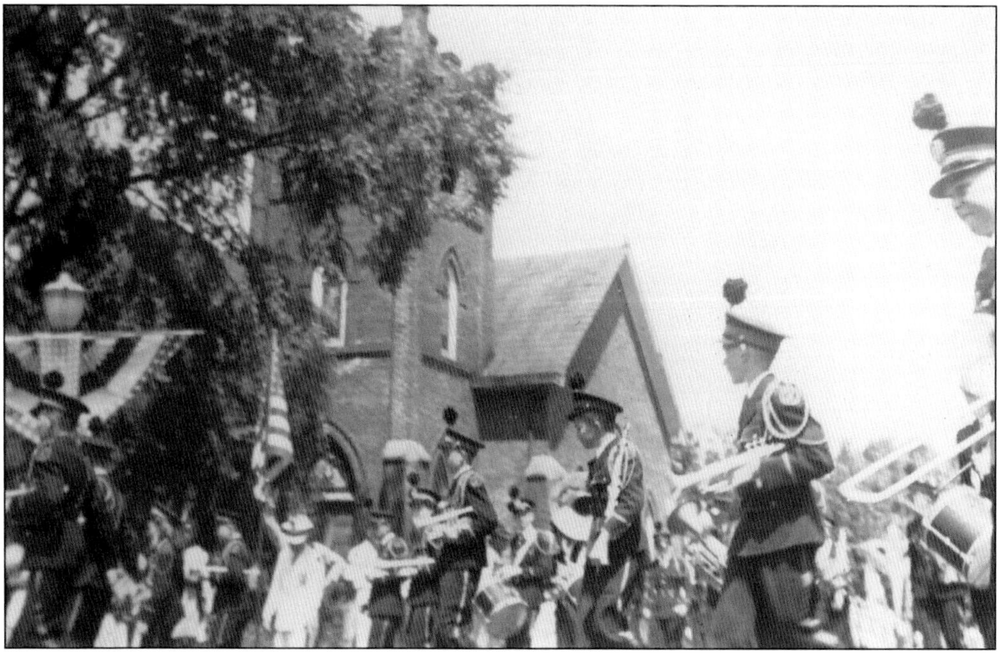

During the early 1940s, the Kings Mountain Marching Band was the pride of the town. They performed concerts for the residents and participated in parades through the streets, as seen in this photograph. In the background is the First Presbyterian Church of Kings Mountain. (Courtesy of Mary Lewis Nantz.)

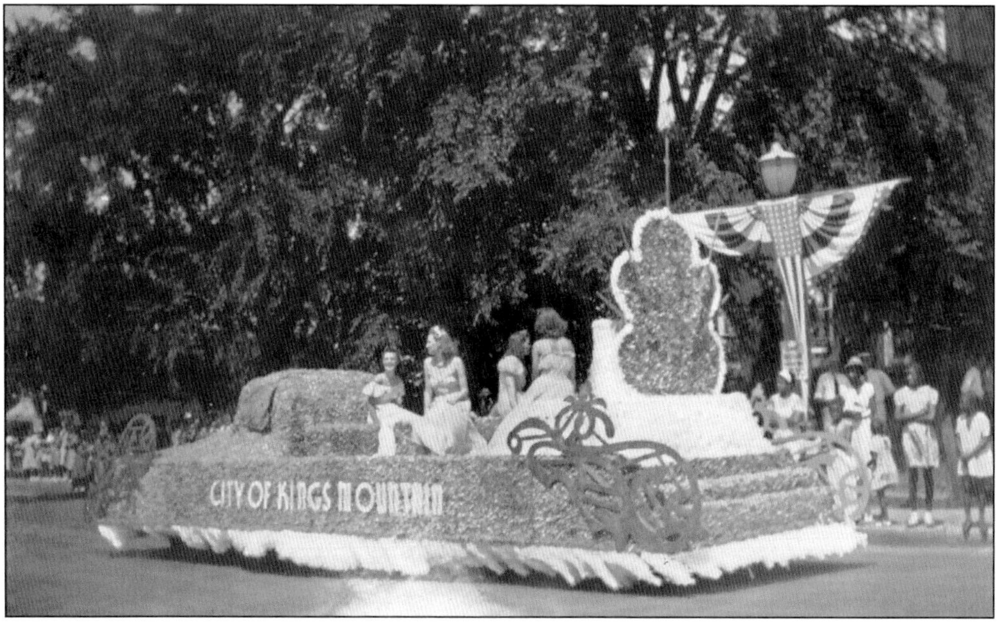

Early in the 1840s, Cleveland County emerged as its own county from the larger Rutherfordton and Lincoln Counties. The new county was named Cleveland after a Revolutionary War hero, Gen. Benjamin Cleveland. In honor of the county's centennial, a parade was held in the streets of downtown Shelby. In August 1940, the City of Kings Mountain entered the Cleveland County Centennial Celebration parade. (Courtesy of Mary Lewis Nantz.)

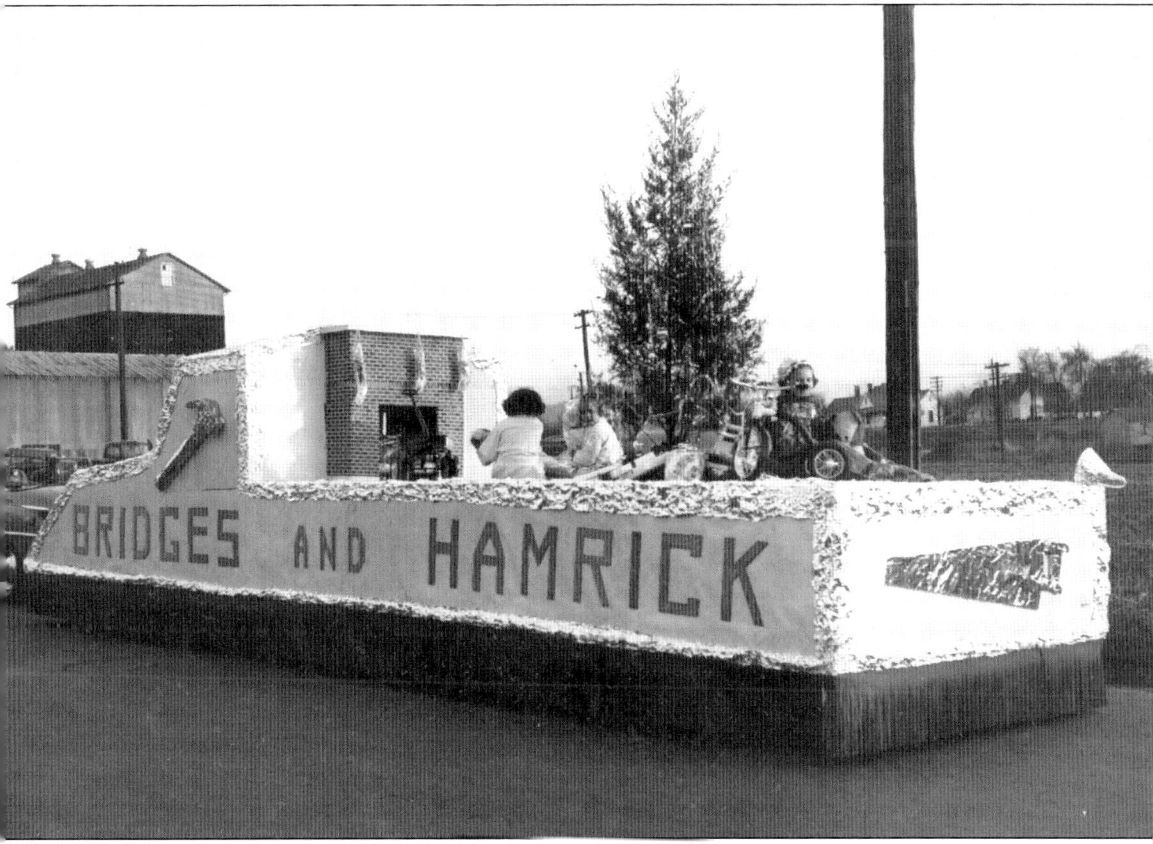

In 1949, this float sponsored by the Bridges and Hamrick Hardware Store participated in the annual Kings Mountain Christmas parade. This photograph was taken before the parade began while the float was queued up on West Gold Street. Sitting on the float are, from left to right, Sara Hendricks, Brenda Gail Hamrick, and Norma Hamrick. In the background, at the far left of the photograph, is the Ware Roller Mill. W.A. Ware presided over the wholesale grocery company at the end of the 19th century. After a few years, his son and son-in-law joined him in the business, which was renamed Ware and Sons. In the 1950s, a 50,000-bushel grain elevator was constructed on the property. While in operation, the roller mill ground wheat into flour and corn into cornmeal. The family endeavor operated until 1973, when it was sold after 91 years of operation. (Courtesy of Norma H. Drewery.)

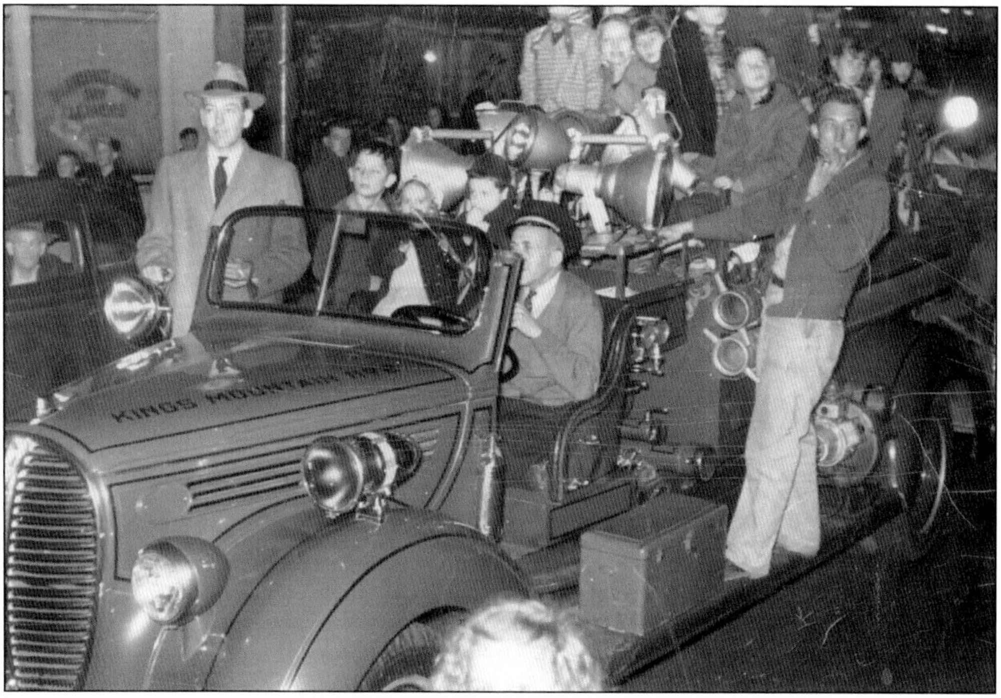

Fire chief Grady King drives the Kings Mountain Fire Department's second fire truck through town during the 1950s. The 1938 Ford fire truck was purchased by the fire department in 1939. The existing 1930 fire truck also remained in service until it was sold to the newly formed Bethlehem Fire Department in 1960 for $1.

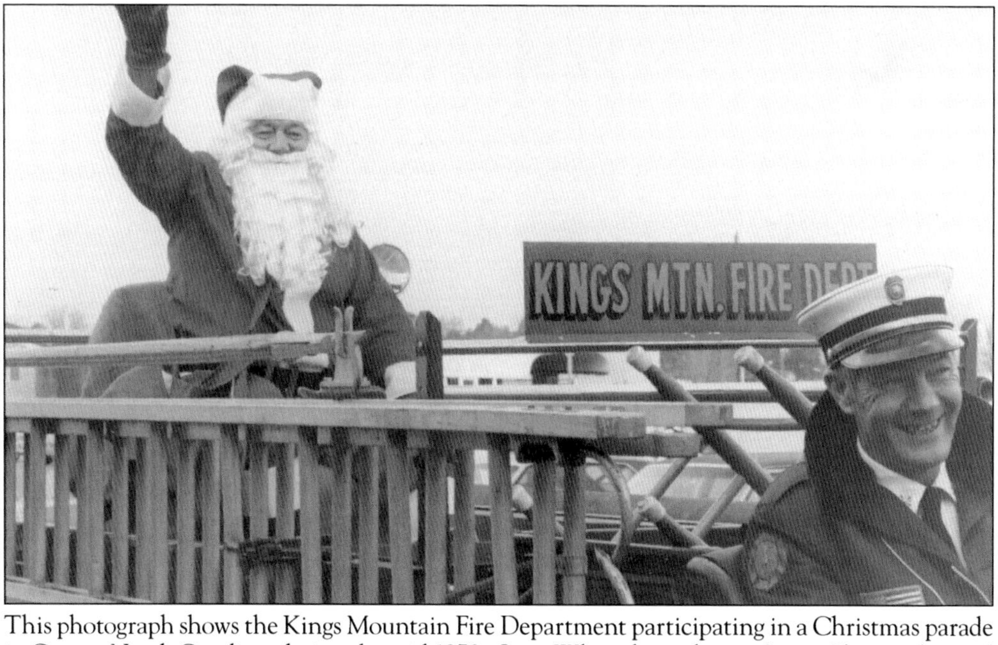

This photograph shows the Kings Mountain Fire Department participating in a Christmas parade in Grover, North Carolina, during the mid-1970s. Jerry White dressed up as Santa Claus and waved to the crowd, while fire chief Eugene Tignor rode along in the front seat of the department's fire truck. (Courtesy of the Kings Mountain Fire Museum.)

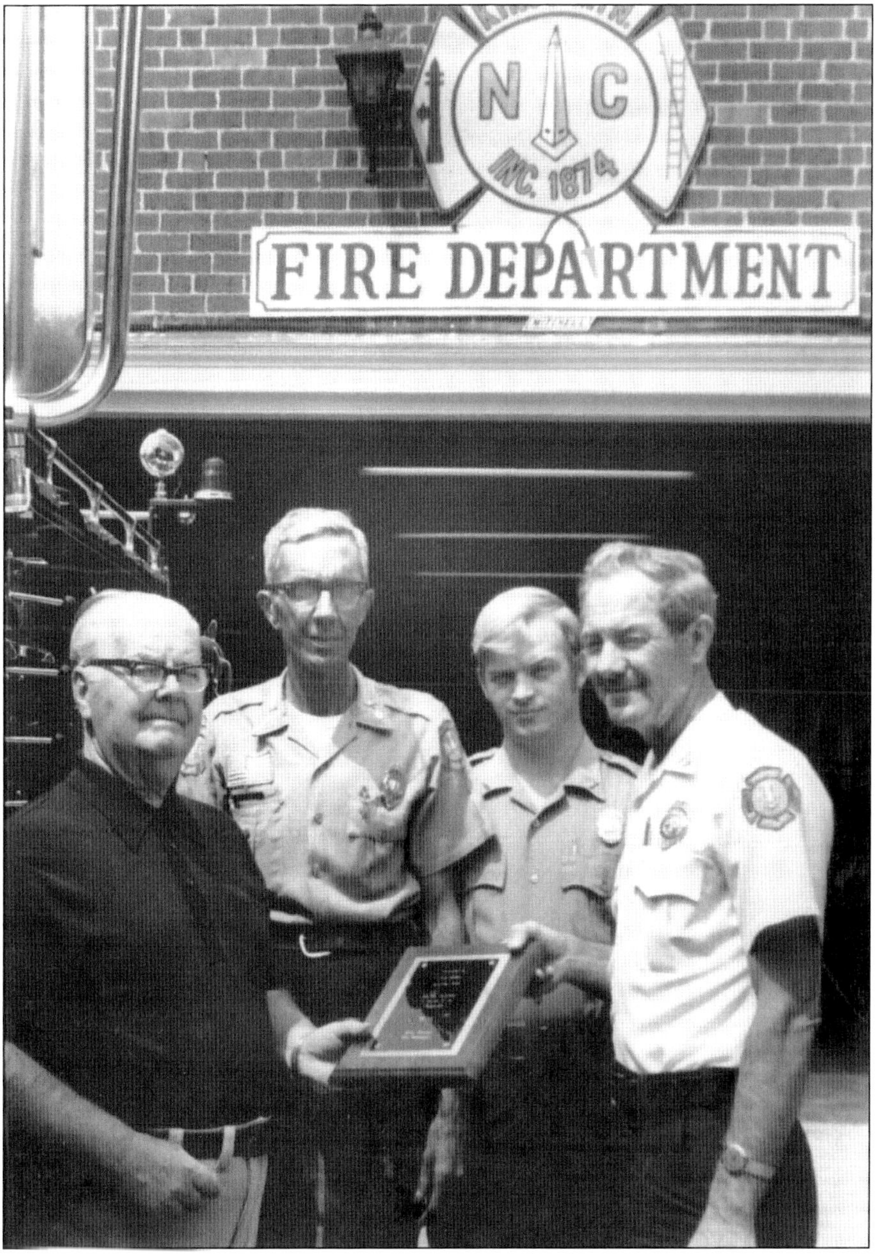

The Kings Mountain Fire Department began as a completely volunteer organization. In April 1931, the City of Kings Mountain organized a municipal department. That same month, city council members authorized the purchase of a 600-gallon fire truck, engine, and hose. Eugene Tignor was the city's first paid fire chief. He became the first full-time chief in 1973. Prior to his appointment as fire chief, three other Kings Mountain residents (Floyd Thornburg, Pat Tignor, and Grady King) had held the position. This photograph was taken approximately a year later when C.D. Ware retired from the fire department. Ware had served with the Kings Mountain Fire Department for over three decades. Shown in the photograph are, from left to right, C.D. Ware, Charles "Pete" Peterson, Frank Burns, and Eugene Tignor. (Courtesy of the Kings Mountain Fire Museum.)

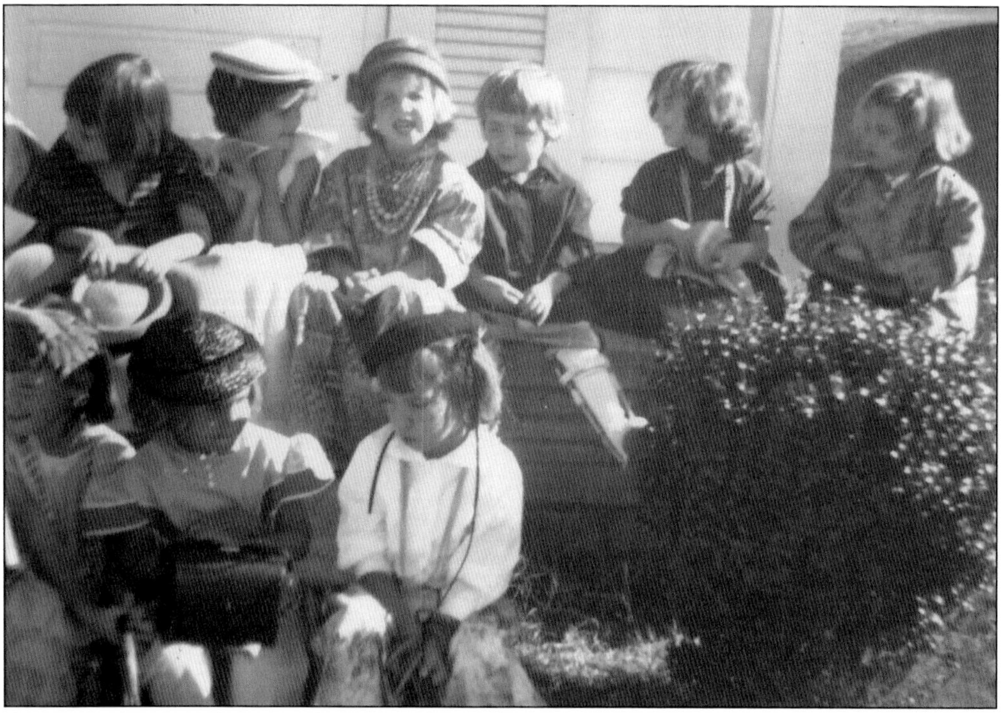

On November 9, 1961, Laura Carpenter (second row, third from left in necklace) celebrated her fifth birthday with a party at her family home on Crescent Hill Road. Shown in the photograph are Robin Dickey, Ellen Neal, Donna Blanton, Terry Harmon, Sharon Timms, Laura Carpenter, Julie Durham, Tricia Herndon, and Myra Griffin. (Courtesy of Laura Carpenter Bingham.)

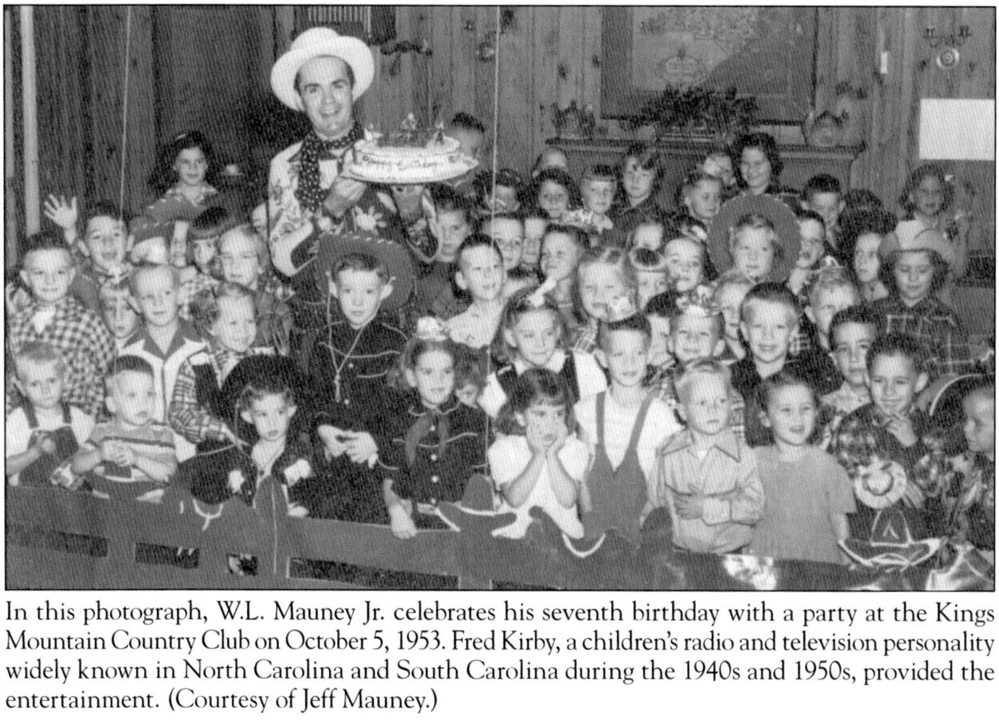

In this photograph, W.L. Mauney Jr. celebrates his seventh birthday with a party at the Kings Mountain Country Club on October 5, 1953. Fred Kirby, a children's radio and television personality widely known in North Carolina and South Carolina during the 1940s and 1950s, provided the entertainment. (Courtesy of Jeff Mauney.)

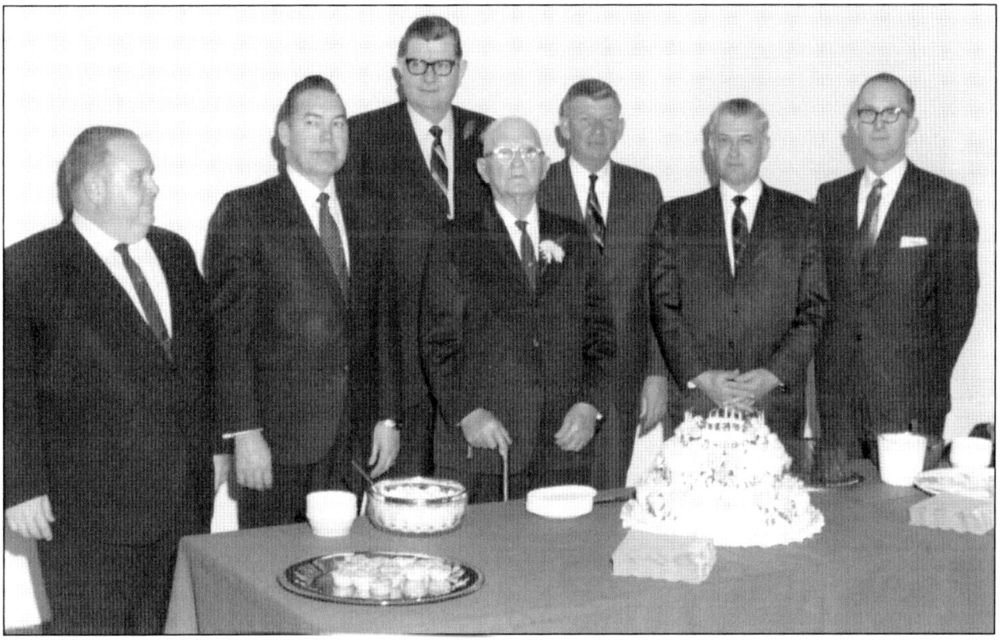

B.M. Ormand celebrates his 100th birthday in this photograph taken by Carlisle Studios. Ormand served as a conductor on the Southern Railway. Shown from left to right are W.K. Mauney Jr.; Mayor John Henry Moss; US congressman Basil Whitener; B.M. Ormand; R.G. Esteppe, trainmaster for the Southern Railway; H.R. Moore, general manager for Southern Railway; and Dr. Paul K. Ausley, minister for the First Presbyterian Church in Kings Mountain.

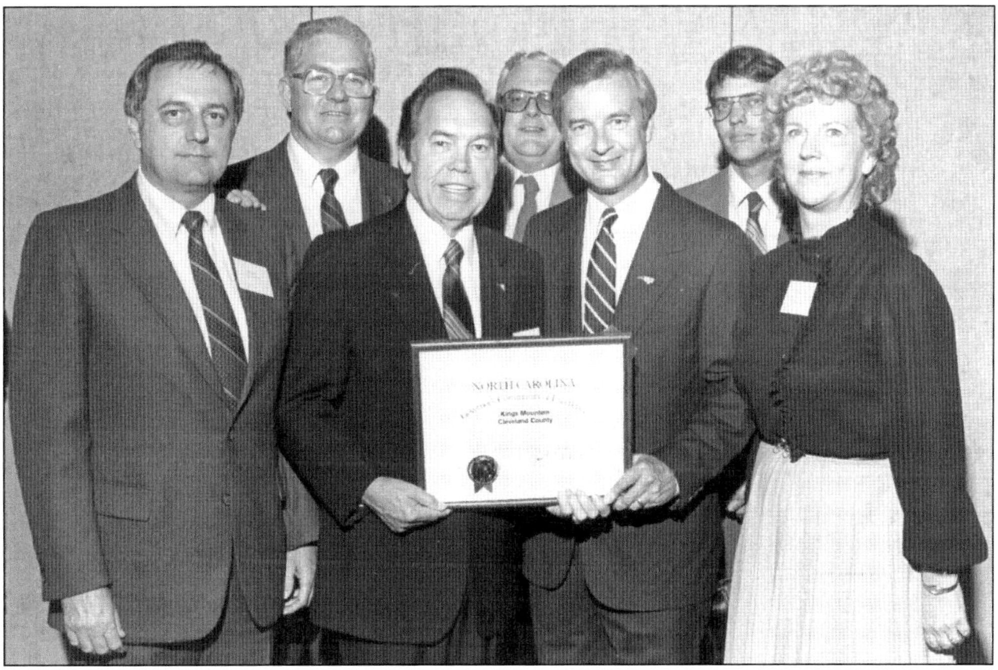

The Governors Community Excellence Award was presented to the City of Kings Mountain in the 1970s. Pictured from left to right are Jerry King, Larry Hamrick Sr., then mayor John Henry Moss, Charles Hamilton, Gov. Jim Hunt, Danny Dilling, and Ruby M. Alexander.

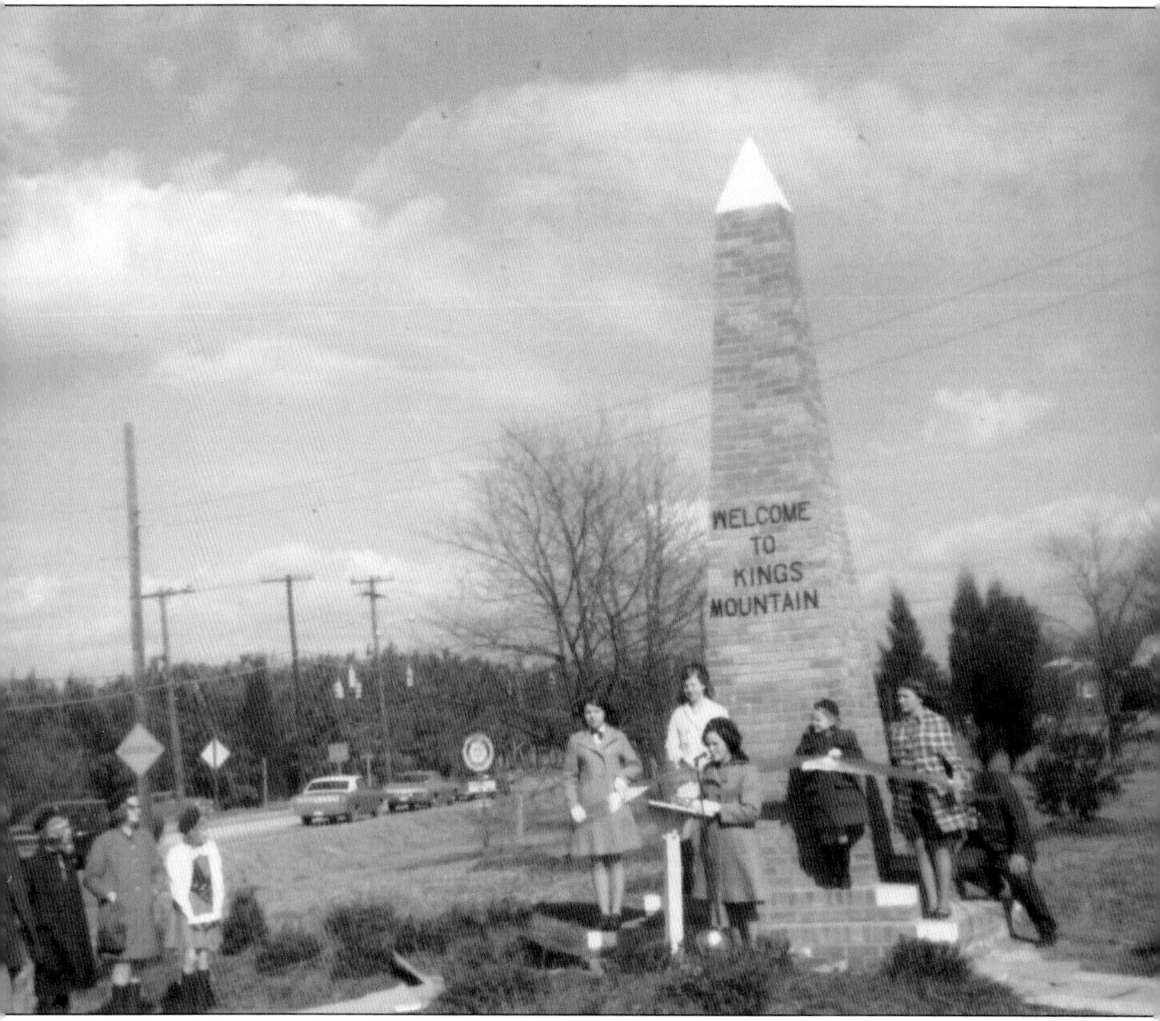

Dedicated on March 9, 1969, Girl Scout Troop 200 received approval from the Kings Mountain City Council to help with a beautification project for the west entrance to the city. The monument is a replica of one of the Kings Mountain Military Park monuments. Construction of the sign (whose message reads, "Welcome to Kings Mountain, the Historical City") was made possible with funds awarded to the Girl Scouts by a Reader's Digest Foundation Grant. This grant was one of 18 awarded in the United States that year. Evelyn Stepp Blanton was the troop leader. The business community aided the Girl Scout project as well. Clyde Bridges of Spangler Ready Mix assisted with the concrete. Dorus Bennett of Bennett Brick gave the brick, and Dean Spears laid the brick. Dan Finger of Hoke Electric assisted with power. Carolina Farm and Garden Center of Gastonia helped with the landscaping. Pictured by the monument are, left to right, Carol Goforth, Laura Bingham Carpenter, Francis McGill (at the podium), Lindsay Holmes Meakin, and Jane Yates.

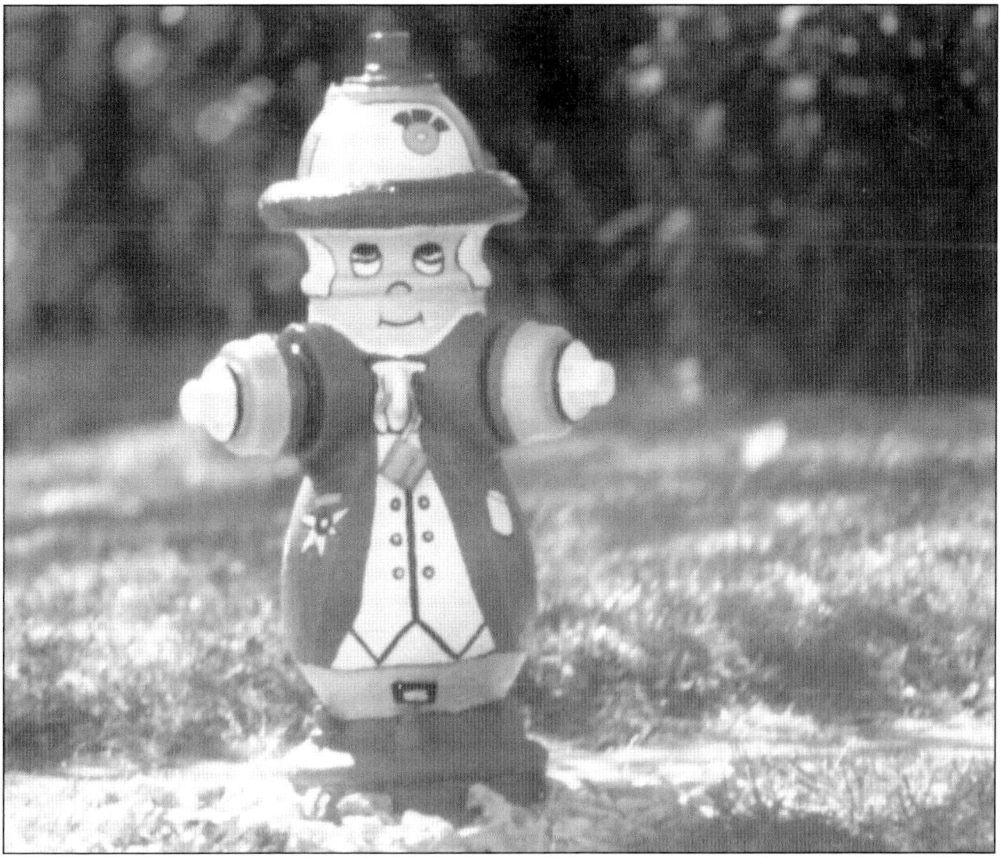

Kings Mountain celebrated its 100th birthday in conjunction with the October 6, 1974, celebration of the Battle of Kings Mountain and with a grand series of events. A Centennial Commission created fun events, such as men growing long beards or being able to purchase buttons for the privilege of partaking in certain liberties otherwise denied during the event. There was also a 100-unit parade and a visit by then governor James Holshouser, Jr. and other dignitaries. In preparation of the festivities, 20 local artists painted 25 fire hydrants in the city to depict five American Revolutionary patriots. As part of the "Paint a Plug for America" national movement starting in Indiana, the group had hoped to extend the project with more designs for the bicentennial celebration in 1976.

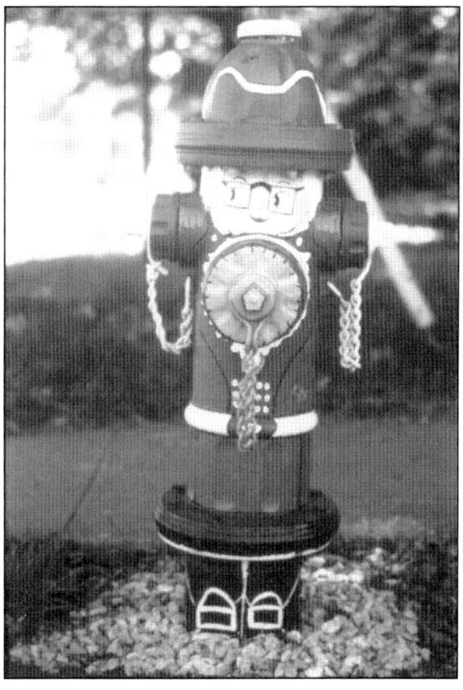

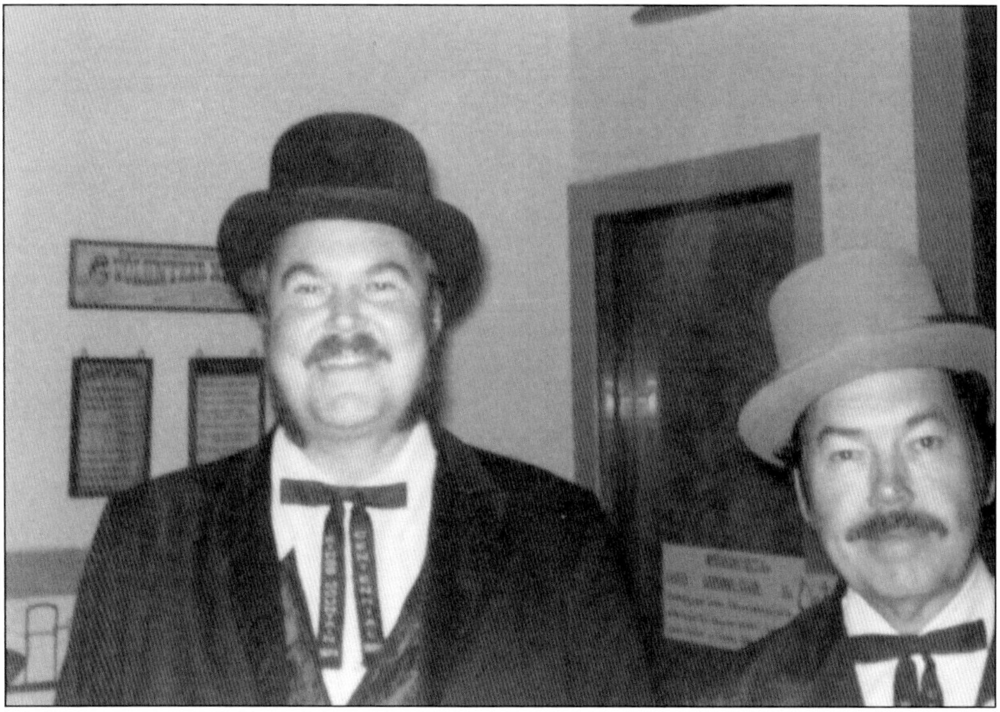

Charles F. Mauney (left) and then mayor John Henry Moss (right) pose for this portrait at the 1974 Kings Mountain Centennial Celebration. The celebration, held in October 1974, honored both the 194th anniversary of the Battle of Kings Mountain and the 100th anniversary of the city of Kings Mountain, established February 11, 1874. Charles F. Mauney served as both president and cochair of the Kings Mountain Centennial Commission.

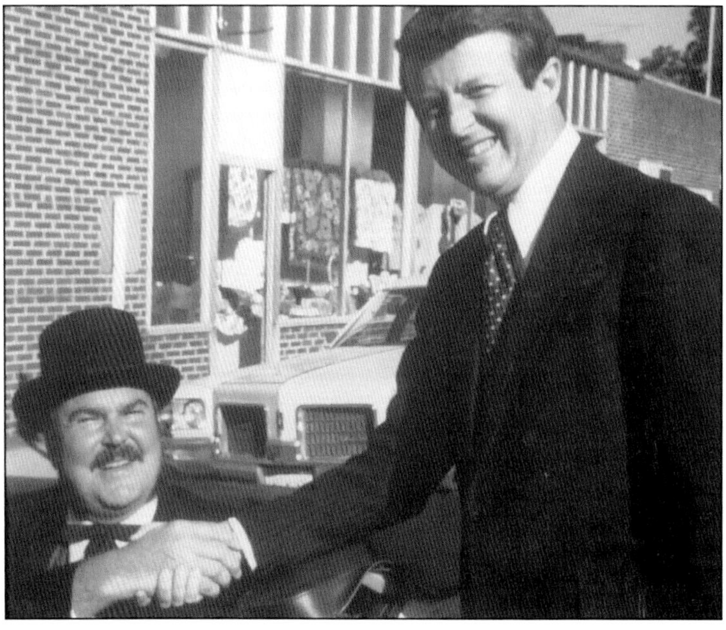

This photograph of Charles F. Mauney (left) and North Carolina governor James E. Holshouser Jr. (right) was taken during the Kings Mountain Centennial Celebration. Holshouser was one of several dignitaries from throughout the United States who attended the weeklong celebration. On October 5, he addressed the community at the centennial luncheon held at the Royal Villa Motel.

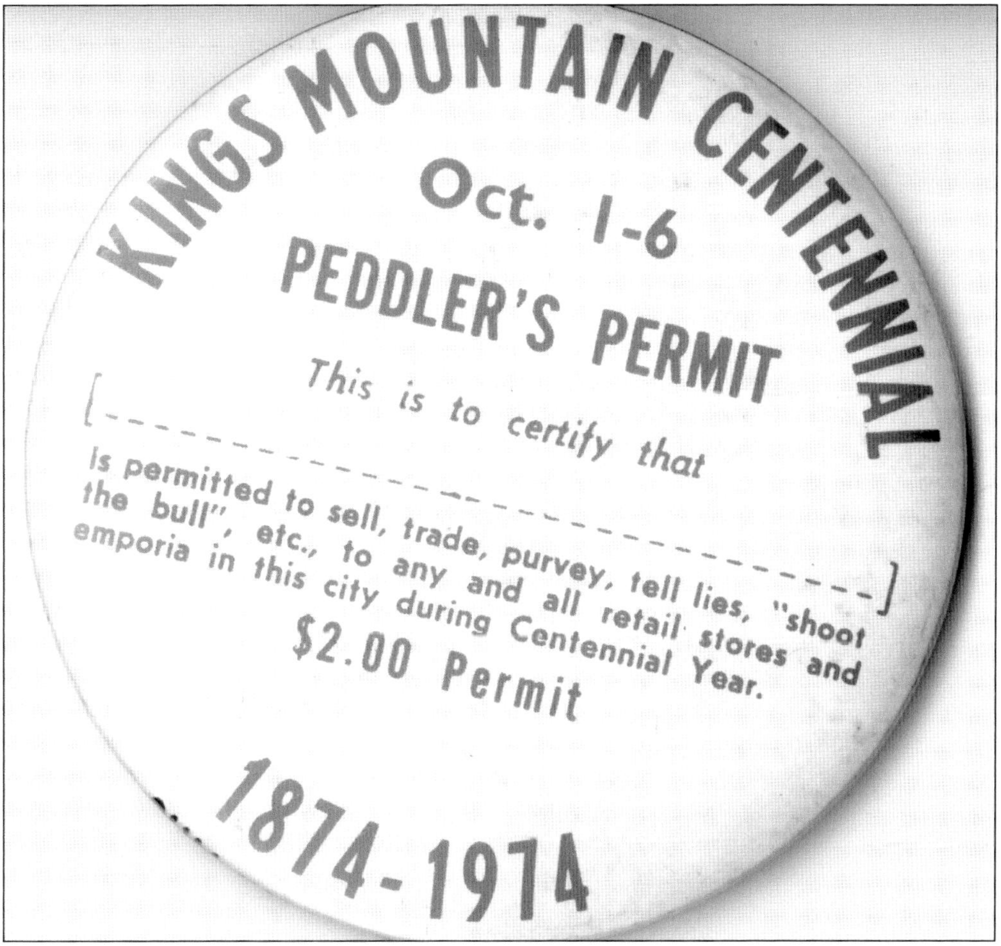

During the week of events and programs that made up the 1974 centennial celebration in Kings Mountain, various buttons could be purchased. These buttons, such as the two seen here, allowed the purchaser certain liberties otherwise denied during the multiday event. Men around town began growing out their beards for the festivities in order to fit the role of an early settler to the area. Shaving before the designated time at the end of the week was "forbidden" without a permit. On the Monday after the event, all the men gathered together, with their permits, to have their beards removed at the makeshift barbershop set up in town as a part of the festivities. The buttons were one of several planned revenue programs employed to help finance the event.

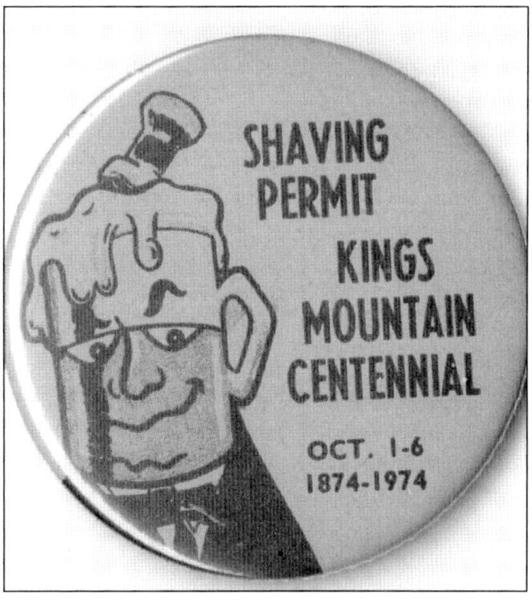

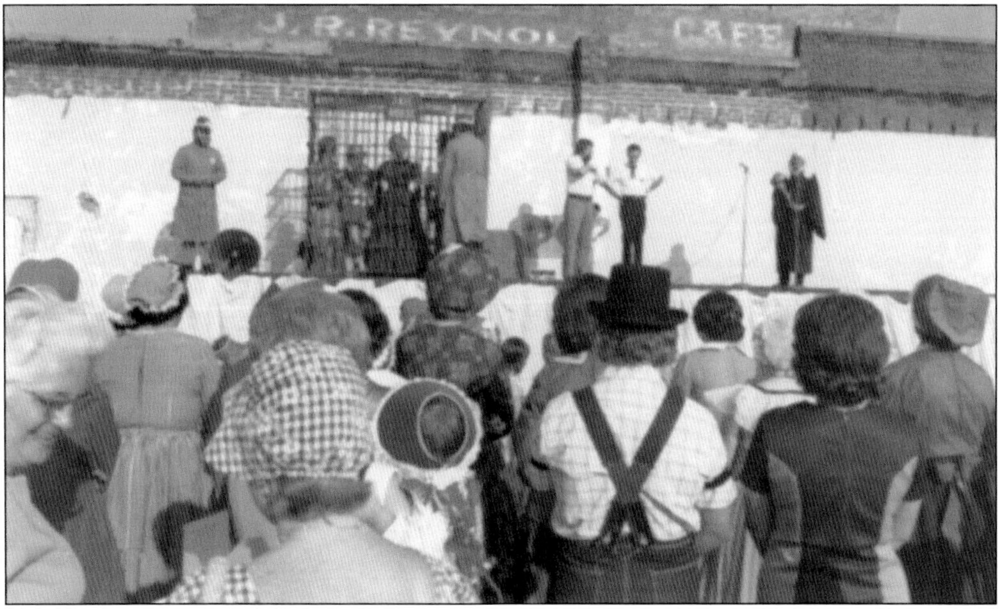

In 1974, the City of Kings Mountain established the Centennial Kangaroo Court for use during the centennial celebration. It was held each Thursday at 5:30 p.m. leading up to the October festivities. Judge George Thomasson, the Kings Mountain Recorder's Court judge, also presided over the Kangaroo Court. Residents could be placed "in jail" or given a shaving cream pie in the face for crimes considered to be against the centennial.

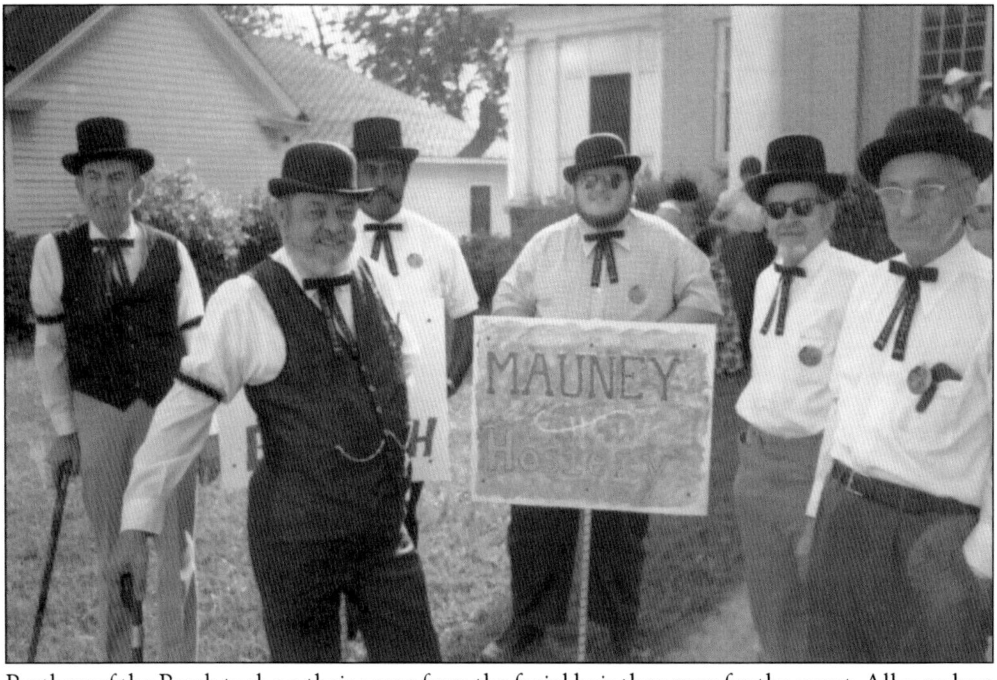

Brothers of the Brush took on their name from the facial hair they grew for the event. All members were required to sign a letter promising "to do [their] civic duty and grow a mustache, full beard, goatee, or sideburns as a part of the Centennial Celebration." The Mauney Mills, Inc., Brothers of the Brush Charter No. 11 stand in front of the Jacob S. Mauney Memorial Library.

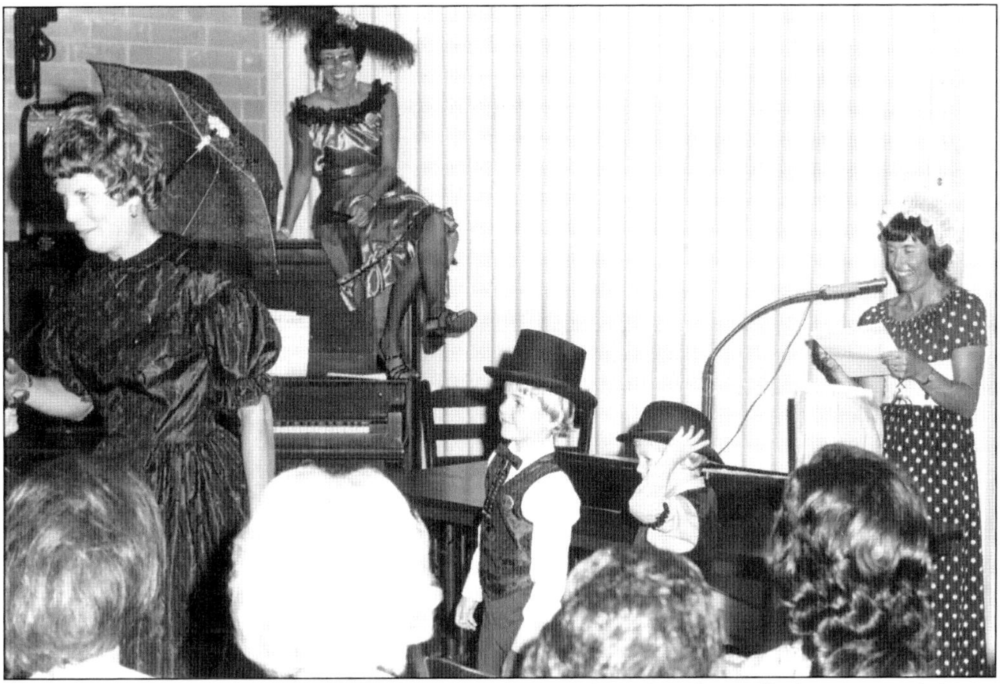

During the 1974 centennial celebration, residents dressed in what they called "centennial dress." Various Kings Mountain civic groups and businesses wore costumes to represent a particular time in the town's history. Throughout the week, one might run into a "Centennial Belle," a "Kingston Kop," or a "gold-digger." Shown in this photograph are, from left to right, Lynn Mauney (in black dress), Yvonne Greene (on piano), and Sylvia Holmes (at podium).

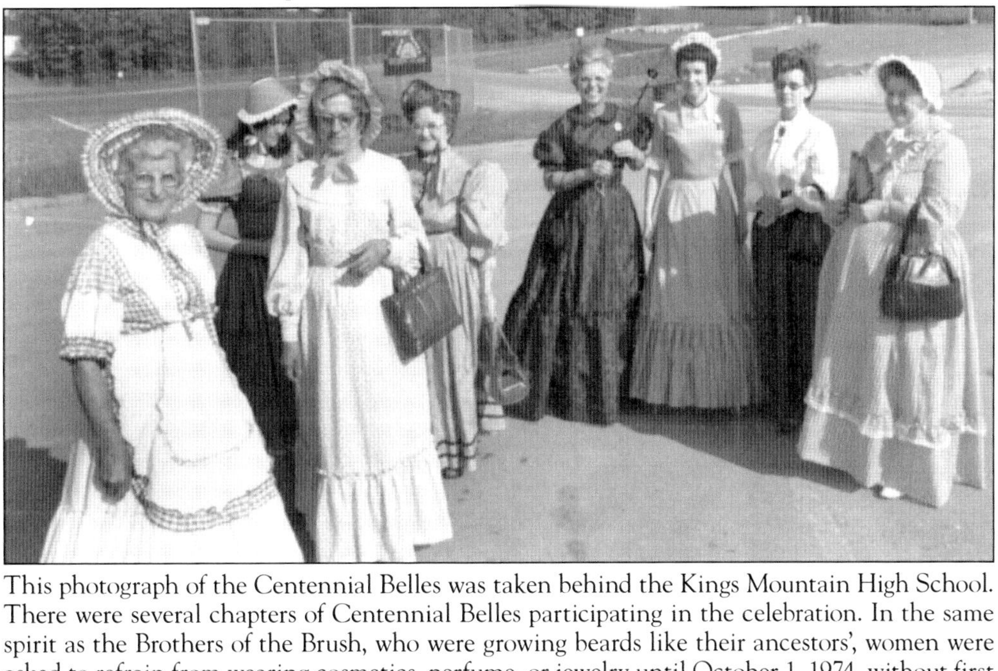

This photograph of the Centennial Belles was taken behind the Kings Mountain High School. There were several chapters of Centennial Belles participating in the celebration. In the same spirit as the Brothers of the Brush, who were growing beards like their ancestors', women were asked to refrain from wearing cosmetics, perfume, or jewelry until October 1, 1974, without first joining the Centennial Belles and obtaining the Official Centennial Celebration Button.

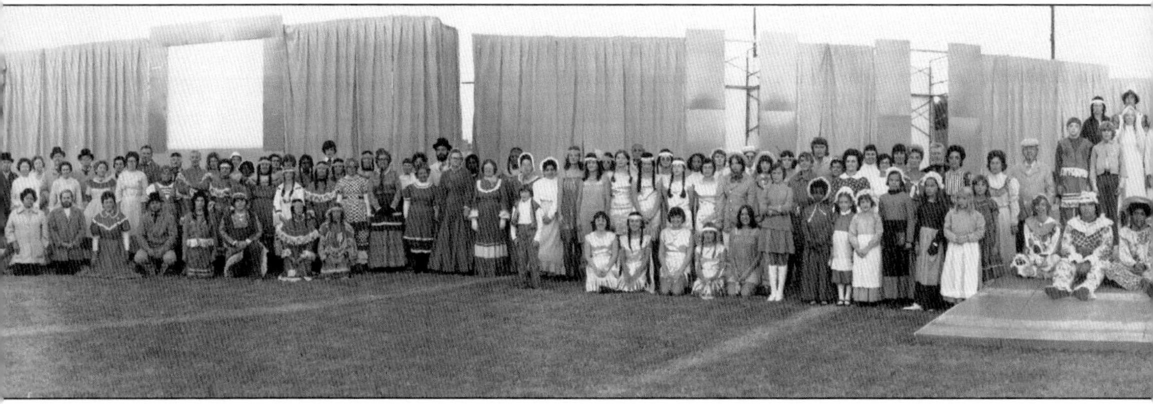

Look to the Mountain, a spectacular presentation of the area's history, was commissioned by the Kings Mountain Centennial Commission and written by Gary L. Welz. Over 200 cast members posed in the commemorative collectible photograph. Note that many on the left also appear on the right, due to the fact that they ran around to be photographed twice. Appearing in the image are, from left to right, JoAnn McDaniel, Ellen McCurdy, Diane Gamble, Fred Weaver, Dot Weaver, Martha Nell Dunlea, unidentified, Peggy Hord, Ada Bridges, Tommy Bridges, Fred ?, unidentified, Reba Humphries, Scott Wells, Ollie Wheeler, Lesia Hughes Wilson, Helen Biddix, Penny Biddix, Ed Anthony, Brenda Biddix, Ethel McGinnis, Winnifred Fulton, Margaret Harmon, LouAnn Blaylock, Rheta Jackson, Fred ?, Lois Mabry, Cindy ?, Sereta Ayers, unidentified, Sheila Blanton, Shannon ?, Peggy Baird, Janet Alexander Edwards, Dana Clemmer Wray, Ann Thomasson, Roxanne Scism Bridges, Dennis Falls, Ethel Williams, Holly Dellinger, Laura ?, Caroline Harper,

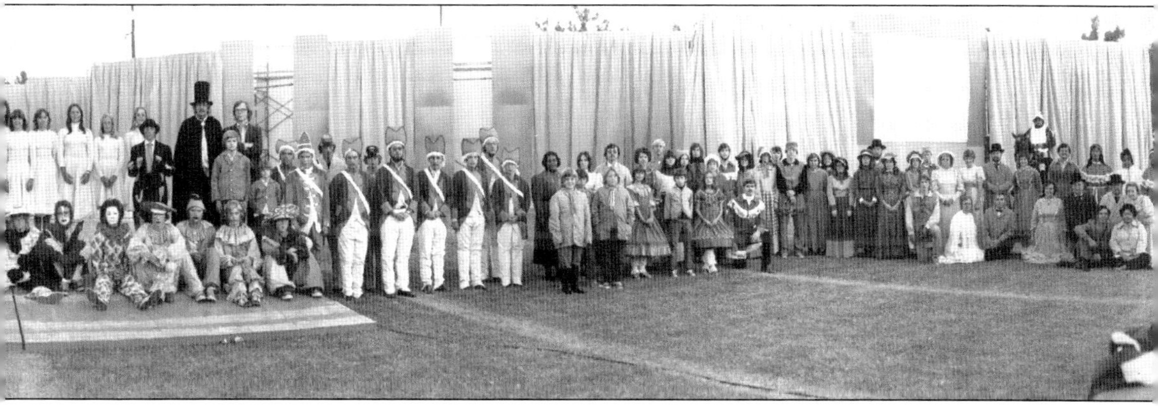

Yvonne Green (Boggs), Rainey ?, Becky Barun, unidentified, Dot Dixon, Joe Smith, Joni Smith, Mark Howell, ? Bennett, Mark Dixon, Gary Howze, K. Wilson, Gina Patterson, Terry GG, Beverly Lynch, Denise Collins, Nikki ?, Jennifer Mauney, Howard Bryant, Kelly Adams, Robin Spears, Lindsay Holmes, Greg McGinnis, Jane Campbell, Beth Bates, Myra McGinnis, Sylvia Holmes, Jeff Crawford, Ray Holmes, Mike Sisk, Robert Swafford, Barbara Harper, Joel Kidd, David Kidd, John Gamble, Ronnie Whetstone, John MeDir, Stanley Bridges, John Grant, Barbara Fulton, Corky Fulton, David Grant, Jennifer Campbell, Hilda Leonard, Dennis Bolin, Anna Lester, David Jones, Chris Holmes, Jamie Humphries, Scott Moss, Jeff Jones, Cindy Bridges, Lisa Bridges, Steve Walker, two unidentified, Jeff Bridges, Karla Bennett, Libby Blanton, Lina ?, and Annette Parker. (Courtesy of James M. McKeown.)

BIBLIOGRAPHY

Baity, Dave. *Tracks through Time: A History of the City of Kings Mountain, 1874–2005.* Charlotte, NC: Jostens Books, 2005.

Black, C.J. *History of the First Baptist Church of Kings Mountain, NC.* Kings Mountain, NC: The Herald Publishing House, 1926.

Broad River Genealogical Society. *Cleveland County Heritage—North Carolina Volume 2.* Marceline, MO: Walsworth Publishing, 2004.

Cleveland County Historical Association. *Cleveland County Heritage—North Carolina Volume 1.* Winston Salem, NC: 1982.

Fryer, Hazel Herndon. *A Sense of Delight.* Kings Mountain, NC: Herald Publishing House, 1984.

Jolley, Reba Odom. *My Life, Dirt Farmer's Daughter.* Kings Mountain, NC: Reba Odom Jolley.

Kings Mountain Centennial Commission, Inc. *History and Program Commemorating the Centennial of Kings Mountain, 1874–1974.* Kings Mountain, NC: Kings Mountain Centennial Commission, Inc., 1974.

Lohr, Lawrence. *And Then They Stood: Old Textile Mills of the Carolina Piedmont.* Ann Arbor, MI: The Shadford Press, 2010.

Mauney, Jack. *Paul and Lillian: Real People.* Kings Mountain, NC: Jack Mauney, c. 2000.

Tarpley, Cassie, Heather Barr, et. al. *Century Stories: The History of Cleveland County in the 20th Century*, Shelby, NC: Westmoreland Printers, 2000.

Weathers, Lee B., *The Living Past of Cleveland County: A History*, Shelby, NC: The Shelby Daily Star, 1956.

www.presidency.ucsb.edu

About the Authors

Mauney Memorial Library began as a dream of Haywood and Liz Lynch, a young couple that moved to Kings Mountain. Lynch purchased the local newspaper and began to write articles pressing for the need to establish a public library. In 1937, the Kings Mountain Library began its operation in the basement of city hall on Piedmont Avenue. In October 1947, children of Jacob S. and Margaret Juletta Mauney purchased the Hord mansion and donated it to the City of Kings Mountain to be used as a library. The library operated in the front two rooms, while the remainder of the building was used as a boardinghouse for young, unmarried teachers. Additions in 1987 and 2000 facilitated the library's growth. Today, it is an award-winning, full-service municipal library funded by the citizens of Kings Mountain. Sharon Stack is the director of the Mauney Memorial Library.

Chartered in 1986 as a nonprofit corporation, the Kings Mountain Historical Museum Foundation is the result of Hazel Herndon Fryer with assistance from former mayor John Henry Moss. In 2000, the Kings Mountain Historical Museum opened to the residents of Kings Mountain and surrounding communities. Prior to that time, the museum had consisted only of storage space in the attic of the old city hall as well as many home and office basements. The museum eventually found a home in the city's vacant 1939 post office building. Today, the museum's permanent collection contains over 3,000 objects, including 1870s vintage clothing, military memorabilia, and textiles, in addition to archival collections of documents and photographs. Also included within the collection is a 1926 delivery truck from the Ware Mill and two historic houses—the Robert Barber House (c. 1830–1850) and the George Washington Cornwell House (c. 1870). Stephanie Walsh is the director and curator of the Kings Mountain Historical Museum.

The authors' royalties from the sale of this book will be divided between the library and the museum.

The City of Kings Mountain and the Kings Mountain Historical Museum hold the copyright to the publication.